Woody Allen
A Retrospective

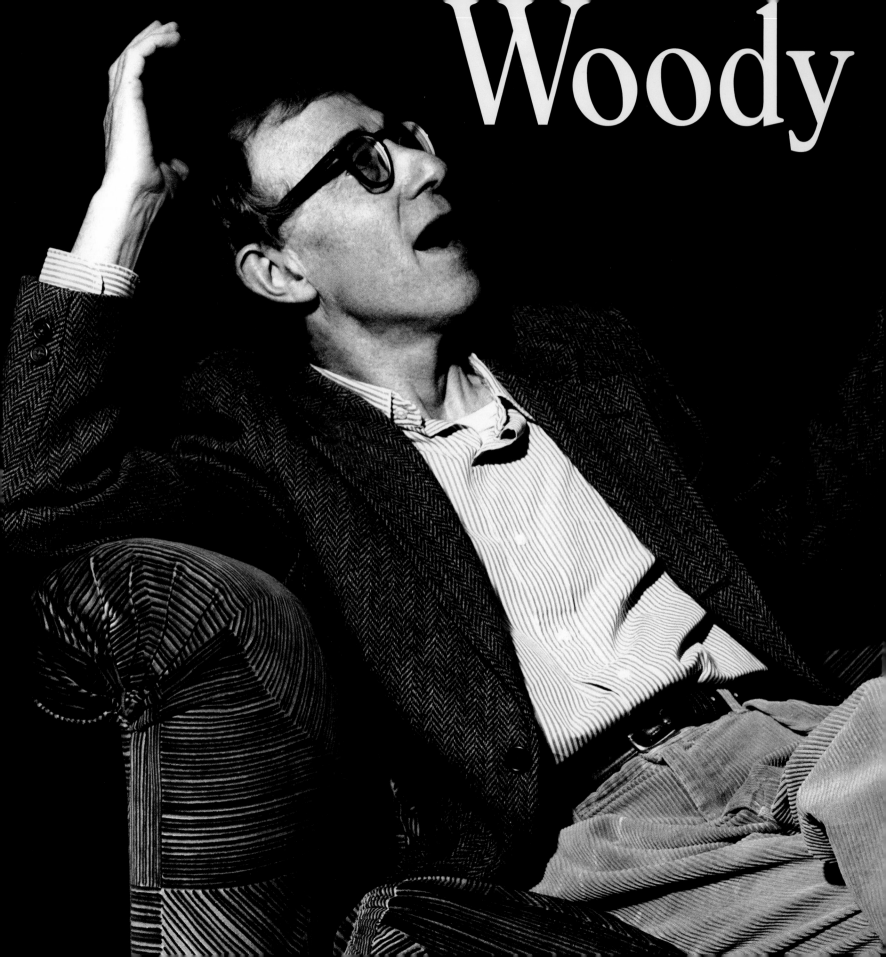

Woody

Allen A RETROSPECTIVE
BY TOM SHONE

Abrams, New York

For Kate
TS

Published in 2015 by Abrams, an imprint of ABRAMS.
All rights reserved. No portion of this book may be reproduced, stored in a retrieval system, or transmitted in any form or by any means, mechanical, electronic, photocopying, recording, or otherwise, without written permission from the publisher.

Text © 2015 Tom Shone
Design and layout © 2015 Palazzo Editions Ltd
Cover design by John Gall

The moral right of the author has been asserted.

Library of Congress Control Number: 2014959569

ISBN: 978-1-4197-1794-9

Created and produced by
Palazzo Editions Ltd
2 Wood Street, Bath, BA1 2JQ, United Kingdom
www.palazzoeditions.com

Publisher: Colin Webb
Art Director: Bernard Higton
Managing Editor: Joanne Rippin
Editor: James Hodgson
Photo Editor: Emma O'Neill

Printed and bound in China by Imago.

10 9 8 7 6 5 4 3 2 1

Abrams books are available at special discounts when purchased in quantity for premiums and promotions as well as fundraising or educational use. Special editions can also be created to specification. For details, contact specialsales@abramsbooks.com or the address below.

Author's note
I'd like to thank Woody Allen, who graciously agreed to answer some of my questions for the purposes of this book; Leslee Dart for her assistance; the *Sunday Times*, for sending me to interview Allen in Paris in 1997; *Elle* magazine for again putting me in contact with the filmmaker in 2011; Rachel McAdams for her insights into the making of *Midnight in Paris*; and Eric Lax, whose biography and book of interviews with the director proved an invaluable resource.

Also helpful were *The Complete Prose of Woody Allen* by Woody Allen; *The Reluctant Film Art of Woody Allen* by Peter J. Bailey; *Woody Allen on Woody Allen* by Stig Björkman; *Woody Allen: Interviews*, edited by Robert E. Kapsis and Kathie Coblentz; *Then Again* by Diane Keaton; *What Falls Away* by Mia Farrow; *Woody: Movies from Manhattan* by Julian Fox; *Woody Allen on Location* by Thierry de Navacelle; *When the Shooting Stops…The Cutting Begins* by Ralph Rosenblum; *Woody Allen* by Richard Schickel; *The Films of Woody Allen: Critical Essays*, edited by Charles L. P. Silet; and *Critical Mass* by James Wolcott.

Tom Shone was the film critic of the *Sunday Times* in London from 1994 until 1999, when he moved to New York. His articles have appeared in many newspapers and periodicals including the *New Yorker*, the *New York Times*, the *TLS*, *Intelligent Life*, *Areté*, and *Vogue*. He is the author of *Blockbuster: How Hollywood Learned to Stop Worrying and Love the Summer*, *In the Rooms*, and *Scorsese: A Retrospective*. He currently teaches film history and criticism at New York University.

Pages 2–3: Portrait by Nicholas Moore, 2003.
Front cover photograph © John Minihan/Evening Standard/Getty Images. See picture credits on page 287 for further image copyright information. Source for quote on the back cover: *On Being Funny: Woody Allen and Comedy* by Eric Lax (New York: Charterhouse, 1975).

ABRAMS
THE ART OF BOOKS SINCE 1949
115 West 18th Street
New York, NY 10011
www.abramsbooks.com

Contents

Introduction

A creature of tidy habit and unerring routine, Woody Allen likes to rise every morning at 6.30 a.m. He gets his children out to school, endures a short spell on the treadmill, then sits down to write at his manual Olympia SM-3 typewriter, which was bought when he was sixteen and still works. Actually, his preferred writing position is not sitting but sprawling on the four-poster bed in his writing room, unless he is collaborating with another writer, in which case he decamps to the living room. "I would come over and for several hours a day we would work," recalled Douglas McGrath, his collaborator on *Bullets over Broadway*. "By four, our energies dipping, we slouched in our seats. It was with the sun setting that the outline of the West Side replaced my view of his eyes. I could tell what time it was by Woody's glasses."

The length of time it takes him to write a script varies. "On average the comedies write more easily for me as they come more naturally, but there is really no precise time," he tells me. "I've written scripts in a month and dramas in two months, other comedies in three months. It varies with only a general observation that the comedies move more easily for me." Preproduction is similarly speedy, about two months, during which time his casting director, Juliet Taylor, will supply him with a long list of possible actors for each role. Casting calls are notoriously brief, with Allen usually trying to head the actors off at the threshold of the screening room before they can occupy a chair. "You shouldn't be offended,"

Taylor will explain, "he does this with everyone." And: "This can be very brief." With pauses and a few cordial nods of the head, it can all be over in a minute.

"I did have the classic, three-minute conversation when he offered me the job," says Rachel McAdams, whom Allen cast in his 2011 film *Midnight in Paris* after seeing her in *Wedding Crashers*. "He said, 'Well, if you don't want the job, we'll do something else some other time.' I couldn't tell if he was offering me the job or giving me an out in case I didn't want it, which of course I did. I was very happy to be a part of his canon. It's funny—you hear such ridiculous stories. 'He hates the color blue! Don't ever show up wearing blue!' And I wear a very clearly blue shirt at one point. When the costume designer put it on me, I said, 'But he hates blue, what are you doing? I'm just going to have to wear something else.' She's like, 'Well, this is a gray blue.' And we debated over how blue the blue was and in the end I'm sure he didn't notice that I was there that day."

A Woody Allen set is chaotic but quiet—so hushed, in fact, you would never guess that he was shooting a comedy. He doesn't yell "Action!" or "Cut!" himself—his assistant director does it. Sometimes playing chess with the technicians between shots, Allen stands apart from his actors, watching, judging, mulling, and very occasionally making suggestions, mainly to encourage departures from the script. "You know, I sit on the bed and write the dialogue, but the first thing I'll

"I would hardly call it genius, but I do sometimes have a sudden flash."

say to the actors is, 'Forget the script,'" Allen told me when I first interviewed him in the mid-1990s. "He doesn't give a lot of direction, and he does give quite a lot of freedom," says McAdams. "I kind of felt as if I was in the theater sometimes. He would set the stage, light this room quite beautifully and you could go anywhere in it, and pick up any prop; you could light a cigarette. He said, 'You know, if you think your character would do that, then give it a try.'"

Allen cuts within scenes as little as possible, preferring to construct them from longer master shots, sometimes handheld, sometimes not. "Don't save your best stuff for the close-ups," Michael Caine advised actress Gena Rowlands after appearing in *Hannah and Her Sisters*. "He's not going to shoot any close-ups." Occasionally, he has replaced an actor when something is not working, as he did Michael Keaton in *The Purple Rose of Cairo*, but on the whole he is quicker to find fault with his script than with an actor, and always budgets for reshoots, sometimes of entirely new material: The second Thanksgiving dinner in *Hannah and Her Sisters* was just such a scene, written on the hoof when Allen realized he needed another dinner to balance the movie out. Filmmaking thus allows him much the same level of control as writing does, finding his way through to the finished work through successive drafts. He has the unusual luxury of second thoughts. "I have always personally referred to movie making for me as writing with celluloid," he says. "To me

it's just like writing with a typewriter except you're dealing with a different substance. Someone agrees to finance me, knowing from my reputation what to expect and what the pitfalls are, and after putting the money in the bank I show up some months later with a film. They never see a script, or have anything to do with the project except, of course, out of courtesy I keep them informed on the cast and where we will be shooting, but that's really it."

The original deal that his managers Jack Rollins and Charles Joffe hammered out with United Artists all those years ago has needed some protection—in today's fractured cinematic landscape Allen has had to hustle, moving from Miramax to DreamWorks to Fox, like any other independent filmmaker—but the basics remain intact. Not since Charlie Chaplin has a comic artist been such a master of his own fate, although in truth it is Chaplin who does well out of the comparison. If Chaplin had survived the transition to sound, managed to evolve from comedian to dramatist, succeeded in replacing himself in his own films, expanded his filmmaking universe to feature ever more layered ensembles spanning a career lasting fifty years as opposed to Chaplin's twenty good years, then his achievement might merit comparison with Allen's. *Vanity Fair* recently asked "How Few Outstanding Films Are Necessary to Create the Reputation of Being a Great Director?" Terrence Malick secured his reputation with two (*Badlands*, *Days of Heaven*); Martin Scorsese, three (*Mean Streets, Taxi Driver, Raging Bull*); Francis Ford Coppola, three (*The Godfather, The Godfather Part II, Apocalypse Now*); Robert Altman, three (*M*A*S*H, McCabe & Mrs. Miller, Nashville*). Allen has directed at least ten films that can hold their own in such company—*Annie Hall, Manhattan, Zelig, The Purple Rose of Cairo, Hannah and Her Sisters, Radio Days, Husbands and Wives, Manhattan Murder Mystery, Bullets over Broadway, Blue Jasmine*—and can boast of a bench of subs that is almost as dazzling: *Sleeper, Love and Death, Stardust Memories, Broadway Danny Rose, Crimes and Misdemeanors, Sweet and Lowdown, Match Point, Vicky Cristina Barcelona*.

This assessment may come as a surprise to those whose view of him is occluded by the clouds of media speculation surrounding his private life. He has been pronounced the beneficiary of a "comeback" more times than seems logically possible. Allen's very ubiquity has brought its own form of invisibility, his sheer productivity a little exhausting to contemplate, his reputation hidden in plain sight. He's just "Woody"—*there*, like a landmark building or tourist sight, putting out a film a year for the best part of five decades, but somehow entirely absent from the pages of *Easy Riders, Raging Bulls*, Peter Biskind's account of American cinema's great golden age in the late 1960s and 1970s, when maverick directors like Altman, Scorsese, and Coppola, high on equal parts pot and French auteur theory, stormed the Hollywood citadel and produced one wild, ragged masterpiece after another, full of handheld camerawork, Godardian jump cuts, self-conscious narration and raw, improvised acting riffs that dared to question America's headlong pursuit of the happy ending.

But enough about *Annie Hall*. Fondness has fogged our view of that film: no rom-com template, but the opposite, a bittersweet account of love's transience in which everything is thrown at the screen—split-screens, empty frames, black frames, subtitles, sudden bursts of animation—much like its two central characters, riffing like crazy, trying to find a chord in all that mental jazz, two notes that together can briefly sing. Until Allen came along, comedies did not look or sound like this—which is to say, like Jean-Luc Godard films. As Allen himself remarked, "Mostly the good-looking stuff is stuff without laughs in it." The *look* of comedy—its status as cinematographic artifact, as cinema—was not really something anybody got too bothered about. Nobody talks about the *mise-en-scène* of the Marx Brothers. Film students do not look to Chaplin for lessons in composition. The average Hollywood comedy, when Allen started making movies, was shot and lit like a car salesroom: bright and boxy, in medium shot, so you could see everything. "I don't see any reason why movie comedies can't also look pretty," insisted Allen, employing Belgian cinematographer Ghislain Cloquet, who had worked with Jacques Demy and Robert Bresson, to

Opposite: Portrait by Michael O'Neill, 1994.

Overleaf: Ten of Allen's best, spanning more than three decades—from *Annie Hall* in 1977 to *Blue Jasmine* in 2013.

shoot *Love and Death*, and *The Godfather*'s cinematographer Gordon Willis to shoot *Annie Hall*, beginning a daring experiment in modernist composition that reached its angular apotheosis in *Manhattan*. "Cinematography *is* the medium," he insisted.

Allen may cut an odd figure against the rogue's gallery of mavericks and movie brats who make up our mental picture of the Hollywood seventies—the bespectacled nebbish at the orgy, his glasses held in place by frown lines mourning the passing of America's previous golden age, the one with Cole Porter and the Marx Brothers—and yet he proved to be that decade's one genuine auteur success story, avoiding flame-out to survive with his independence intact, his fogyishness a kind of gym-prep for posterity, tow-roping him out of the pot haze. His great subject, first glimpsed through the rococo fabulism of his short stories, fleshed out in the Borgesian frames of his high-concept farces, has turned out to be nothing less than the imagination itself. No American dramatist has done more to document the pleasures, pitfalls, and withdrawal pains, of imagining the world other than it is. If his early work gave full vent to Allen's most Mitty-ish imaginings, his mature work, from *Annie Hall* on, drew rueful comedy from reality's refusal to play ball, crafting dramas in which the need for illusion and the urge toward disillusion found an immaculate, porpoise-like balance.

He is our great disappointed dreamer, his escapism tinged with the melancholy of one who knows he or she must awake. That is the signature Allen tone, as distinctive as Lubitsch's. It is the look of deflation on Allan Felix's face when the house lights come up in *Play It Again, Sam*; it is the late afternoon blue that greets Mia Farrow when she exits the theater in *The Purple Rose of Cairo*; it is the shot of the empty street that awaits Alvy once Annie has departed the frame at the end of *Annie Hall*. "The consolations of an over-fertile imagination help a little in the same way that band-aids help, but to mix a metaphor, the house always wins," he says. "In my work, I've tried to make it clear that reality is an extremely ugly and horrific experience and that any respite from it or alternative is welcome. Existing in any fictional world, particularly of my own creation, would be greatly preferable for me but unfortunately the best we can do is temporary escapes into the pages of a book or more vividly into the wonderful alternate reality (which is fantasy) that Hollywood so skillfully provided in the decades when I grew up. I agree I am productive, but none of my films has the depths of Chaplin's best, certainly Keaton's best. The brilliant illusion that I think I have pulled off over the last fifty years has been somehow, with a minor gift, to be able to entice shrewd businessmen to finance me and audiences to turn out in sufficient numbers for me not to have been thrust out to wait on tables."

WOODY
ALLEN

DIANE
KEATON

TONY
ROBERTS

CAROL
KANE

PAUL
SIMON

JANET
MARGOLIN

SHELLEY
DUVALL

CHRISTOPHER
WALKEN

COLLEEN
DEWHURST

"ANNIE HALL"

A nervous romance.

WOODY ALLEN
DIANE KEATON
MICHAEL MURPHY
MARIEL HEMINGWAY
MERYL STREEP
ANNE BYRNE

MANHATTAN

"MANHATTAN" Music by GEORGE GERSHWIN
A JACK ROLLINS-CHARLES H. JOFFE Production
Written by WOODY ALLEN and MARSHALL BRICKMAN Directed by WOODY ALLEN
Produced by CHARLES H. JOFFE Executive Producer ROBERT GREENHUT Director of Photography GORDON WILLIS

United Artists R

A JACK ROLLINS and CHARLES H.

Editor SUSAN E. MORSE Costume Designer SANTO LOQ
Director of Photography GORDON WILLIS Executive Producer CHARLES H.
Written and Directed by WOODY ALLEN

ORION PICTURES / WARNER BRO

A Jack Rollins and Charles H. Joffe Production "Radio Days"
Costume Designer-Jeffrey Kurland Editor-Susan E. Morse, A.C.E. Production Designer-Santo Loquasto
Director of Photography-Carlo Di Palma A.I.C. Musical Supervision-Dick Hyman Associate Producer-Ezra Swerdlow
Executive Producers-Jack Rollins and Charles H. Joffe Produced by Robert Greenhut Written and Directed by Woody Allen
An ORION Pictures Release

HUSBANDS AND WIVES

Woody Allen Blythe Danner Judy Davis Mia Farrow Juliette Lewis Liam Neeson Sydney Pollack

TriStar Pictures Presents A JACK ROLLINS AND CHARLES H. JOFFE PRODUCTION "HUSBANDS AND WIVES" CASTING BY JULIET TAYLOR CO-PRODUCERS HELEN ROBIN AND JOSEPH HARTWICK
COSTUME DESIGNER JEFFREY KURLAND EDITOR SUSAN E. MORSE, A.C.E. PRODUCTION DESIGNER SANTO LOQUASTO DIRECTOR OF PHOTOGRAPHY CARLO DiPALMA, A.I.C.
EXECUTIVE PRODUCERS JACK ROLLINS AND CHARLES H. JOFFE PRODUCED BY ROBERT GREENHUT WRITTEN AND DIRECTED BY WOODY ALLEN

A TriStar RELEASE TRI STAR

ALAN
ALDA

WOO
ALLE

ANJE
HUST

DIAN
KEATO

MAN
ER
MYS

THE PURPLE ROSE OF CAIRO

...pure enchantment.
—VINCENT CANBY, NEW YORK TIMES

...an event...
—GENE SHALIT, NBC-TV, THE TODAY SHOW

...a gem...
—JACK KROLL, NEWSWEEK

...it's a jewel...perfect.
—MICHAEL WILMINGTON, LOS ANGELES TIMES

...it deserves a medal.
—REX REED

...an enduring classic.
—PETER TRAVERS, PEOPLE MAGAZINE

...masterpiece...
—RICHARD SCHICKEL, TIME MAGAZINE

...funny and charming...
—SISKEL AND EBERT, AT THE MOVIES

...I love this movie.
—JOEL SIEGEL, ABC-TV, GOOD MORNING AMERICA

...inventive, funny and magical...
—PAT COLLINS, CBS-TV, CBS MORNING NEWS

HANNAH AND HER SISTERS

WOODY ALLEN   MICHAEL CAINE
MIA FARROW   CARRIE FISHER
BARBARA HERSHEY   LLOYD NOLAN
MAUREEN O'SULLIVAN   DANIEL STERN
MAX VON SYDOW   DIANNE WIEST

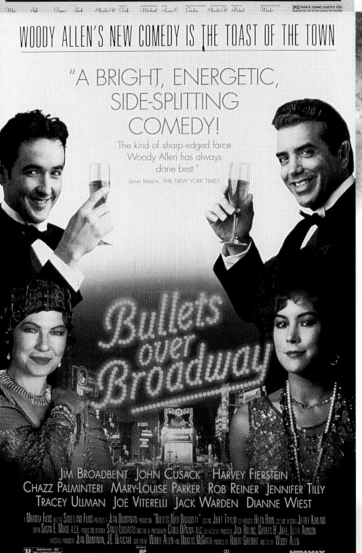

WOODY ALLEN'S NEW COMEDY IS THE TOAST OF THE TOWN

"A BRIGHT, ENERGETIC, SIDE-SPLITTING COMEDY!

The kind of sharp-edged farce Woody Allen has always done best."

Janet Maslin, THE NEW YORK TIMES

Bullets over Broadway

JIM BROADBENT   JOHN CUSACK   HARVEY FIERSTEIN
CHAZZ PALMINTERI   MARY-LOUISE PARKER   ROB REINER   JENNIFER TILLY
TRACEY ULLMAN   JOE VITERELLI   JACK WARDEN   DIANNE WIEST

Alec Baldwin
Cate Blanchett
Louis C.K.
Bobby Cannavale
Andrew Dice Clay
Sally Hawkins
Peter Sarsgaard
Michael Stuhlbarg

Blue Jasmine

Written and Directed by
Woody Allen

The Early Years

In 1952, during his last year at Midwood High School, Woody Allen's daily routine was as follows. He would get out of class at one o'clock, head straight for the subway station and catch the BMT train from Flatbush, in Brooklyn, over the Manhattan Bridge to Sixtieth Street and Fifth Avenue, all the while writing jokes with a pencil. It was always crowded and Allen would have to straphang, but he would scribble away, and by the time he got to Manhattan he'd have at least twenty-five jokes. He would walk east a few blocks, past the Copacabana nightclub to the office of show-business publicist David Alber at 654 Madison Avenue, a slightly ramshackle place in need of a paint job where six or seven men worked in four offices, cranking out gags to run under the name of this or that celebrity in the tabloids. For the next three hours he would sit there and write until he had fifty jokes—ten pages, five jokes to a page. For this, he was paid $20 a week. "There was nothing to it," he said. He was sixteen.

Allen had always had a facility with gags, the same way some people had a facility with a paintbrush, or perfect pitch. "If you're a joke maker it's hard *not* to make jokes," he told CBS's *The Way It Is* in 1967, with a young man's cocky *sprezzatura*. "I'm always amazed when I see somebody that can draw a horse. I can't figure out how they can possibly do it. Because they actually reproduce the horse with a pencil and paper and it's terrific. Now I can't draw a horse or anything else. But I can write jokes. It's hard not to write them. I mean if I walk down the street it's almost my normal conversation. It just comes out that way."

The job had come about after Allen was pushed by his mother, Nettie—the way most things got done in the Konigsberg household. He'd always done terribly at school, a joyless place of rigid discipline ruled by unpleasant, humorless teachers. "I hated it more than rat poison," he told biographer

Eric Lax. "I paid attention to everything but the teachers." The only subject he did well in was English Composition, where his inventive riffs on such topics as what presents he hoped to receive if sick in bed always drew a laugh in class. When he told his mother he was thinking of becoming a joke-writer she took him to buy an Olympia SM-3 typewriter that sold for $40 and looked like a small tank. "This typewriter will last longer than you will," promised the sales clerk, and on the suggestion of a cousin, he submitted samples of his work to some of the big newspaper gossip columnists of the day—Walter Winchell at the *Daily Mirror*, Earl Wilson at the *New York Post*—always with the same note, "Enclosed are some gags for your consideration and sent exclusively to you." To his amazement, he opened the *Mirror* one day, turned to Nick Kenny's column and found he had used one: "*The happiest man I know has a cigarette lighter and a wife—and they both work.*"

Kenny was soon followed by the more widely read Earl Wilson ("*Says Woody Allen: A hypocrite is a guy who writes a book on atheism, and prays it sells.*"), an "astonishing touch of fame" from a world in which he presumed to figure not even as the tiniest speck. "I was just this jerky little kid in high school and suddenly my name appeared," not Allen's own—Allan Konigsberg—but a *nom de plume* because he didn't want to be embarrassed in Math class the next day. His talent was soon pushing him forward faster than his shyness could pull him back. One night, at a Peggy Lee concert at the La Vie en Rose café in Manhattan, a personal manager for David Alber asked one of Wilson's assistants if he could recommend a good gag writer. The assistant told him about this high-school kid in Brooklyn who was being quoted so much the readers were confused—who was this Woody Allen? At their first meeting with the sixteen-year-old wunderkind, Alber's writers—all in their thirties and forties—were nonplussed. "He was full

A portrait of the artist as a young man. By the age of sixteen, Allen was already earning a living as a gag-writer.

"I took great pains to sign a different name, 'cause I thought, God, if anyone ever used this it would be so embarrassing to have my name printed in the newspaper. So I changed my name to Woody."

of exclamations," said Mike Merrick "He was always saying 'Wow!' or 'Gee!' He was overwhelmingly likable. He was personable, he was sweet, he was curious…the antithesis of a smart ass. He would come in completely unassuming and never make any noise and knock out these original, funny lines for, say, Sammy Kaye. We'd read them and say 'Sammy Kaye should be so clever.'"

At the end of a day's work, Allen would take the half-hour subway ride back to Brooklyn, getting off at the elevated station at Sixteenth Street, and walk the block home, a small, wood-frame, two-family building with cement steps on Fifteenth Street in Midwood, south of Flatbush, deep in the heart of Brooklyn, where he lived with his parents, Nettie and Martin, his younger sister, Letty, and his grandparents. There were always so many people around the apartment— his Uncle Cecil, Uncle Abe, Nettie's sister Sadie, and Sadie's husband, Joe, any one of seven aunts, plus assorted strays in various states of pre-marital or ex-marital woe—that Allen frequently bunked in an army cot. It was a boisterous environment, very similar to the one portrayed in *Radio Days*. The dominant impression was of too many people, living in too small a space, all yelling at one another in a mixture of Yiddish, German, and English, "always very lively, people doing things and yelling at each other and activity," recalled Allen. "It was a madhouse all the time." A perfect grounding, one might say, in the stage mechanics and emotional temperature of farce.

The main attraction was always the Konigsbergs and their Amazing Harmony-Free Marriage. "They did everything but exchange gunfire," said Allen. "They were on the verge of breaking up, I would say, every single night for the first thirty of those years, certainly the first twenty. It was astonishing." They argued over everything, but particularly Martin's

reckless spending and rocky business fortunes. Husbands, to Nettie's way of thinking, were supposed to earn money and pay the bills, but Martin, who told everyone he was a butter-and-egg salesman, moseyed from job to job—selling mail-order jewelry, working in a pool hall, running bets to the racetrack in Saratoga for some racketeers. He was a cab driver, a bartender, an engraver, a waiter at Sammy's Bowery Follies; coming home he always found time, and money, to splurge on a new suit, or a toy for Allen, sending Nettie into a fury. The boy was wide-eyed, silently absorbing it all, much later to fill his comic universe with an array of ne'er-do-wells, chancers, grifters, petty scammers, and con artists, from Virgil Starkwell in *Take the Money and Run* to Murray the pimp in John Turturro's *Fading Gigolo*. The *primum mobile* of this universe is the hustler.

"There was so much aggression in my house and everybody hustling, my father particularly. He would promote or hustle anything," said Allen. "I learned all my father's street, suspicious, tough attitudes toward everything. He couldn't go for a car ride without getting into a fight with another driver. He was just difficult that way and always ready to hustle someone out of a buck. From watching him I didn't know people ever behaved nicely toward one another…I thought that was how you dealt with the world." When Allen found a counterfeit nickel on the street, he tried to fob it off on his grandfather, on the grounds that he was too old to know the difference, but was caught by his mother, who was very much the disciplinarian of the house, with a hot temper and a firm right hand. She "was always taking a whack at him," said boyhood friend Jack Freed, "whenever he got her goat, she'd start howling and yelling before taking a good swipe at him. He had an amazing ability to restrain his emotions. His mother couldn't control herself at all."

Again, it doesn't take a psychoanalyst to locate the source for all the shrews, scolds, and nags that form one thread among the female characters in Allen's work—"she slapped me every day of my life," he told the makers of Barbara Kopple's 1997 documentary *Wild Man Blues*—but at the time the only tactic he knew and practiced with any degree of ingenuity was escape. There was a side of him that seemed hatched from a Damon Runyon short story. He dreamed of being a gambler, a cardsharp, a hustler, and practiced sleight-of-hand tricks endlessly in his room, or else sat on the stoop with his friends hatching schemes to scam his schoolmates with rigged card games or crooked dice. "Never play cards with Konigsberg," advised the editor of Midwood's school paper, the *Argus*. On Saturday mornings he and his friends would make the pilgrimage to Irving Tannen's Circle Magic Shop on West Fifty-Second Street in Manhattan, or else head down to Red Hot Peppas at Victor's record store over on Kings Highway, to spend their pocket money on 78 rpm records by Jelly Roll Morton to play at his friend Elliott Mills's house where they would listen to jazz for hours and hours on his twelve-and-a-half-dollar phonograph. "We never stopped listening, I mean obsessively to note after note," said Allen. "I can't tell you how

obsessive it was." It always amazed his friends that he never had to ask for permission to be away from the house the way they did. He simply ran loose.

Above all, there were the movies, which were like a compendium of all his favorite obsessions—Manhattan, magic, music, girls, illusion, petty crime, escape—rolled into one. Allen was three when his mother took him to see his first movie, *Snow White*, in 1939; he ran up to touch the screen until she pulled him away. The first time his father took him into the city, he was six; they took the J train from Brooklyn and got off at Times Square. "It was the most astonishing thing you could imagine. As far as the eye could see there were movie houses in every direction. Now I thought there were a lot, and there were, where I grew up in Brooklyn, but here, every twenty-five feet or every thirty feet, there were movie houses—up and down Broadway, and it appeared to me the most glamorous kind of thing. It was the configuration of all those signs, the Howard Clothes sign and the Camel sign, all those things that have become icons now. And there were streets mobbed with soldiers and sailors, and they all looked great in their uniforms. And the women at that time had the Betty Grable, Rita Hayworth, Veronica Lake look—that's what

"When I was a little kid, I loved comedy and I loved Bob Hope and Groucho Marx. I grew up with that. Right up until my teens, I tried to act like Hope and make the jokes and snap off the one-liners effortlessly."

Bob Hope and Groucho Marx, two of Allen's childhood comedy heroes.

they were all aspiring toward. And they'd be walking around the streets and holding hands with sailors, and there would be guys up against the building selling apparently string-less dancing dolls, you know, and papaya stands and shooting galleries. I mean it was not terribly unlike where Fred Astaire is walking in *The Band Wagon* at the beginning. That was not exaggerated…It was an astonishing thing to see. And the minute I saw that, you know, all that I ever wanted to do was live in Manhattan and work in Manhattan, I mean I couldn't get enough of it."

It's easy to forget that when Isaac Davis makes that famous list of things that make "life worth living" in *Manhattan* ("Okay, for me, I would say Groucho Marx, to name one thing, and Willie Mays, and the second movement of the *Jupiter* Symphony, and Louis Armstrong's recording of "Potato Head Blues," um Swedish movies, naturally, *Sentimental Education* by Flaubert, uh Marlon Brando, Frank Sinatra…"), Allen is not indulging in fogyish nostalgia for the culture of a previous generation. He's talking about the stuff of his childhood. The Marx Brothers were still in theaters when he was born, in December 1935; "Potato Head Blues" was on jukeboxes. When Willie Mays joined the New York Giants and Marlon Brando appeared in *A Streetcar Named Desire*, Allen was fifteen. He was nineteen when Sinatra signed with Capitol Records. Even leaving aside the overtly autobiographical films he has made—*Broadway Danny Rose*, *Radio Days*—Allen's films are, to an extraordinary degree, steeped in his childhood, and the culture by which he sought to escape it. "I've never felt Truth was Beauty. Never," he told John Lahr in 1997. "I like being in Ingmar Bergman's world. Or in Louis Armstrong's world. Or the world of the New York Knicks. Because it's not *this* world. You spend your life looking for a way out."

If the route to Hollywood seemed notional at best, Allen was perfectly positioned to take advantage of the satire boom that swept America in the late 1950s. All over the big cities, coffee houses and jazz clubs were sprouting like mushrooms, nowhere more so than in New York's Greenwich Village where in venues like the Figaro and the Reggio musicians like Pete Seeger and Beat writers like Jack Kerouac and Allen Ginsberg played to hip, young audiences eager for someone to help them shake off the absurdities of the McCarthy era. In Chicago, the Compass players brought together Mike Nichols and Elaine May for the first time; in California, Mel Brooks and Carl Reiner performed their skit about a two-thousand-year-old man recounting all the famous people he'd met (Jesus: "I knew him well. Thin, beard. Came in the store. We gave him water.") on an LP that sold more than a million copies. In 1954, Allen saw Mort Sahl perform stand-up for the first time at the Blue Angel nightclub. Dressed not in a tux but wearing slacks and a sweater, the *New York Times* under his arm, absent the usual jokes about wives and women's underwear but instead riffing on "the dilemma of metropolitan man drowning in the surroundings he himself fashioned," to use Jonathan Miller's formulation, Sahl was spellbinding.

"It was like when Charlie Parker came along, it was just an automatic revolution in jazz. He was absolutely like nothing anybody had seen before. And he was so natural that the other comedians became jealous. They used to say, 'Why do people like him? He just talks. He isn't really performing.' But his jokes came out of a stream-of-consciousness, in a kind of jazz rhythm. And he would digress. He would start to talk about Eisenhower and then he would digress from that to the FBI and mention something that happened to him and then something about electronic surveillance and then he would talk about hi-fi equipment and women and then come

back to his point about Eisenhower. It was a spectacular format." Above all, Sahl's act represented a triumph of voice. He didn't sound like a performer performing, he sounded like someone catching up with his own thoughts— quick, cerebral, candid, intemperate—a sound that would feed into Allen's own voice, less cantankerous than Sahl's but animated by the same casual rhythms.

The other key influence of this period was Danny Simon, brother of playwright Neil, and the head writer of NBC's *Colgate Comedy Hour*, where Allen won a rookie placement as part of NBC's writers development program. The show was canceled almost as soon as Allen arrived, but Simon was to prove an invaluable tutor and lasting friend. "Everything I learned about comedy writing I learned from Danny Simon," he told Eric Lax. He taught him about the importance of a clean line—an unforced set-up—and the difference between stand-up comedy, which relied on one-liners, and sketch comedy, which relied on situations that you set up and then explored with characters; he taught him to push every concept through to its extreme: "And then what?" He also gave him work, recommending him for a gig at the Tamiment resort near Stroudsburg, Pennsylvania. Tamiment was a lakeside summer retreat, a kind of Jewish Catskills, where young Jewish men and women could meet and enjoy staged entertainment by the likes of such fledgling talents as Sid Caesar, Carl Reiner, Mel Brooks, Danny Kaye, Neil Simon, all of whom had made their starts there before going on to Broadway.

Allen's typewriter sounded from his cabin like a buzz saw. Every Monday the performers needed new material, they would rehearse it through Wednesday, with a run-through in the theater on Thursday before performing it on Saturday and Sunday nights. "You couldn't sit in a room waiting for your muse to come and tickle you," said Allen. "You had to get that thing written." His shows at Tamiment included a convict awards ceremony in which thugs present annual prizes for Best Murder, Best Robbery, and Best Assault with a Deadly Weapon; also a skit about psychological warfare, in which adversaries meet on a battlefield and creep up behind one another, whispering, "You're short, you're short and you're unloved." They were an instant hit, and led to work on a 1958 TV special *The Chevy Show with Sid Caesar*, where he wrote a spoof of *Playhouse 90* for Caesar called *Hothouse 9D* and a take-off on *American Bandstand* with Art Carney plugging hot new rock groups like "The Sisters Karamazov." Allen didn't much like writing for Caesar, then in irascible decline; the other writers carped and inveigled against one another. "A little red-haired rat," was Mel Brooks's description of Allen. "Woody looked to be all of six years old," said fellow writer Larry Gelbart. "His previous writing credit, I assumed,

Groundbreaking comedian Mort Sahl, seen here at Mister Kelly's, Chicago in 1957, was another major influence.

Mel Brooks, Woody Allen "the little red-haired rat", and Mel Tolkin pitching ideas to Sid Caesar. Allen worked as one of Caesar's writers in the mid-1950s.

must have been learning the alphabet. He seemed so fragile, a tadpole in horn-rims."

An Art Carney show followed, with Allen writing a spoof of Bergman's *Wild Strawberries* (1957) called *Hooray for Love*, which involved Carney speaking pseudo-Swedish with preposterous subtitles. "Parodies on Tennessee Williams and Ingmar Bergman," wrote one critic. "Man, this is getting pretty far out for this mass audience." Allen's intellectual sphere was widening. Two years earlier, in March 1956, he had married Harlene Rosen, the daughter of a shoe-store owner he'd met through the Flatbush Jewish social clubs. In the fall of 1957, Harlene enrolled at Hunter College to study philosophy and her husband, anxious to keep up, arranged for a tutor at Columbia to guide him through a course of Great Books—Plato, Aristotle, Dante, Joyce—which they would read and discuss. Allen hadn't started reading until he was in his late teens, regarding it as "a chore," but he was as diligent and methodical in his self-tuition as he was in everything. At four o'clock every afternoon, he would walk the four blocks from his apartment to the Metropolitan Museum of Art and spend half an hour studying a different exhibit until he had worked his way around the whole museum. Allen's adventures in higher education were largely sexual-romantic in motivation: He wanted to keep up with Harlene, and then, when that marriage was over, in 1962, he wanted to attract a different type of woman. "They weren't interested in me, because I was

a lowlife culturally and intellectually," he said, "I had to start trying to make some sort of effort to explore interests they had; all I knew about was baseball. I used to take them out and they'd say 'Where I'd really like to go tonight is to hear Andrés Segovia' and I'd say 'Who?' Or they'd say 'Did you read this Faulkner novel?' and I'd say 'I read comic books.'"

By the late 1950s, most of the elements that would make up Woody Allen's comedy were in place: a light-fingered ability to set up a joke invisibly that owed something to the studied casualness of Mort Sahl; a delight in puncturing the intellectual aspirations of metropolitan café culture; an attitude toward women that was shedding some of its second-hand adolescent callowness ("*My first wife got a traffic violation. Knowing her it couldn't have been a moving violation.*") to mine candid seams of male insecurity; and an increasingly agile ability to develop conceits over the long distance, thanks to his workouts in the comedy mills of Tamiment and network television under the tutelage of Danny Simon. There was only one element lacking: a persona, a flair for performance, or any sense that Allen would one day front his own material.

"We *smelled* that this shy little guy could be a great performer," said Jack Rollins, after he and his partner, Charles Joffe, saw Allen in their newspaper-scattered offices on West Fifty-Seventh Street in 1958. Allen read through a series of his sketches. "He'd be dead serious when he read a sketch of his but it hit us funny. He didn't know why we were laughing. He'd give a what's-so-funny look. Very removed, he was. Quiet and shy." Rollins and Joffe were then the Rolls-Royce of show-business management, the men who had brought Lenny Bruce to New York, who handled Harry Belafonte, Nichols and May. They were both instantly smitten with Allen's unassuming personality—his shrugging, apologetic sense that the real

performer would be along at any minute. Both men sensed the potential for a "triple threat"—an Orson Welles, capable of writing, directing, and performing his own material—and decided to sign him up.

After a period of prevarication, during which Allen was hired and fired by the long-running *Garry Moore Show*, the threat of impecuniousness served to sweeten Rollins and Joffe's offer, and they booked him his first stand-up gig, in October 1960, after comedian Shelley Berman's Saturday night late show at the Blue Angel. It was a notoriously difficult venue to play, a red-carpeted footpath leading patrons down a corridor to a small black room filled with smoke, with low ceilings and a pocket-sized stage, at the base of which were a string of circular tables, crowded with a mixture of bohemians and TV bookers. Larry Gelbart was in the audience on Allen's first night and described him as looking like "Elaine May in drag." He dodged and darted through his routines—the one in which he enrolled in college courses like Advanced Truth and Beauty and Death 101 but cheated in exams by looking into the soul of the boy sitting next to him—hitting words hard, biting off syllables, his right hand clutching the mike until his knuckles were white, his left hand gripping the top of the stand as if it were glued there. He looked naked, helpless—like a skinned rabbit.

"He would get up there and wrap that cord around his neck," recalled Rollins of that first, frightful season. "You thought he was going to choke himself. Oh and filled with nervous tics. Nervous, nervous. It was a sight. I mean you just had to see him." Said Joffe, "Woody was just awful." What followed was, according to Allen, "the worst year of my life." Every morning he'd wake up with a fear in his stomach that wouldn't abate until he fled the stage, hands over both ears to block out the response from the audience. Both Joffe

and Rollins would drive him to the show, afraid he would bolt. Once there, said Rollins, "he would walk like a small caged lion, up and back, up and back," wearing out a path in the carpet. A few times he vomited before going onstage. They literally had to push him on. "There were many times Woody and I stood back there and he shook like a leaf," said Jane Wallman, who ran the nightclub and introduced the performers. "That little body would be quivering and I would be holding him. He came up to about here on me. I'd pat him on the back and say, 'Come on, you're going to be great.'"

Afterward they would all go to the Stage or the Carnegie Deli, where Rollins and Joffe would perform an autopsy, pointing out lines that needed work or mannerisms that needed reining in, while Allen pleaded with them to let him quit: "I'm not funny, I'm not a comic, I can't do this, I hate it, I don't like the hours, I'm shy, I don't like standing in front of an audience," he would say and Rollins would always quietly remonstrate with him, "Give it a little time." Then at 3 a.m. he would go home to sleep, wake up and repeat the cycle. Allen almost quit five or six times. Eventually, something clicked. Instead of burrowing through his material as if hoping to uncover an exit, he realized: *They have paid to see me*. The gulping delivery and nervous mannerisms, once turned through a ninety-degree angle, gradually took on the outline of a persona: "A slight man with a startled look about him, as if just caught in an unspeakable act," in the words of Phil Berger.

Above: "We *smelled* that this shy little guy could be a great performer." Jack Rollins (center) and his partner Charles Joffe (left) seized the chance to manage Allen. Here pictured in the 1970s.

Overleaf: Allen's full range of onstage tics and twitches are here captured by photographer Rowland Scherman during a mid-1960s stand-up performance in Washington, DC.

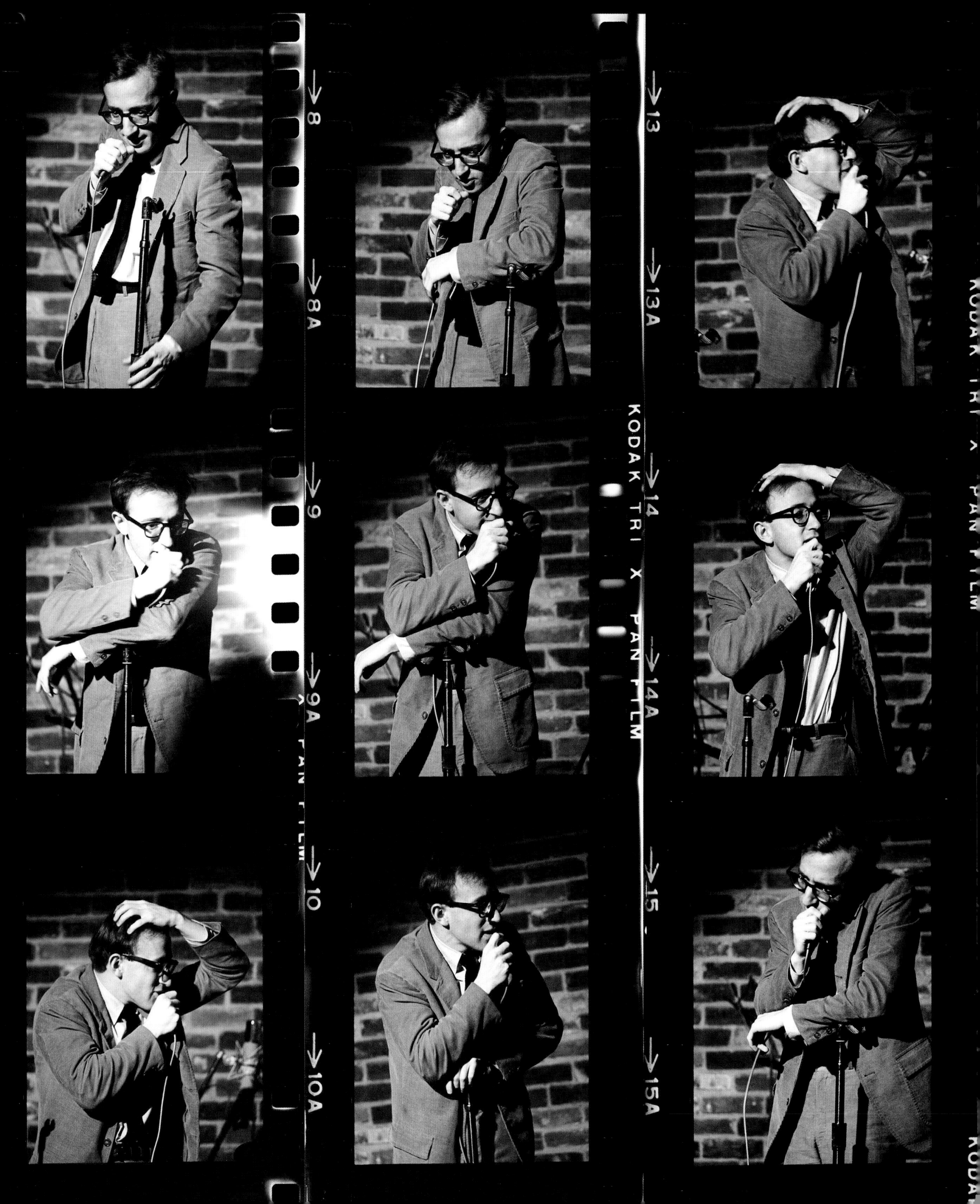
8
8A
13
13A
KODAK TRI X PAN FILM
9
9A
14
14A
10
10A
15
15A

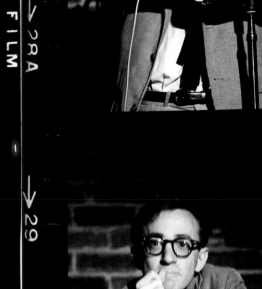

KODAK TRI X PAN FILM → 23 → 23A KODAK TRI X PAN FILM → 24 → 25 → 25A KODAK SAFETY

ODAK TRI X PAN FILM → 28 → 28A → 29 → 29A KODAK SAFETY FILM → 30 → 30A

NOTED STARS, WOODY ALLEN AND MONIQUE VAN VOOREN, ENJOY THEIR SMIRNOFF MULES TOGETHER.

On the mule train with Monique Van Vooren in this 1960s Smirnoff vodka ad.

The circularity was performative: That's what Allen's act was *about.* Unspeakable dread. Performance anxiety. Existential shakedown. So it made perfect sense for the audiences to see just that up on stage: a performer caught in his own funk, hanging on to the mike as if for dear life, picked out by the lights as if by oncoming headlights. Allen turned his fear of performing into its own performance. Much later, when he appeared on *Saturday Night Live,* he explained something to Lorne Michaels that Michaels remembers vividly: "He said that *he* is his premise."

"When I started out, I thought just the opposite. I just wanted to go out and do my jokes because I felt that was what the audience was laughing at. But Jack Rollins kept saying to me, 'You have it backwards.' I didn't know the first thing because I was totally oriented as a writer. I thought if S. J. Perelman goes out and reads 'No Starch in the Dhoti, S'il Vous Plait' they're going to howl. But that's not what it is at all; it's that the jokes become a way for a person to display a personality or an attitude. Like Bob Hope. You're laughing not at the jokes but at the guy who's vain and cowardly and full of false bravado. You're laughing at character all the time."

By the end of 1961 Allen was really hitting his stride. He was such a hit at the Bitter End that he had to do four shows on Friday and Saturday to keep his fans satisfied, and over the weekend more than four hundred had to be turned away. An article in the *New York Times* had the lines running all the way down to MacDougal Street. "What Allen projects— and his work has been called fresh, bright, individual—is wistful futility," wrote Arthur Gelb, in November 1962. "He is a waif in schnook's clothing—bedeviled always by the world and society…He is a Chaplinesque victim with an S. J. Perelman sense of the bizarre and a Mort Sahl delivery despite the fact that he steers clear of topical material." In the *New York Journal,* Jack O'Brien praised Allen's "marvelous modern wit which unlike Mort's…is aimed straight at himself, his own pint-sized ineffectiveness, his owlish face and what he maintains is his disaster-prone capability for hilarious social and physical indignities." The comments go a long way to explaining why Allen's achievement has been the longer lasting, while Sahl's reputation has been largely eclipsed by those who followed in his disgruntled wake: Lenny Bruce, Bill Cosby, Richard Pryor, Bill Hicks. "When we see his films, all our emotions attach to him," Pauline Kael

would note of his films. "His fear and his frailty are what
everything revolves around."

This is true of all great comedians, but Allen's self-
absorption was to strike a particular chord with an era of
national solipsism defined by Watergate on the one hand
and therapy on the other. "The new alchemical dream is:
changing one's personality—remaking, remodeling, elevating,
and polishing one's very *self* ... and observing, studying, and
doting on it. (Me!) ..." wrote Tom Wolfe in an article for
New York magazine in which he reported on the growth of
Freudian analysis, Shutzian encounter sessions, group therapy,
and primal scream treatments by which Americans sought
to strip away their defenses and facades, face the truth and
realize their potential. Allen, who began analysis in 1958
for a "terrible and terrifying" feeling he had been unable to
shake—the date matches up with his first exposure on network
television—was to be the Me Decade's pint-sized court jester,
a Chaplin for the era of Freud, a wriggling under-mensch in
whose shrimpish frame audiences found a physical rebuke
to the outdated macho mindset then being critiqued in
everything from the movies of John Wayne to the Vietnam
War. "When he uses his wit he becomes our D'Artagnan,"
observed Kael. "It's a comedy of sexual inadequacy. What
makes it hip rather than masochistic and awful is that he
thinks women want the media macho ideal, and we in the
audience are cued to suspect, as he secretly does, that that's
the real inadequacy. Woody Allen is a closet case of potency;
he knows he's potent but he's afraid to tell the world—and
adolescents and post-adolescents can certainly identify with
that ... He isn't a little fellow for college students; he's a hero."

Throughout 1962 and 1963, Allen continued to draw
acclaim and, increasingly, TV bookings, appearing on *The
Merv Griffin Show*, *Candid Camera*, *The Ed Sullivan Show*,

The Steve Allen Show, and *The Tonight Show*, where he became
the first of Johnny Carson's countless guest hosts. Hollywood
was beginning to pay attention. Watching him perform at
the Blue Angel one night in 1964 were Shirley MacLaine
and film producer Charles K. Feldman, who saw the young
comic convulse the audience with laughter. The next morning
Feldman approached Rollins and Joffe with an offer of $35,000
for Allen to adapt a story he owned, a frothy bedroom farce
about an inveterate Don Juan. The story, entitled *Lot's Wife*,
would eventually become *What's New Pussycat?* It was "the
quintessential Hollywood production, almost a satire on itself,"
Allen would later say. "I couldn't bear the picture when it
came out. I was completely embarrassed and humiliated by the
experience. I vowed I would never write another film script
unless I could direct it. And that's how I got into films."

"If it's really gray and raining, it's fine. If it's bright and sunny, I have trouble dealing with the day, personally."

Blue skies ahead? Portrait
by John Minihan, 1971.

Breaking into Hollywood

1965–1967

"What's new, pussycat?" was the phrase Warren Beatty used to greet his girlfriends on the phone. "*Title!*" Charles Feldman yelled when he heard it. Tan and mustachioed, with houses in Beverly Hills and the French Riviera, Feldman was the gleaming embodiment of Hollywood bling. A lawyer turned agent turned producer, he had helped bring *The Seven Year Itch* and *A Streetcar Named Desire* to the screen, and was known for dispensing outsized gestures of largesse—a house, a Rolls-Royce—to his friends and associates. "Charlie was generous, the kind of guy you could go to when you needed a favor," said Allen. "He would go over to the baccarat table and lose a hundred thousand dollars the way you'd lose your Zippo lighter, [but] he just had a block, a psychological block which prevented him from telling the truth. It made it very hard to work with him."

Preproduction on *What's New Pussycat?* resembled Alice's descent down the hole of the white rabbit. They would be shooting in Paris with Beatty in the lead role. And could Beatty's new girlfriend Leslie Caron have a part, too? Actually, no, Beatty can't make it. How about Peter O'Toole in Rome, with Peter Sellers playing the rake's psychiatrist? Except Sellers refuses to shoot in Italy. How about Paris after all? And could Sellers's part be bigger? Initially recovering from a heart condition, Sellers had signed on for a small role, but once production was underway, he sought a much bigger one, taking over scenes Allen had written for him and improvising new ones. O'Toole, meanwhile, came to the set fresh from *Becket*, where he had played opposite Richard Burton. Could Burton have a cameo?

"I had written what I thought was a very offbeat, uncommercial film," said Allen. "And the producers I turned it over to were the quintessential Hollywood machine…People putting their girlfriends in roles. People writing special roles just to accommodate stars, whether those roles worked or not. The worst nightmare you could think of." He would sit in the screening room, while everyone viewed the rushes, going "This is *terrible*," only to be shushed. "Woody was a nobody on set," said actress Louise Lasser, who was to become Allen's second wife a year after the film was released. "He was totally eclipsed by Sellers and O'Toole. Nobody was listening to a word he said."

He amused himself as best he could. Installed in the George V Hotel just off the Champs-Élysées, he wrote and practiced his clarinet, eating the same identical dinner at Le Boccador every night for six months—*soupe du jour*, fillet of sole, crème caramel. He tracked down a boyhood idol, clarinetist Claude Luter, at the Slow Club, ran into Samuel Beckett in a café, visited the Louvre. But as production wore on, the arguments

At the center of this *What's New Pussycat?* cast photo, though Allen felt increasingly marginalized during production.

with Feldman got worse. The producer wanted a big *Pink Panther*–style chase-cum-demolition-derby with police cars and go-karts for the ending; meanwhile, Allen's co-star Romy Schneider objected to being married off to him in the final reel; and Sellers was angry that Allen appeared in the ending and not him. Finally, during a viewing at which the opinions of Feldman's entourage filled the air—"Oh, I don't think that's funny…," "I think what should happen is he should be more crazy in that scene…"—Allen snapped and, in a rare display of temper, told Feldman to fuck off. If the producer was insulted he didn't show it. "My outburst just slid right off him," noted Allen. "Probably he'd been cursed out so often that it was not a bothersome moment to him."

Much could be said of Allen's impact on the finished film, a frantic, overlong, and intermittently funny sex farce in which

O'Toole blinks his blue eyes innocently as Michael, a magazine editor exhausted by his success with women, tales of which have his psychiatrist's (Sellers) eyes on stalks. As Pauline Kael noted, "Sellers is in the Woody Allen role, but Woody turns up, too," as Michael's best friend, Victor, hopelessly in love with Michael's fiancée, Carole (Schneider). His hair neat and schoolboyish, Allen gets to try out his Bob Hope impression for the first time in a scene set in a library in which Victor defends Carole's honor from a muscle-bound blond ("Have you seen the guy's knuckles? They're *huge*…"), but in the battle of the comic foils, it's Sellers who is the victor. Allen's graceful comic curlicues pale when set next to the sight of Sellers in a Beatles wig, sporting a Dr. Strangelove–style Teutonic accent—a riff on Freud turned up to Wagnerian volume. They have one scene together, in which Sellers attempts

Receiving instruction from *What's New Pussycat?* director Clive Donner on location in Paris with Peter O'Toole and Nicole Karen.

to commit suicide, Viking-style, on board a burning boat wrapped in a huge Bavarian flag, only to be interrupted by Allen, consuming a chicken dinner on the banks of the Seine. He ends up prone in the funeral boat being psychoanalyzed by Sellers, while tossing his drumsticks nonchalantly over his shoulder into the river. Strange to say, but Allen is almost the calmest thing in the movie.

The big, gaudy film was a big, gaudy success, raking in $17 million, momentarily setting a new box-office record for a comedy. Away from the chat-show circuit, Allen consoled himself with devising clever, rococo insults for the film, describing it as "the result of a two-hundred page manuscript that blew out of a taxicab window and was never put back in its original order." He later would arrive at the following formulation: "Left to my own devices, I could have made the film twice as funny and half as successful," a paradox in which self-deprecation and ambition are beautifully balanced, but at the center of which can be found the small worm of dissatisfaction that would eventually eat away at Allen's relationship with the audience. "I was not in a position to tell

the public, 'It's not my fault this is not what I would make as a picture,'" he said. "*Pussycat* was born to work. There was no way they could screw it up, try as they might they couldn't. It was one of those things where the chemicals accidentally flow right."

What's New Pussycat? gave Allen the break he needed, and in 1965 he availed himself liberally of the offers that came his way. In August he appeared in a *Playboy* feature titled "What's Nude, Pussycat?," a nebbish in a sea of strippers. Having released a self-titled comedy album the year before, he saw his follow-up, *Woody Allen Volume 2*, reach number five in the comedy charts. He was invited to the Lyndon Johnson White House, changing into his tuxedo in the bathroom at Washington National Airport. By far the strangest offer, however, came from a TV producer called Henry G. Saperstein who, inspired by Roger Corman's habit of redubbing and rereleasing foreign sci-fi films on the cheap, asked Allen to write new dialogue for a Japanese, Toho-produced Bond rip-off called *Kagi no Kagi* ("Key of Keys"), with a view to turning the spy saga into an hour-long comedy for television.

> "They made What's New Pussycat? into a film that I was very unhappy with. I didn't like it at all. And I vowed at that time that I would never write another film script unless I could be the director of the film."

Easy, tiger! Responding to the charms of Akiko Wakabayashi during the end credits of the "stupid and juvenile" *What's Up, Tiger Lily?* (1966). Allen would reprise the snarl nearly thirty years later in the final frame of *Manhattan Murder Mystery* (1993).

Renting a room at the Stanhope Hotel on Fifth Avenue, Allen filled it with half a dozen friends including Lenny Maxwell and Frank Buxton and ran the film several times with everyone kibitzing as they went. "If Woody liked it, he put it in," said Maxwell. Maybe you had to be there. The resulting film is conceptually brilliant, even ahead of its time, with Allen and his fellow dubbers paving the way for such couch-potato wiseacres as Beavis and Butthead, but it's let down in the execution—an act of lazy, and at times condescending, cinematic karaoke. In Allen's retelling the film's Bond-ish spy hero becomes "lovable rogue" Phil Moskowitz, hell-bent on beating his evil, mustache-wearing rivals to a recipe for the ultimate egg salad. "Name three presidents," whispers an Asian hottie in a towel. "Would you like to see my collection of off-color Italian hand gestures?" Like a lot of early Allen projects, the movie has sex on the brain, but the Japanese original was semi-parodic to begin with—the hero's hand creeping along the shoulder of every woman he meets—and the suspicion that some of the laughs were intended stops Allen's fun dead in its tracks. By the time Moscowitz confronts the evil mastermind Shepherd Wong, and promises to bring "joy and fulfillment in its most primitive form" to his playmates Suki and Teri Yaki, the single entendres have wilted, and the comedy gods taken their bow and left the building. "A sophomoric exercise," Allen was later to call it, "stupid and juvenile." Sensing some easy money, Saperstein added some songs from the Lovin' Spoonful, slapped on an extra twenty minutes culled from other Japanese B-movies, and released the results, now titled *What's Up, Tiger Lily?* to catch some of *What's New Pussycat?*'s success. Allen sued the studio to have it pulled from theaters, but once the film started attracting crowds, and even praise from critics, he dropped the lawsuit. Even he could see he would have a tough time convincing a court that he had been damaged by the film's success at the box office. He seemed doomed to meretricious success.

It was a slightly more jaded Allen who flew to London in the spring of 1966 to appear in another James Bond spoof, this time based on the one Ian Fleming novel not owned by the Broccolis, *Casino Royale*, and featuring Orson Welles, David Niven, William Holden, and Peter Sellers and produced by Charles Feldman. Any misgivings Allen had about making another film with Feldman and Sellers so soon after *Pussycat* were steamrollered by Joffe. "Just shut up and be in the movie," he was told. "You're trying to get into the film business. It's going to be a big picture and you'll be in it with a lot of stars so it will help get you launched."

What was supposed to be six weeks of work soon turned into six months, as the troubled production metastasized and spread across three soundstages, burned through the talents of twelve writers and six directors, with Sellers running sabotage as he had on *Pussycat*, holding everyone up while

"Just shut up and be in the movie." Manager Charles Joffe overrode Allen's reluctance to appear in the James Bond spoof *Casino Royale* (1967).

he went shopping for a new record stylus, or ordering forty-five suits from a fashionable tailor and charging them to the production. This time, Allen, who didn't start a day's work until he was already on overtime, sat back and enjoyed his per diem, which he used for marathon poker sessions with the cast of *The Dirty Dozen*, Lee Marvin, Charles Bronson, Telly Savalas, who were also staying at the Hilton while shooting their film. "*Casino* is a madhouse," he wrote his friend Richard O'Brien. "Saw rushes and am dubious to put it mildly, but probably film will coin a mint…my part changes every day as new stars fall in."

He never saw the finished film, in which he delivered his most surefooted comic performance to date as young Jimmy Bond, the nephew of James Bond (Niven). In the final reel, Jimmy is unmasked as the villain Dr. Noah, head of S.M.E.R.S.H. Dressed in a gray *Dr. No*–style Nehru tunic, performing balletic pirouettes, miming Debussy on the piano, Allen delivers a fluting, descant riff on the artistic pretensions of megalomaniacs that is the forerunner for Mike Myers's Dr. Evil in the *Austin Powers* movies, and Steve Carell's Gru in *Despicable Me*—"his best moments yet on film," said Kael, although the film is probably as significant for the work of Allen's it facilitated off screen as much as on. Holed up in his room at the Hilton, he finished a play, *Don't Drink the Water*, also his first draft of what would become *Bananas*, and had his first occasional piece published by the *New Yorker*, "The Gossage-Varbedian Papers," about an increasingly hostile exchange of letters between two intellectuals playing a game of chess by mail. "I could be happy doing nothing but writing for them," said Allen of the magazine, which over the next

decade would publish several dozen such pieces, including "The Whore of Mensa," about a call girl who specializes in pseudo-intellectual chit-chat for husbands whose wives won't talk about T. S. Eliot with them, and "The Kugelmass Episode," about a professor of humanities who slips into the pages of *Madame Bovary* to enjoy a passionate affair with the book's heroine, confounding scholars: "First a strange character named Kugelmass, and now she's gone from the book. Well, I guess the mark of a classic is that you can read it a thousand times and always find something new."

Allen's prose offers a fascinating peek into the boiler room of his imagination, an absurdist palace of Perelmanesque flourishes where high and low culture trade places and fantasy and reality overlap, overtake and shunt into the back of one another like railway carriages. It is easily the most consistent theme of his career. "It comes up very frequently in my films. I think what it boils down to, really, is that I hate reality," he once said. "And, you know, unfortunately, it's the only place where you can get a good steak dinner." It is only a short step from the meta-fictional adventuring of Kugelmass to the fourth-wall-breakage of *The Purple Rose of Cairo*, *Play It Again, Sam*, and *Annie Hall*, or to *Deconstructing Harry* and *Midnight in Paris*, all films straddling the gap between fantasy and reality—at times a gulf, at others, so membrane-thin that the slightest whisper will carry its own echo, summoning spirits, characters, whole plots from the ether. No other living director has proven quite so preoccupied with tracing, not his dream life, but his daydream life, as well as the Thurber-ish bump by which reality finally and inevitably intrudes. The heir of Thurber as much as Fellini, Allen is American cinema's great escapologist, the dolorous clerk of dashed hopes and stumbling dreams—Harry Houdini caught in his own zipper. As his directorial debut would prove.

Take the Money and Run

1969

A comedy about a compulsive but inept thief named Virgil Starkwell, *Take the Money and Run* drew in spirit if not to the letter on Allen's experience as a wannabe teenage grifter, hatching scams and schemes from his parents' stoop in Brooklyn. It was the first of two films he co-wrote with his old school friend Mickey Rose, who used to play on the same baseball team and who had helped out on *What's Up, Tiger Lily?* The two men took turns on the typewriter, going through the script joke by joke by joke. "Nothing was sacred," said Allen, "The [jokes] could be anachronistic, they could be surrealistic. It didn't matter. We didn't care about anything else except that each progression of the story, every inch of the way, was a laugh."

The film would mark his debut as director—by the skin of his teeth. Thinking it too early to launch Woody Allen as the new Orson Welles, Rollins and Joffe, now acting as producers for the first time, went to Val Guest, who had directed parts of *Casino Royale*, to see if he would take it on. They also tried Jerry Lewis, but Lewis was busy with his own work. It was only after they hooked up with a newly formed company, Palomar Pictures, the subsidiary of ABC that was backing Allen's hit 1969 play *Play It Again, Sam* on Broadway, that they secured the $1.7 million and assurance of creative control, including final cut, that would be the hallmarks of Allen's legendary autonomy.

"They never bothered me," he said. "It was a very pleasant experience. And from that day on I never had any problems in the cinema from the point of view of interference in any way."

"It never occurred to me for a second that I wouldn't know what to do. For the joke to be funny, the camera had to be here. It's common sense." He had lunch with the *Bonnie and Clyde* director, Arthur Penn, and gleaned some basic technical information about color correction, crowd control and the like. For his cast and crew he screened *Blow-Up* (1966), *Elvira Madigan* (1967), *I Am a Fugitive from a Chain Gang* (1932), and *The Eleanor Roosevelt Story* (1965) to give them some idea of what he was trying to achieve. Even so, the night before the first day of shooting, Louise Lasser walked into their bedroom to find Allen perched on the bed, cross-legged, reading a book entitled *How to Direct*. The next morning, he cut himself shaving.

Opposite: The usual suspect. As hapless criminal Virgil Starkwell.

Right: Finally given the opportunity to direct his own script, Allen thrived on both sides of the camera.

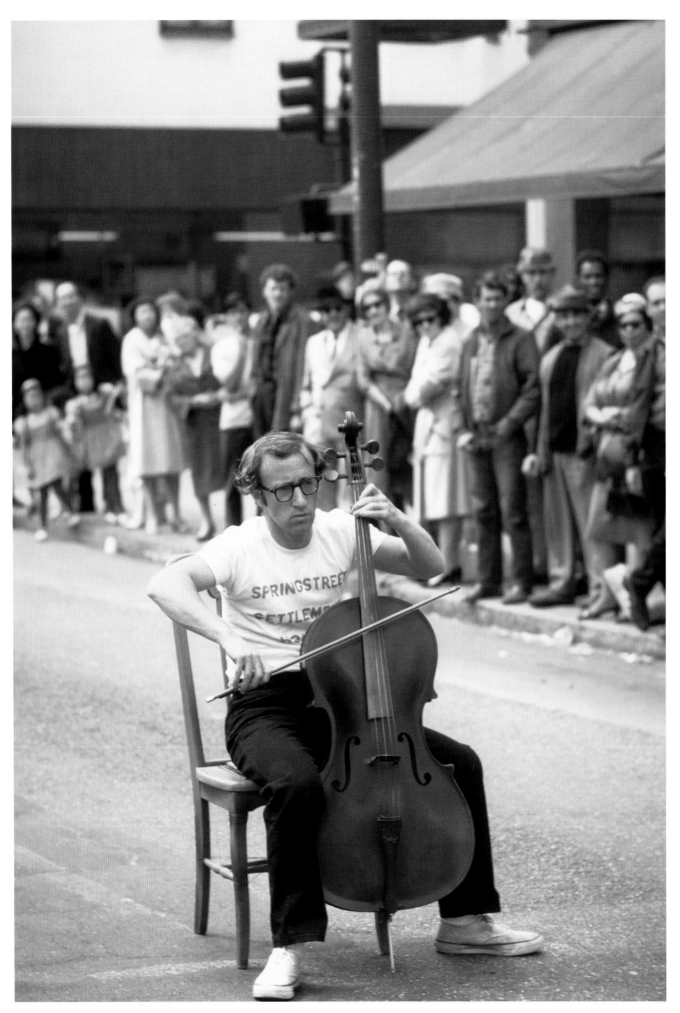

Left: Virgil's attempt to play cello in a marching band is one of many inspired visual gags in *Take the Money and Run*.

Opposite: A perplexing discovery in the prison laundry.

> "I got final cut, everything I wanted to do. It was a very pleasant experience. And from that day on, I never ever had any problems in the cinema from the point of view of interference in any way."

The film shot for ten weeks in the San Francisco area, chosen for its cheapness, and thus the only place where Allen felt confident of completing eighty-seven scenes within budget. Driving himself to work every morning in his brand new red convertible—a hair-raising sight "better than the movie," according to assistant director Fred Gallo—Allen shot a lot of footage as insurance, but even with improvisations he managed to get through as many as six setups a day, sometimes wrapping as early as four o'clock, with a break for lunch so that he could call his analyst from a phone booth. "It would be a hot sunny day and stifling in the phone booth and I'd be free-associating in a standing position," he recalled.

He finished a week ahead of schedule, and nearly a half million dollars under budget. It was while editing the picture that he hit a wall. Panicked by how unfunny everything seemed, he cut and cut and cut until he had virtually no film. He showed a rough cut—with no music, and crayon marks from the editing process—for a dozen soldiers hauled from a USO club into a screening room on Broadway. They sat stone-faced throughout. At the first screening for four Palomar executives, one turned around after the first reel and asked, "Are the rest of the reels like this?" After the final scene, a grotesque shootout in the style of *Bonnie and Clyde* that leaves Virgil riddled with bullets, Allen recalled they said, "'Is that really how you want to end the film?' They were very nice about it, they were being very polite, but they couldn't hide their disappointment. I knew they were talking about not releasing it."

Allen sought help from veteran editor Ralph Rosenblum, who had cut Mel Brooks's *The Producers*. A burly man with thick black-rimmed eyeglasses and a salt-and-pepper beard,

Rosenblum found Allen despondent. "Of course you're going to die if you show a rough cut with no music to twelve servicemen from Montana," he told him and asked to see all the material that had been cut out. A truck delivered two hundred boxes of film to his office; watching them, Rosenblum felt like a publisher stumbling across the lost notebooks of Robert Benchley. The material was "so original, so charming, so funny in absolutely unexpected ways that it made this period one of the most pleasurable in all my years in editing." While Allen was appearing in *Play It Again, Sam*, Rosenblum restored much of the footage the director had cut, extended or recut scenes, using the interview with Virgil's parents as bridge material, and ran a new temp score—a piece of Eubie Blake ragtime here, a bossa nova there—to liven up the film's maudlin patches, "the worst side of Chaplin," Allen would later agree. At Rosenblum's request he also shot a new ending for the film, recounting the events leading up to Virgil's arrest in a parody of TV journalism. "It was like opening the doors and letting in a fresh burst of air," said Allen. "I feel Ralph saved me on that picture."

Told in the form of a fake documentary, or "mockumentary" —a form enjoying a small vogue in the late sixties thanks to the Beatles' *A Hard Day's Night*, and to which Allen would return with *Zelig—Take the Money and Run* is a quickly flicked scrapbook of sketches, sight gags, fake cinéma vérité interviews, and old newsreel footage, all looped together with

Jackson Beck's *Dragnet*-style deadpan. "On December 1, 1935, Mrs. Virginia Starkwell, the wife of a New Jersey handyman, gives birth to her only child. They name it Virgil…" The birthday is Allen's own. In initial drafts the character's name was "Woody." What follows is a comic extrapolation and exaggeration of Allen's years as an aspirant teenage con artist, fooling his school friends with card tricks, fake dice, and betting scams—A Portrait of the Artist as a Young Sneak Thief.

Virgil fails at pretty much every job he turns his hand to, from shoeshine boy to cellist ("He really had no conception of how to play. He blew into it.") before turning to a life of crime. He robs his local pet shop, only to be chased away by a gorilla. He holds up a butcher's shop and "gets away with 116 veal cutlets," which means he then has to steal "a tremendous amount of breading." Finally he holds up a bank, but the teller cannot read his handwritten holdup note ("That looks like 'gub'…," "No it's *gun*…"). His career as a criminal is dogged, in other words, by the same ineptitude which drove him to a life of crime in the first place—a rubbery paradox that would also energize everything from Wes Anderson's *Bottle Rocket* to the Coen brothers' *Raising Arizona* and *Fargo*. So many directors, from Kubrick to Allen to Anderson, have kicked off their careers with heist movies that it is tempting to see the genre almost as an allegory for neophyte film directors. An act of creative daring, months in the planning, requiring meticulous execution, an illusion of normalcy, and an attention to the tiniest detail. And something always goes wrong.

For Allen, the attraction is the gulf between plan and execution, dream and reality, with the criminal as dreamer—a strain of Mitty-ish lyricism which lends the film, for all its string-of-gags skitter, the lift and buoyancy of a stone skimming across a lake. "I'm going to be late for the robbery," complains Virgil when he finds his wife (Janet Margolin) hogging the shower, in what is basically the film's main joke—that a criminal career is just like any other—and while some gags are better than others, the film as a whole subscribes to the double-decker-bus theory of comedy: If this joke misses, another will be along in a second. "I can't wear *beige* to a robbery," protests Virgil, thus marking the world debut of *that* particular color in the Allen oeuvre.

The Allen persona is remarkably well formed. We see him cowering in a fistfight; donning a rabbinical beard; making come-hither eyes at himself in a mirror; licking envelopes like a lizard; doing his lying-with-palpitations act—all the elements of the lily-livered, lustful schlemiel he would reprise and perfect in subsequent films. "This is a robbery, not a movie," Virgil tells one member of his gang, a Langian film director who wants everyone to practice their lines, but he directs as if there is no difference, pick-pocketing *Cool Hand Luke*, *I Am a Fugitive from a Chain Gang*, *Elvira Madigan*, and the gauzy soft-focus romanticism of Claude Lelouch's *A Man and a Woman* as he goes. "I do not want this film to be eclectic," Allen was overheard by Margolin telling an interviewer in San Francisco. "I don't want people to say I've borrowed a little bit from this director and a little bit from that director…" only for Margolin to interrupt, "But Wooood," she said. "That's *exactly* what you've been doing."

"The idea of doing a documentary, which I later perfected when I did Zelig, was with me from the first day I started movies. I thought that was an ideal format for doing comedy, because the documentary format was very serious, so you were immediately operating in an area where any little thing you did upset the seriousness and was thereby funny and you could tell the story laugh by laugh by laugh."

Interviewer: How did you come up with the idea?
WA: I was high from smoking Polish corn flakes. It suddenly came to me.
Interviewer: I see. How would you rate it as a film?
WA: It's better than Fellini's masterpiece "How Sweet My Finger" but not
as good as Bergman's Greek tragedy "Beyond Dandruff."

On August 18, the film opened at the Sixty-Eighth Street
Playhouse, a small art-house movie theater more used to
showing foreign films, where it ended up breaking all records
and winning a wider release. The critics were delighted.
Newsweek called the film "a silly symphony that can put the
zing back into life." In the *New York Times*, Vincent Canby
described it as "something very special and eccentric and
funny." Only Pauline Kael nit-picked, thinking she could
detect in Allen's failure to keep his wife a strain of masochism
that smacked of Chaplin's lonely-heart pathos. "We want
you to get the girl at the end," she told Allen after she had
seen the film. "We don't want you to fail. You have a different
conception of yourself."

Allen's self-conception was undergoing a revolution from
another direction, too, after he met the collaborator who,

perhaps more than any other, would reorder his comedy,
his career, the very shape of his films. Her impact would
be so great, in fact, that you can divide his career in two:
Before Keaton and After Keaton. He first met the twenty-
two-year-old actress when she auditioned for the role of
Linda in the Broadway run of *Play It Again, Sam*. Fiddling
with her hair, rubbing her nose, she was dressed in a football
jersey, with a skirt over combat boots and wore mittens—
"real hayseed, the kind that would chew eight sticks of gum
at a time," he said. "I wasn't attracted to her, but I wasn't
unattracted to her." Diane Keaton was instantly smitten by
the comedian—a household name by that point. "My game
plan was really to force Woody to like me," she said, "so I was
always plotting and scheming about how he could grow to see
me as an attractive woman."

One night during a break in rehearsals they went to dinner at Frankie and Johnnie's Steakhouse. It wasn't a date per se—Allen had a date the next night with another girl—but he had such a great time with Keaton he found himself thinking: *Why am I going out with this other girl tomorrow night? What am I doing? This girl is great. She's wonderful.* At one point Keaton caught her fork on plate, causing a scraping sound that made Allen yelp. "I couldn't figure out how to cut my steak without making the same mistake," Keaton wrote her mother afterward, "so I stopped eating and started talking about women's status in the arts, like I know anything about women and the arts. What an idiot."

Allen later wrote to reassure her:

"Humans are clean slates. There are no qualities indigenous to men or women. True there is a different biology, but all

defining choices in life affect both sexes & a woman, any woman, is capable of defining herself with total FREEDOM…"

A touch of Zelig, perhaps, in Allen's feminism, but the conversation that started that night, about men and women and art was one they would continue, over several decades, through the eight films they subsequently made together. After eight months in the editing room, it was to Keaton that he turned with his near-final cut of *Take the Money and Run*. "You know, this is good. It's funny. It's a funny film," she said. "I somehow knew at that moment, at that second, that it was going to be OK with the audience," Allen recalled. "Her imprimatur was very meaningful to me, because I felt she was in touch with something deeper than I was in touch with. So over the years we went out together. We lived together and we've remained friends to this day."

"If I didn't make movies, if I didn't work, then I'd sit at home and brood and think and my mind would drift to unsolvable issues that are very depressing."

The Woody Allen persona by now remarkably well formed. Portrait by Philippe Halsman, 1969.

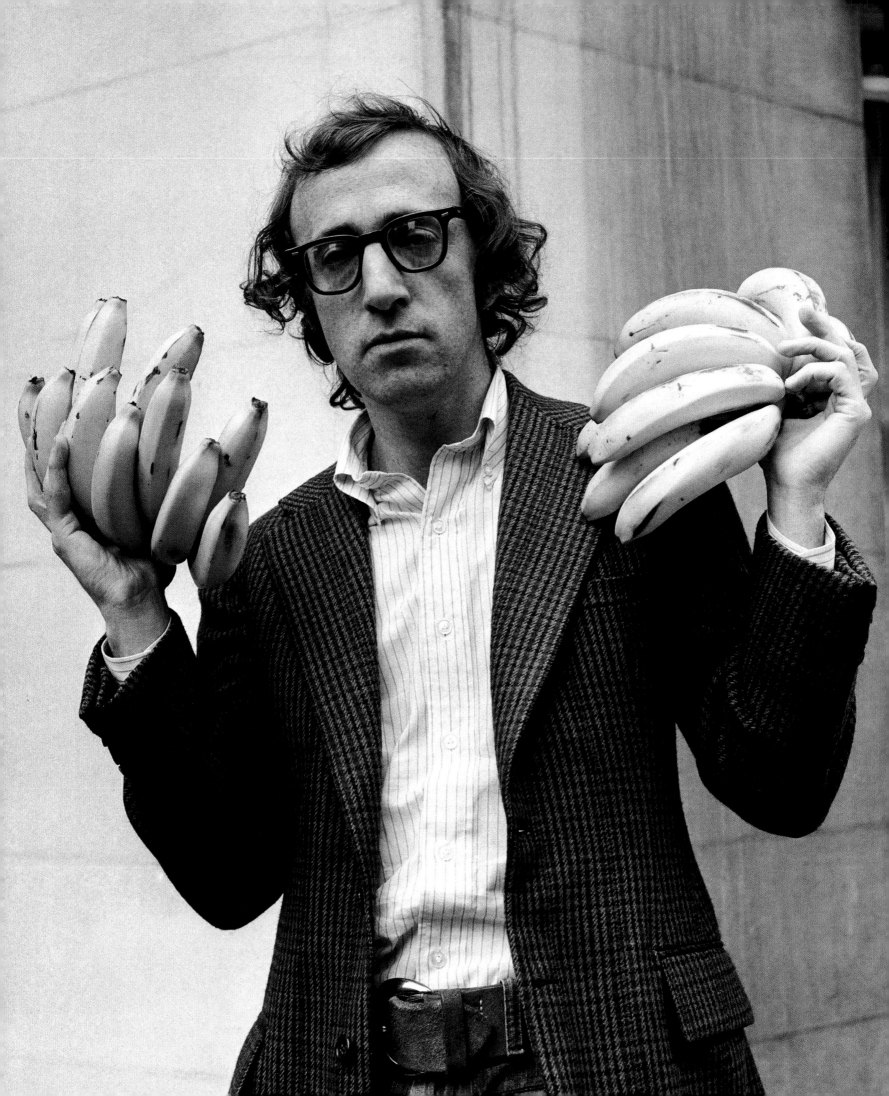

Bananas

1971

United Artists executives were so impressed by *Take the Money and Run* that they approached Charles Joffe to make a deal. "I want Woody to make pictures for my company," David Picker told him on behalf of UA's chairman, Arthur Krim. "What will it take?" The deal that Rollins and Joffe hammered out—for three pictures with a budget of $2 million, fees of $350,000 for Allen's writing, directing, and acting, and final cut, with no script approval for UA, no casting approval, nothing—was unprecedented. Although the seventies was the so-called era of the auteur, in which directors such as Martin Scorsese, Francis Ford Coppola, and Michael Cimino would fight for and sometimes win such prerogatives, only Allen would retain creative autonomy as a contractual right, in film after film. "From my first movie," he said, "when I certainly had done nothing to earn complete control—nothing—I had complete control and haven't done a movie in my life where I didn't have complete control."

The first thing he brought them was a script called *The Jazz Baby*, about a jazz guitarist in New Orleans in the twenties—an early, more downbeat version of *Sweet and Lowdown*. The executives at UA were "white-faced" reading it, said Allen, who cut them short. "If you guys don't want to do this, I won't do it. I'm not going to make you do a picture you don't like." He went back to his writing partner Mickey Rose, telling him, "We've got to write something. These guys definitely want a film from me."

"What about the South American dictator thing?" said Rose.

The "South American dictator thing" was something Allen had knocked out during those interminable days holed up in his London hotel room shooting *Casino Royale*. He'd been asked by B-movie impresario Sam Katzman to turn Richard Powell's *Don Quixote, USA*, a satirical novel about a naïve American Peace Corpsman adrift in a Caribbean dictatorship,

into a comedy for actor Robert Morse. The book was so boring he just dumped it and went with his usual freeform style: joke, joke, joke, joke, joke.

Morse hadn't liked it, and when Allen dug it out of his drawer it wasn't in great shape, but together with Rose he spent the next two weeks in his apartment reworking it. It became the story of Fielding Mellish, a frail, sly New York product tester who becomes embroiled in the revolution of San Marcos, a fictional South American dictatorship, in order to win the heart of a pretty idealist named Nancy and returns to the United States as the bearded Castro-like leader of the country. The script met with swift approval from UA for the production to begin shooting in Puerto Rico, with Louise Lasser in the role of Mellish's inamorata Nancy.

Allen and Lasser had divorced by the time they shot the movie, but in what was to become something of a habit, he got the best performance from his female lead after they had separated. "And of course I got her much cheaper," he was to joke on *The Dick Cavett Show*. "I went down fully prepared for *anything*," said Lasser, and while that might have included the improvisation and ad-libs Allen was keen, as ever, to do, it did not include Diane Keaton, ensconced in the director's hotel room with her own drawer. Since meeting on *Play It Again, Sam*, their relationship had followed its own fitful stop-start rhythm. "We went together, on and off, never sure, just on and off until it was time to go away and make *Bananas*," he said, although the shoot was no romantic idyll. Venturing out to San Juan's one movie theater, they found themselves having to zigzag from seat to seat to avoid a leaky roof. "It was boring being in Puerto Rico," complained Allen. "There wasn't anything to do. The food wasn't good. The weather was hot and humid. The movie house leaked and I found a dead mouse in my room."

Interviewer: Why did you name the movie *Bananas*? WA: Because there are no bananas in it.

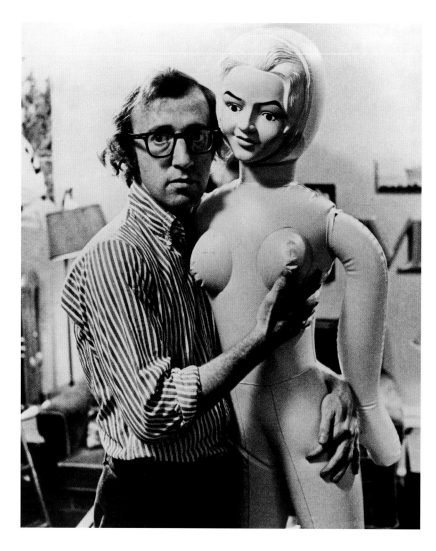

Left: In *Bananas*, Allen played Fielding Mellish, a frail, sly product tester.

Opposite: Mellish travels to the fictional South American republic of San Marcos and returns to the United States as the bearded, Castro-like leader of the country.

The shoot saw much improvisation, both intentional and enforced. A surprise attack on the rebels by government troops disguised as a rumba band doing the cha-cha-cha was drenched by a sudden downpour. When the instruments for the chamber quartet that was to play in the palace of the dictator failed to arrive, Allen quickly improvised the gag where the quartet sit empty-handed, playing thin air. Having learned from *Take the Money* how many of his sequences would fail to make the film, Allen packed *Bananas* "so full of jokes that another movie could have been made from its outtakes," said Ralph Rosenblum, who traveled to Puerto Rico in his new capacity as associate producer. "If he thought he needed 150 jokes in an hour and a half, he wrote and photographed 300."

When looking at Allen's early films it's tempting to see each through the prism of his influences. If *Take the Money and Run* was Allen at his most Chaplinesque, *Sleeper* would add Buster Keaton to the mix, while *Love and Death* would

see him perfect his Bob Hope impression. In which case, the provenance of *Bananas* is easy to spot. With its fictional tin-pot dictatorship of San Marcos, its cigars, its nonstop gags, and sense of anarchy—it's Allen's *Duck Soup*. Cornered by police, Mellish even performs a version of the rubber-limbed dance Groucho does in *A Day at the Races*, where his arms do the Egyptian while his legs turn into corkscrews. "I've often made this comparison but if you get someone like Picasso and he draws a little rabbit, a simple rabbit, and then the kids in class draw the same rabbit, there's just something in his line. He doesn't have to do anything fancy, no explosive idea. But it's just something in his line, the feeling in his line on the paper that's so beautiful."

By this measure, *Bananas* is a beautiful film. Not to look at. The lighting is possibly the worst of any of Allen's films—a cheap, single bulb turns Fielding Mellish's bachelor apartment into an unexpected exercise in neorealist grunge, while the

revolution takes place beneath washed-out skies the color of a dirty sock. Allen's direction is still over-fussy, with too many clever angles and tracking shots and a stab at Godardian montage-editing during the presidential assassination. But Allen's line as a writer—the line between setup and gag—has never been simpler or more straightforward, while his line as a performer—the physical line his body traces on screen—is a marvelous, omnidextrous ballet of bends, cringes, flinches, and ellipses.

Embellishing his nebbish persona with intellectual aspirations for the first time, Allen's comedy finds its upper register. "Have you read the *I Ching*?" asks the Philosophy major Nancy. "Not the actual *Ching* itself…" bluffs Mellish, a high-school dropout. His movie parodies have gone a notch or two up the brow: this time Bergman (for a dream sequence in which rival crucifixes duke it out for the same parking spot) and Eisenstein (during the storming of the

palace, a baby carriage is sent rolling down the steps). The script is also Allen's most overtly satirical, taking pointed jabs at American foreign policy and goggle-eyed TV culture, with Howard Cosell's coverage of "colorful riots" and promise of "videotape replay of beatings" a literal retort to the Black Panther slogan, later the title of a Gil Scott-Heron song, "The Revolution Will Not Be Televised."

Such topicality has held *Bananas* back from the classic status enjoyed by *Sleeper* and *Love and Death*, but in other ways the film marks a muscular move toward posterity. Few other comedians in 1971 were looking to Chaplin or the Marx Brothers as models, and even though Allen would consistently deprecate his skills of physical comedy they are quite remarkable; whether chasing a brick of frozen spinach around his floor like an ice-hockey puck, or cowering before Sylvester Stallone's thug in a subway car, Fielding Mellish seems a man born without a bone in his body. The business

"Bananas was still a film where I only cared about being funny ... I wanted to make sure that everything was funny and fast-paced. That was really what I was concentrating on. So if I shot or edited certain scenes almost cartoon-like, it was for that reason."

with Stallone is worked out to perfection, Mellish ejecting him from the carriage and, as the doors close, turning to the camera to bask in the gratitude of the other passengers, only for Stallone to prize the doors open behind him and descend on Mellish at his moment of greatest triumph. It's peerlessly executed, a gag dreamed up in the movie camera, relying as much on camera placement and framing as it does Allen's mercurial performance, and shows for the first time just how seamlessly he would eventually meld the roles of writer, actor, and director.

Another first: Heeding Kael's advice, Allen finally gets the girl. Originally the film was to have ended with Mellish being bombed while speaking at Columbia, emerging from the soot in black face, only to be mistaken for a brother by black revolutionaries. "Woody, the end doesn't work," said Rosenblum, in what was now becoming a familiar refrain. "Why not do something that relates to the beginning of the picture?" Allen sat and thought and the next morning he came in with a new ending, echoing the first scene in which Cosell narrates a presidential assassination, *Wide World of Sports* style ("Well, you've heard it with your own eyes"), except this time Cosell narrates Mellish's wedding night. "The two are working together," he says, "it is swift, rhythmic, coordinated …" Mellish's arm pops out from under the bedcovers, his fingers in a "V." "That's it!" announces Cosell, "It's over! It's all over! The marriage has been consummated!"

Play It Again, Sam

1972

Allen very much enjoyed performing onstage in *Play It Again, Sam* during its run at the Broadhurst Theatre on West Forty-Fourth Street in 1969. "There is no easier job than being in a play," he said. "I mean, you have the whole day off and you do

Right: Onstage during the 1969 Broadway run of Allen's original play. Photograph by Dennis Brack.

Opposite: "I was very happy that Herb Ross directed *Play It Again, Sam*. I didn't want to make it into a movie."

whatever you want. You can write, you can relax… You just drop over to the theater at eight o'clock at night." He used to stroll there from his apartment with Diane Keaton, wearing his everyday clothes, and walk straight onstage. He was so relaxed about his performance he frequently blew it, flubbing a line and then, catching the eye of one of his co-stars, Keaton or Tony Roberts, would collapse in stifled laughter. "If Woody blew a line he just went up," said Keaton, "He couldn't continue the scene. Tony and I could mess up a line and go on but not Woody. And then you started laughing. The discipline some nights was really bad." Allen's inability to improvise had an interesting cause, said Roberts. "We were pretending to be these people he's invented and he *was* one of them. So when the story didn't continue for a moment, it was existentially dumbfounding to him."

Written in Chicago in 1968 while Allen was playing at Mister Kelly's nightclub, as his marriage to Louise Lasser wound down, the play drew on his experience being introduced to girls by his married friends—"Oh, we know a nice girl for you…"—only to clam up around them, in a way he never did when he was with the wives of his friends. "I'd be natural around them and real, and they would find me much better company than the women I pressed to impress," he said. "And that's what gave me the idea: You're pressing with a stranger and you're totally at home with your friends because you don't give a damn." There was no thought of including Humphrey Bogart as a character at first, but while staying at the Astor Tower hotel he found himself typing the words, "Bogart appears…" Then he did it again. By the end Bogart had appeared six times—a major character.

Rollins and Joffe sold the film rights to Paramount, who initially wanted Dustin Hoffman, fresh from *The Graduate*, in the role of Allan Felix, the divorcé who can't relax around

The central character was Allan Felix, a movie fan who takes his romantic cues from an imaginary Humphrey Bogart (Jerry Lacy).

any girl except the wives of his friends; Richard Benjamin, who would later appear in *Deconstructing Harry*, was also suggested. "They didn't want me in it until *Bananas* started doing well," said Allen, who edged out of directing it because he was already at work on *Everything You Always Wanted to Know About Sex* (*But Were Afraid to Ask)*. With Herbert Ross, who had just done *Funny Lady*, brought in as director, Allen adapted the play in just ten days, opening it out to include some party and disco scenes and a few fantasies in which he imagines his ex-wife (Susan Anspach) exploring her sexuality with some Aryan bikers, and shifting the action from New York to San Francisco, after New York film workers went on strike in the summer of 1971. They started shooting that October.

Of all Allen's works, *Play It Again, Sam* is the one you could most easily imagine being directed by Nora Ephron, its movie-love-versus-the-real-thing conceit a clear precursor for *Sleepless in Seattle*. It opens with a shot from *Casablanca* reflected in Allen's glasses, his mouth slowly dropping as he drinks in Bogie's noble goodbye to Ingrid Bergman. The lights come up, Allen gives a little look to either side of him as if to say, where'd they go? and gives a little puff of disappointment—a lovely touch of naturalism in a performance that is more rooted in character than anything he had done to this point, while also recapping his skills as a physical comedian. Watch out for his entanglement with a hairdryer, and the moment when, trying to impress a date set up for him by his friends Dick (Roberts) and Linda (Keaton),

Allan interrupts his stream of misjudged conversational entrees ("I love the rain") to oh-so-casually send an LP frisbee-ing one way across the room, its cover another—an unimprovable piece of bachelor-pad slapstick.

On dates, Allan's face snarls up in a nervous rictus as he grinds through cheesy seduction routines. Only autopsying the dates with Linda afterward does he relax into himself. It's interesting how the shyness of the Woody Allen persona shades imperceptibly into a setup for, and justification of, adultery—the script is a doctoral thesis in romantic Machiavellianism. Bonding over pharmaceuticals ("Apple juice and Darvon is fantastic together!" "Have you ever had Librium and tomato juice?"), Allan and Linda are two pills from the same prescription, although Allen hasn't quite figured out how to make the plot work from any perspective other than his character's. He catches Allan's adolescent delusion perfectly ("Who am I kidding, I was dynamite in the sack last night"), but he can't write women yet. Keaton is doe-eyed and passive, merely a dupe during the scene in which Allan takes his romantic cues from Bogart ("Tell her she has the most irresistible eyes you've ever seen"), a device uniting him and the audience but leaving Keaton out in the cold ("She *bought* it!"). It's the only role she plays in a Woody Allen project that wasn't written for her specifically, and it shows. He had yet to tune in to Keaton's particular cadence—that sing-song mixture of the dizzy and the caustic that he would capture so well in *Annie Hall.* "The chemistry between Diane and me developed over time," said Allen. "It was something that happened offstage as well as on. In fact, our relationship offstage became the chemistry that translated for us accurately into movies… I got to look at things through her eyes very frequently and it really upgraded and broadened my perception. She was a major influence on me."

Above: "She *bought* it!" Having acted opposite each other on Broadway, Allen and Diane Keaton now appeared on screen together for the first time.

Left: The true start of a beautiful friendship, an homage to the last scene of *Casablanca*.

"I rarely think in terms of male characters, except for myself only. I have a tremendous attraction to movies or plays or books that explore the psyches of women, particularly intelligent ones."

Allan: You were fantastic last night in bed.
Linda: Oh, thanks.
Allan: How do you feel now?
Linda: I think the Pepto Bismol helped.

Everything You Always Wanted to Know About Sex* (*But Were Afraid to Ask)

1972

Allen underestimated the itchiness of his spider costume and the fragility of a fifteen-foot fabric breast.

One night, after coming home to his apartment from a Knicks game with Diane Keaton, Allen happened to catch *The Tonight Show* on TV, featuring an interview with Dr. David Reuben about his best seller *Everything You Always Wanted to Know About Sex (But Were Afraid to Ask)*, which had sold over 100 million copies worldwide. "Is sex dirty?" Johnny Carson asked, to which the doctor replied, "It is if you're doing it right." First

Allen thought: That was his line, from *Take the Money and Run*. Then he thought: Wouldn't it be funny to do a series of sex sketches based on the book? "I thought I was going to have a million comic ideas on sex," he said later, "but it wasn't as fertile a notion as I imagined, and I had about six."

Working with cinematographer David M. Walsh, who initially didn't want the job after viewing the drabness of Allen's previous efforts, and set designer Dale Hennesy, who had previously worked on *Fantastic Voyage* (1966), Allen faced sizable logistical problems while shooting. An Old Testament spoof about masturbation was scripted but not filmed, because the budget would not stretch to a passable re-creation of the period. The marauding fifteen-foot-tall breast was built of fabric so thin it ripped when the wind picked up. Another sequence, "What makes men homosexuals?," featuring Louise Lasser as a black widow and Allen, in a reddish-brown spider suit, as her soon-to-be ex, was "one of the most hateful experiences of my life and hers," he recalled. "I couldn't sit up without itching, my costume was terribly uncomfortable, she hated her costume, we fought all the time. Sitting on that steel cable web hurt. Still, you think you'd be able to get a few-minutes sequence out of that. We shot more than a hundred thousand feet of film over two weeks of filming, two or three cameras, all for six-and-a-half minutes. I had a great subliminal joke to back up the whole sequence with music from *The Nutcracker Suite*—but it wouldn't work."

Throughout the shoot Allen remained dour. "It was like walking on a Bergman set," said Gene Wilder, cast in the segment about a doctor who falls in love with a sheep. "The way Woody makes a movie it's as if he's lighting ten thousand safety matches to illuminate a city." He tinkered with the film right up to its final release, switching the order of the segments, before finally deciding to cut the spider sketch

The first two sketches in the film revolve around an Elizabethan court jester who uses an aphrodisiac to seduce the queen, and a love triangle between a doctor (Gene Wilder), his patient, and a sheep.

in favor of the Lou Jacobi sequence in which Jacobi plays a transvestite. He cut the deadline so fine they had to run the wet print through the projector twice to dry it out.

As cynically conceived as any studio cash in, *Everything You Always Wanted to Know About Sex* (*But Were Afraid to Ask)* was a massive hit, taking $18 million at the box office, enough to make it the second biggest comedy of 1972 after *What's Up, Doc?* with Barbra Streisand. But so what? By that measure Allen's career has never recovered from the mighty peak

represented by *What's New Pussycat?* and *Casino Royale* (his two biggest hits, adjusted for inflation). As Allen realized, sex was not nearly as productive a source for his comedy as he had thought—his great subject is sexual anxiety—and too many of the sketches here feel like the tail end of the *Run for Your Wife* era, with leering jokes about homosexuality, cross-dressers, and kinky lingerie that seem to cry out for a nudge and a wink from some Borscht Belt comedian. Nothing dates so fast as another era's smut.

The first sketch—"Do Aphrodisiacs Work?"—about an Elizabethan court jester (Allen) who uses an aphrodisiac to seduce the queen, is mainly an opportunity for some Perelmanesque fun with linguistic anachronism ("With most grievous dispatch I shall open the latch to get at her snatch!"). The second—"What Is Sodomy?"—concerns a doctor (Wilder) who sees a patient who has fallen in love with his sheep, only to fall in love with her himself. Wilder is terrific, insinuating and deadpan, going through the full gamut of emotions—tender, bashful, fond ("I'll never forget these afternoons, Daisy"), sly, angry, hurt, abandoned—without once betraying any sign that the material is comic.

The third sketch, "Why Do Some Women Have Trouble Reaching Orgasm?," featuring Allen as a Felliniesque Italian sophisticate—shades, comb-over, cigarillo—whose lover (Lasser) can reach orgasm only in public places, is notable chiefly for the pastiche of Michelangelo Antonioni's minimalist *mise-en-scène*, but Allen speaking Italian, minus his yo-yoing Brooklyn intonations, turns out to be only half as much fun. "Are Transvestites Homosexuals?," the fourth sketch, about a middle-aged married man (Jacobi) who excuses himself during a dinner party to dress in women's clothes, is possibly the film's weakest segment: so overexcited by the comic possibilities of transvestitism ("She's my husband!") that,

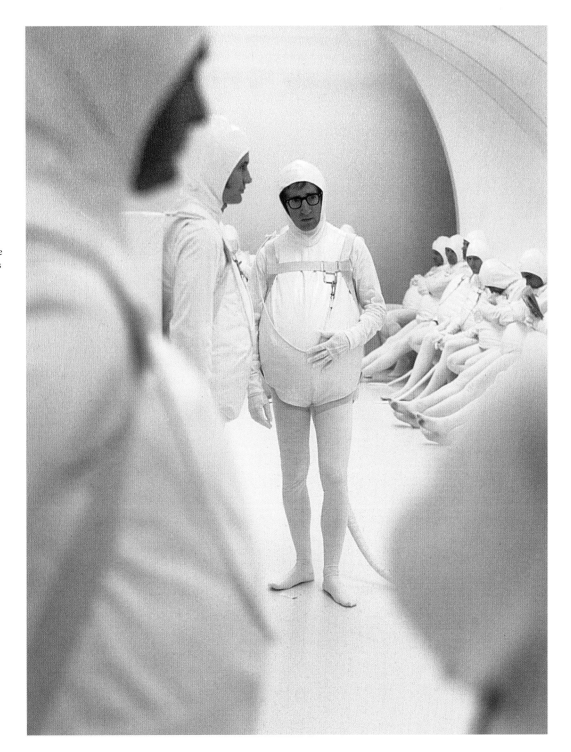

As a sperm cell preparing for the great unknown in the final sketch, "What Happens During Ejaculation?"

in terms of dramatic development, it exhausts itself with a single puff. The humor is Allen at his most conservative, without his self-deprecating nebbish persona to take the edge off what now seems stodgily illiberal.

Things pick up for the fifth sketch—"What Are Sex Perverts?"—a TV game-show parody in which four panelists, Regis Philbin, Toni Holt, Robert Q. Lewis, and Pamela Mason, attempt to guess a contestant's perversion ("Likes to expose himself on subways"). The sixth segment, "Are the Findings of Doctors and Clinics Who Do Sexual Research and Experiments Accurate?," climaxes with the famous chase of Allen by a giant runaway breast—a parody of *The Blob* by

way of Philip Roth—and the seventh, "What Happens During Ejaculation?," is a deserved classic, in which a dinner date is observed by a NASA-like control center situated within the man's body ("Fettuccine Alfredo processing nicely"). It ends with the couple having sex in a car ("Erection angle forty degrees and climbing") and a queue of sperm, one of them played by an extremely nervous Allen, preparing for what lies ahead. "What if he's masturbating?" worries Allen. "I'm liable to end up on a ceiling somewhere." The white sets and costumes, the game played with scale, the mind–body polarity, the hilariousness of Allen wearing any kind of skullcap or helmet: All point the way of *Sleeper*.

Sleeper

1973

"I don't know what the hell I'm doing here. I'm 237 years old, I should be collecting Social Security." Having been cryogenically preserved after a botched operation, health-food-store owner Miles Monroe is revived 200 years in the future.

The release of *Sleeper* found Allen in an unusually bullish mood. "*Sleeper* is a picture every kid in America could see and find funny," he said. "It's exactly the kind of picture that I used to see as a kid and love. I don't want to be confined to intellectual humor, especially since I have zero intellectual credentials. Chaplin had some very hip jokes in his stuff. I'm tired of being thought of as special for that Third Avenue crowd."

The initial idea was even more ambitious: a three-hour movie, divided in two. In the first half we would meet Miles Monroe, owner of the Happy Carrot health-food store on Bleecker Street in New York, who goes in for a routine operation on a peptic ulcer, only to fall into a vat of cryogenic nitrogen. Then there would be an intermission and when the audience came back it would be two hundred years in the future. Allen got forty pages into it, then ground to a halt. "Do I really want to write a film just so I can fall in a vat of freezing juice?" he asked. "I figured, let's just do the second half, let's just do the future, when the guy wakes up."

He mentioned the idea to Marshall Brickman, a TV writer whom he had seen playing banjo at the Bitter End back in Allen's stand-up days. Brickman's great strength was narrative—getting from A to B to C. They'd sit in Allen's living room and talk for an hour, an hour and a half, then one of them would say, "Come on, let's go for a walk," and they'd take a walk around and get some fresh air all the time pitching ideas. Allen wanted all the people in the future to be forbidden to talk, making the film a kind of silent movie manqué. He also wanted to shoot much of the film in Brasilia, Brazil's futuristic capital city complex. In the end, he had to settle for Denver, the Mojave Desert, and the old Pathé Selznick lot in Culver City, where Allen holed up in Clark Gable's dressing room, a pretty three-room cottage surrounded by a lawn, a garden full of daisies, and a tall white picket fence. Allen's

"We're all at the mercy of the dailies. I'll watch them and I'll think, None of those walks looks funny, and I'll reshoot them and when I go to edit the film and I cut in those walks, the two worst ones in dailies will get the biggest laughs. That's why film comedies are so hard."

clarinet would sound from the window every day before shooting started at 8.30 a.m.

"Films made for two million are a pain in the ass, and I have to be away from New York," he complained. "Everything in LA is automobiles and has to be done fast—twelve weeks." United Artists wanted the film in time for a Christmas release, with serious financial penalties built in if it went over budget or over schedule. Allen started shooting on April 30 and by August he had already foregone his $350,000 personal fee and was fifty-one days behind schedule. The robots, the mechanized props, the stunt shots all took their toll. An inflatable space suit refused to inflate. A twelve-foot banana looked fake. The wires and tow ropes repeatedly flew into frame. "This is a movie about wires," groaned Allen. "This was still in the getting-to-know-how-to-work-with-me period for United Artists. They sent some people out to Colorado and I showed them some dailies and, as usual, they were nice as can be. They said, 'Leave him alone, he's doing fine.'"

Among the UA contingent was Ralph Rosenblum, whom the studio had asked to begin cutting, seven days a week, as Allen shot. "I sensed the tremendous stress he was under the moment he greeted me on set, and I could see that despite his

efforts he was beginning to show signs of impatience with the production team." By the time Allen and Rosenblum returned to New York in September they had assembled a substantial portion of the film, and by the end of the month the two men, each working with an assistant, editing separate segments and then conferring over the results, had assembled a rough cut running to two hours and twenty minutes. A dream sequence, set in the Mojave, in which Allen is sacrificed as a pawn in a giant chess game—"one of the finest pieces of cinema Allen has ever created," in Rosenblum's eyes—hit the cutting-room floor, as did the original ending, a visual gag which Rosenblum found "corny." One Sunday Allen returned to California with Diane Keaton, by then shooting *The Godfather Part II*, to film a new ending.

"It was only through a whirlwind of overlapping labor that we made the Christmas release," said Rosenblum. The final edit, condensing thirty-five hours of film footage into ninety minutes, was completed just two days before the movie opened.

"*Sleeper* was Woody's first real film," said Rosenblum, meaning that it had more moving parts—more sets, more costumes, more special effects—than any Woody Allen film up until

that point. "To have found a clean visual style for a modern slapstick comedy in color is a major victory," wrote Pauline Kael, although praise came with a sting in the tail:

"*Sleeper* holds together as his sharpest earlier films failed to do; it doesn't spurt and blow fuses like *Bananas* or *Sex*. It's charming—a very even work, with almost no thudding bad lines. But it doesn't have the loose manic highs of those other films. You come out smiling and perfectly happy but not driven crazy … Allen has often been quoted as saying that he wants to stay rough in his movie technique; I used to enjoy reading these quotes because I thought he was right and in *Bananas* his instinct to let the jokes run shapelessly instead of trimming them and asking them to be tidy paid off. The effect was berserk in an original way."

It would be a criticism Allen would hear a lot in the coming years as his films gained in technical proficiency and came on in production value. "Just too beautiful," Stanley Kauffmann would say of *Love and Death*. "The picture was shot in France and Hungary, and some of it is gorgeous. None of it should be." Certainly, until Woody Allen came along, the idea of a good-looking comedy was nearly anathema to the mainstream of Hollywood. Nobody remembers the Marx

Brothers' films for their cinematography. Critics admired Buster Keaton's direction but Chaplin was no maestro. Preston Sturges pulled off elegant tracking shots but, as Allen himself noted, "Mostly the good-looking stuff is stuff without laughs in it." His directorial ambitions would push him into uncharted territory, as he sought out collaborations with *Godfather* cinematographer, Gordon Willis, to make *Annie Hall*, *Manhattan*, and *Stardust Memories*; Bergman's cinematographer Sven Nykvist to make *Crimes and Misdemeanors* and *Celebrity*; and Antonioni's cinematographer Carlo Di Palma to make *Hannah and Her Sisters*, *Radio Days*, *Alice*, and *Manhattan Murder Mystery*—comedies that nonetheless worked as fully formed pieces of cinema, good-looking stuff with laughs in it.

It began, though, with *Sleeper*, where the future populace has devolved into stoned, hippie swingers, pleasuring themselves in smooth, white, ovoid Charles Deaton–designed houses that just cry out for Allen's shrimpy frame to go "splat" against the side of them—windscreens waiting for a bug. The future turns out to be an even better environment for Allen's comedy than the jungle. The rural future, of course: It says something about how rabidly inhospitable an environment

> "I wanted to make a kind of slapstick-style movie, a visual movie in that sense. Mostly I found it very easy."

this is for Allen that this future is one without cities. For the first forty-five minutes or so, the film hits the same manic high of his earlier work. We get a succession of Woody-versus-gadget gags (the space buggy, the jet-pack) followed by a series of Woody-*as*-gadget gags, with Allen disguised as a mute robot, at which point his plundering of silent-movie classics goes into overdrive. He sways around on an unanchored ladder like Harold Lloyd in *Safety Last!*, is chased around, Keystone Cops style, to Allen's own clarinet accompaniment, cowers in a robot-repair shop like Chaplin's boxer in *City Lights*. So far, *plus ça change*. Then Diane Keaton shows up.

It's her first appearance in a film directed by Woody Allen and it's quite a sight. Her face caked in a green mud pack,

cigarette holder cocked, reciting her terrible poetry about caterpillars, Keaton (Luna Schlosser) finds a music in this woman's jangle of nerves that tunes right into Allen's own. Going on the run together, they play their neuroses like two violinists, and for the first time in a Woody Allen movie, his scenes with someone else are better than his scenes on his own, or playing off a foil. Miles teases Luna ("I'm always joking, you know me, it's a defense mechanism."). She confesses to intellectual insecurity ("Do you think I'm stupid?"). Miles then seeks to reassure her ("How can you say that?"), assuaging the anxiety he helped induce. And so to their first kiss, on the stairs of Deaton's egg building, while Allen is fixing up an old clarinet, the first genuinely romantic,

Miles disguises himself as a robot and teams up with Luna Schlosser as played by Diane Keaton in her first role in a Woody Allen–directed movie.

as opposed to sexual-humorous, scene in one of his movies—a significant Rubicon.

Their romance proceeds by a strangely familiar route. First Miles rescues Luna from bourgeois conformity; then after he is captured by the government, she rescues him, now sporting revolutionary khaki and spouting Marxist slogans, much to Miles's dismay ("She's read a few books and suddenly she's an intellectual"). It's the earliest outing, in other words, for the awakened-woman plotline he would later perfect in *Annie Hall*—Pygmalion by way of Erica Jong—in which the male lover-tutor is eventually surpassed and left by his girlfriend-protégée. Allen's films would come back to this theme, again and again, as if fretting over a fatal

flaw, but this is the only time it ends happily, with Miles and Luna hightailing it in their buggy. They are both wearing white surgeon's smocks and hats, against a white backdrop, so it's almost just their faces, hanging there in the frame: two passive-aggressives in love.

"I think you really love me," says Luna.

"Of course I love you," says Miles. "That's what this is all about."

He would use a version of the same line in *Manhattan*, but for the first time in his work it seems entirely true. Allen had met his match, someone whose comic instincts, timing, and gift for mockery were the equal of his own. He would have to learn how to share the screen.

"Sleeper showed me audiences
enjoyed watching me, which
I find hard to believe."

One of the numerous scenes
that failed to make the final
cut of the movie, although
the chicken has a walk-on
role elsewhere.

Love and Death

1975

After completing *Sleeper*, Allen sent United Artists executive Eric Pleskow a note saying that he was almost finished with his next script: a New York murder mystery about a couple, Alvy Singer and Annie Hall, who meet outside a movie theater, argue, and then go back to their apartment building, where a college professor named Dr. Levy has been found dead of an apparent suicide. Alvy, who is familiar with the professor's work and knows suicide to be philosophically repugnant to the great man, sets out to prove that it was in fact murder. "I liked the first half but not the second," said Allen of the screenplay, whose lack of laughs scared him. Pacing his apartment, he glanced up and saw a book on Russian history on his bookshelf and thought: Hey, why not do Love and Death, his two favorite themes?

The idea was basically Tolstoy's *War and Peace* as rewritten by S. J. Perelman, with duels and philosophical debates and village idiots and grand opera, all turned upside down. It flew out of his typewriter. Two weeks after telling Pleskow to expect his Manhattan murder mystery, Pleskow received instead the first draft of a comedy about the Napoleonic Wars in czarist Russia that touched lightly on the meaninglessness of existence.

"What happened?" asked Pleskow.

"I tore it up," said Allen.

In fact he had put the idea back in the drawer, where it would eventually cleave in two, to become *Annie Hall* and *Manhattan Murder Mystery*. Dr. Levy, meanwhile, would migrate over to *Crimes and Misdemeanors* as Louis Levy, the philosophy professor who commits suicide halfway through Allen's character's documentary about him and his work. Such is the strange, timeless economy with which Allen's imagination seems to work, setting aside ideas only to dust them off for use decades later. The executives at United Artists didn't know this, however, and Allen had some explaining to do, at a boardroom meeting he later lampooned for the readers of *Esquire* magazine:

"I found myself in the offices of United Artists' biggest dealmakers, explaining that I had written a comedy about

Opposite: Allen's Perelmanesque pastiche of *War and Peace* flew out of his typewriter.

Right: But harsh weather and communication problems on location in Hungary slowed him down. It would be twenty years before he shot another film outside the United States.

Boris Grushenko overreaches himself during a family celebration.

man's alienation in a world of meaningless existence. They had been led to believe—owing to certain memos I had sent—that I was working on a bedroom farce based on the mistaken identity of two au pair girls and some hens."

The UA execs didn't expect much from the picture, but green-lit it because of Allen's track record: *Sleeper* had just pulled in over $18 million—his biggest hit to date. Hiring Belgian cameraman Ghislain Cloquet, who had worked with such luminaries of the European art house as Louis Malle, Robert Bresson, and Jacques Demy, Allen shot in Paris and Hungary, the latter for the battle sequences featuring hundreds of extras, and special-effects men flown over from London. In ebullient mood he wrote to Diane Keaton from Paris in preparation for her imminent arrival:

"We have enough rehearsal time but not as much as in LA. Still I think *Love and Death* will be easier than *Sleeper* as there are not a lot of falls and spills and water stunts. Our dialogue exchanges should be brisk and lively, but we'll get into that."

Hungary was another matter. By the time Keaton had arrived, Budapest was suffering its coldest weather in twenty-five years—so cold Allen couldn't feel his fingers to play the clarinet. Returning from a day's shooting he used to plunge into the shower, just to warm up. Worried about the food quality, he consumed only canned food and bottled water shipped over from America, and was therefore one of the few among his cast and crew not afflicted with dysentery.

"When good weather was needed, it rained," he wrote. "When rain was needed, it was sunny. The cameraman was Belgian, his crew French. The underlings were Hungarian, the extras were Russian. I speak only English—and not really that well. Each shot was chaos. By the time my directions were translated, what should have been a battle scene ended up as a dance marathon." Returning to New York he swore he would never shoot outside the United States ever again, a promise he kept until *Mighty Aphrodite* in 1995.

It was Ralph Rosenblum who suggested Prokofiev for the score, rather than the Stravinsky proposed by Allen.

Forced to enlist in the Russian army when Napoleon invades, the cowardly Boris is as incompetent a soldier as he is a dancer.

Listening to it in the cutting room, Rosenblum found Stravinsky "too overpowering for the film. He was like a tidal wave, drowning every part of the picture he came into contact with." He played Allen Prokofiev's *Scythian Suite*, *Lieutenant Kijé*, and *Alexander Nevsky* from Eisenstein's film. The jauntiness of the Prokofiev much better suited the tone of the finished film. Allen and Marshall Brickman were downtown having pizza the day it opened. "Come on, I'll go with you to get the reviews," suggested Brickman (this was when Allen still read reviews), and they opened the *New York Times* to Vincent Canby's rave: "Woody's *War and Peace* … as personal a film as any American star-writer-director has made since the days of Keaton, Chaplin, and Jerry Lewis." In the *New Yorker* Penelope Gilliatt called it his "most shapely" film, while in *New York* magazine Judith Crist noted Woody was "going for the character rather than the cartoon" and applauded his acting as "perfection." For once Allen seemed exultant and suggested to UA they run an ad featuring just wall-to-wall praise, bleeding off the page, with no border.

Love and Death took $20 million away from Steven Spielberg's *Jaws*, which in the summer of 1975 was busy eating up the record books. How many parodies of epic Russian literature have *you* seen recently that took a bite out of a blockbuster, and not just any blockbuster but the granddaddy of the form? Critics talk dismissively of the "lowest common denominator," as if what we have in common is, de facto, what is also lowest, but *Love and Death* proves them wrong, pulling off the seemingly impossible task of being both one of Allen's most arcane movies—filled with references to Tolstoy and Gogol and Chekhov—and yet, at the same time, one of his most accessible. It's multi-brow. Just to list the subjects parodied— from Charlie Chaplin to Robert Altman's *McCabe & Mrs. Miller*, *The Brothers Karamazov* to *The Battleship Potemkin*, Vladimir Nabokov to the Marx Brothers, Ingmar Bergman to Bob Hope—is to join one of the most thrillingly eclectic cocktail parties ever thrown inside one man's head.

And it is unreservedly the head at which the movie is aimed. "In *Sleeper*, most of Allen's jokes are about bodies,"

notes Maurice Yacowar in *Loser Takes All: The Comic Art of Woody Allen*. "In *Love and Death*, he kids the mind." From its opening shots of passing clouds, to its spontaneous bursts of *extempore* moral philosophy, which the characters launch into the same way they used to launch into song in Hollywood musicals ("I definitely think this is the best of all possible worlds." "It's certainly the most expensive."), the film finds Allen's humor playing off its most vaulted upper register. The army training scenes are a retooled and slightly better version of the same scenes in *Bananas*, while Allen's performance as the "militant coward" Boris, scurrying from the bayonets and cannon fire of the Napoleonic Wars, or panting dog-like at a frisky countess at the opera, is Allen's most direct steal from

Bob Hope. "Oh no, I can't do anything to the death," he protests upon being challenged to a duel. "Doctor's orders."

A marked man, Boris finally finagles a promise of marriage from his Cousin Sonja (Keaton), with whom he has been unrequitedly in love since childhood. Glassy-eyed, selfish, beautiful, cunning, Keaton is in *Love and Death* no longer the dupe she was in *Play It Again, Sam*, but Allen's comic equal, her powers of deadpan, parody, and timing every bit as sharp as his. This time they *both* get soliloquies to camera, simultaneously, Sonja arguing the pros and cons of marrying Boris, while he rhapsodizes about the wheat harvests he will miss ("Fields of rippling wheat, lots of wheat, a tremendous amount of wheat…"). Their mirrored soliloquies are a potent

"I had, of course, always loved the Russian classics, and I was trying to do a film with philosophical content, if you can believe it. And I learned that it's hard to do a film with philosophical content if you're too broad. It's just like people can't see the structure of a film in a broad film, they also don't take seriously anything that you might be wanting to say in a comedy."

image for what was going on: Allen's method of making movies had effectively cracked in two. Films oriented centrifugally around the persona of one man, a single comic sun, around whom every other planet orbits, had now made room for another, equal presence, whose thoughts and reactions were every bit as important as his and who was busy firing back. Allen had burst his own bubble. Hope had found his Crosby.

Fast-talking their way into Napoleon's palace as a couple of phony Spaniards, reprising and perfecting their fraudster double act from *Sleeper*—completing one another's sentences, tumbling into one another's silences—they seem almost synaptically connected. "What's it like being dead?" Sonja asks Boris after he is executed. "You know the chicken at Tretsky's restaurant? It's worse." Food features heavily in the film, from the inedible dinners Sonja serves Boris ("Oh, sleet!

My favorite!") to Napoleon's determination to develop Beef Napoleon before Wellington invents Beef Wellington, to the French pastries served in Boris's prison cell after his failed assassination attempt. "Gastronomy plays a double role both as a deflator of philosophic pretensions and a conveyor of ultimate questions," as Ronald LeBlanc puts it in his marvelous essay "Love and Death and Food: Woody Allen's Comic Use of Gastronomy." It also prefigured Allen's next film, whose protagonist famously compares relationships to the imaginary eggs laid by someone who thinks himself a chicken ("We keep going through it because we need the eggs…"). Allen wrote to Keaton to prepare her for the script that was coming her way:

"I have decided to let your family make me rich! It turns out they are wonderful material for a film. A quite serious one, although one of the three sisters is a fool and a clown."

"I don't believe in the afterlife, although I am bringing a change of underwear."

Annie Hall

1977

Annie Hall was a breech delivery. The most loved of all Allen's films is also the one which least resembles his initial conception for it, as first devised with Marshall Brickman as they walked up and down Lexington and Madison Avenues in late 1975. "Woody wanted to take a risk and do something different," said Brickman. "The first draft was the story of a guy who lived in New York and was forty years old and was examining his life. This life consisted of several strands. One was a relationship with a young woman, another was a concern for the banality of the life that we all live, and a third an obsession with proving himself and testing himself to see what kind of character he had."

Titled *Anhedonia*, the film was a stream-of-consciousness piece, with lots of narration sealing Alvy off from the events in his life, like a man in a bubble, and it began with a long monologue, delivered to camera, followed by flashbacks to Alvy's Coney Island childhood, his Cousin Doris, a dream about being interrogated by the Nazis, a fantasy sequence involving the Maharishi, Shelley Duvall, and the Garden of Eden, and another set at Madison Square Garden in which the New York Knicks compete against a team of the great philosophers. "It was a picture about me," said Allen. "The thing was supposed to take place in my mind. Something would happen that would remind me of a quick childhood flash, and that would remind me of a surrealistic image … none of that worked."

What *did* work was the love affair. Allen would feign weariness with those seeking an autobiographical interpretation of the film as the story of him and Diane Keaton—"I didn't meet her that way," he insisted, "We didn't part that way"—but as was his habit, his love affair with Keaton's persona, her way of talking and dressing and of ordering pastrami and white bread with mayo, took off only

once they had ended the real affair, sometime before they shot *Sleeper* together. One Thanksgiving dinner with Keaton's family, at which Allen felt like "an alien or exotic object to them, a nervous, anxiety-ridden, suspicious, wise-cracking kind of strange bird," would find its way into *Annie Hall*, complete with Grammy Hall's vision of Alvy in rabbinical beard. "Colleen Dewhurst as me was not a high spot," Keaton's mother would later write. "Annie's camera in hand, her gum chewing, her lack of confidence—pure Diane."

Many years working in theater and movies had left Allen with the memory of seeing actresses coming in to work looking like a trillion dollars, only to climb into the costume provided for them and looking "like my mother's friends," as he put it. This time, when the costume lady protested over some outfit Keaton was due to wear on set—the pants, the scarf, the shirt buttoned up to the collar ("Don't let her wear that")—Allen pushed back. "I think she looks great," he'd say. "She looks absolutely great."

Above all, he would capture the flavor of their verbal interplay—the teasing, slightly needling, passive-aggressive pillow talk of a modern couple in love. "We shared a love of torturing each other with our failures. He could sling the insults but so could I. We thrived on demeaning one another," said Keaton. "The biggest worry I had making *Annie Hall* was whether or not I would get in my own way. I was afraid that unconsciously I might stop myself from showing the truth because it made me uncomfortable. I wanted to do *Annie Hall* fully, without worrying what I did wrong in real life."

Principal photography began on May 19, 1976 at Long Island's South Fork. The first scene shot was the lobster scene. They did seven or eight takes, in one of which Allen and Keaton both broke up. Watching the sequence in dailies with cinematographer Gordon Willis, Allen knew instantly

In Diane Keaton, Allen finally found his comic equal and sparring partner. Having honed their on-screen relationship in *Sleeper* and *Love and Death*, he perfected it in *Annie Hall*.

"It was a picture about me. My life, my thoughts, my ideas, my background."

Above: "Talk to him, you speak shellfish." Alvy attempts to resolve a crustacean crisis.

Opposite: Annie and Alvy visiting their respective analysts looks like a split screen, but was actually shot on one set with a dividing wall.

that was the one they'd be using, all shot in one continuous take. In all there would be only 282 cuts in the picture—the average shot lasting 14.5 seconds. (In any other film released in 1977 the average shot length would have been four to seven seconds, and the average number of cuts closer to a thousand.) "Two things happened on *Annie Hall*," Allen would say when asked about the new-found maturity of his filmmaking. "One was that I reached some kind of personal plateau where I felt I could put the films that I had done in the past behind me. And I wanted to take a step forward toward more realistic and deeper films. And the other thing was that I met Gordon Willis."

Allen almost hadn't hired Willis. He'd heard all the stories about him being difficult, and his nickname—the "Prince of Darkness." "To work with me, and I'd be the first person to say it, is like being locked in a room with Attila the Hun," Willis once admitted. Allen told his line producer Bobby Greenhut to budget for another cameraman in case they had to fire Willis. When Willis asked to see a script, Allen invited him to his apartment, handed him a copy, and disappeared. "He left the

room, and I sat there and read it through, laughing out loud, all by myself," said Willis. "That's how we first met."

It would be the first of eight films they shot together— including *Manhattan*, *Stardust Memories*, and *The Purple Rose of Cairo*—but *Annie Hall* set the stylistic template for what many people would mean by "a Woody Allen film": the long takes, sometimes lasting an entire scene; the shots of people walking on a sidewalk taken from a camera running parallel on the opposite side of the street; the shots of people approaching the camera which then starts to dolly back when they get too close. "Few viewers probably notice how much of *Annie Hall* consists of people talking, simply talking," Roger Ebert would note. "They walk and talk, sit and talk, go to shrinks, go to lunch, make love and talk, talk to the camera, or launch into inspired monologues like Annie's free-association as she describes her family to Alvy… all done in one take of brilliant brinkmanship."

Most groundbreaking of all, there was the sight, or rather just the sound, of two people talking off screen, another Allen/ Willis trick that started with the scene in which Annie and Alvy divide up their books after breaking up. The picture also ends with thirty seconds of empty street scenery, after Annie and Alvy have departed. "I remember we were setting up the shot where Alvy and Annie were breaking up and they were dividing up the books and I said, 'Neither of them is on at the time. Is that OK?' And he [Willis] said, 'Yes, that's great, sure, there's nothing wrong with that at all.' If he had said, 'You can't do that, what are you thinking?' I wouldn't have done it. But as soon as I got his imprimatur, we always managed to do that in subsequent movies, and to this day I'll do it. In every movie there's at least one scene where nobody's on and there's just talking. I throw one in always in honor of Gordon."

The script continued to evolve during shooting. Alvy's sneezing into the cocaine was an unplanned accident that emerged during rehearsal. The scene where Alvy and Annie are at their psychiatrists, which looks like a split screen, was actually shot by Willis on one set with an adjoining wall. "If a scene wasn't working, Woody would do what he always did: rewrite it while Gordon Willis was setting up the shot," said Keaton. But the biggest changes came during editing. The first cut took almost six weeks to assemble and condensed

"I was in analysis. I was suicidal.
As a matter of fact, I would have killed
myself, but I was in analysis with a strict
Freudian and if you kill yourself they
make you pay for the sessions you miss."

Alvy Singer

Above: One of the key influences in Allen's evolution as a filmmaker was Oscar-winning cinematographer Gordon Willis.

Opposite: On set with Shelley Duvall, whose character has a one-night stand with Alvy after his breakup with Annie.

100,000 feet of footage into two hours and twenty minutes, the first twenty-five minutes of which were a "disaster," according to Brickman. The opening monologue was endless, and interrupted by scenes that only amplified Allen's various grievances and hang-ups. Keaton made a brief appearance only to disappear again, lost in the ticker tape of Alvy's thought processes. It was like a highly sophisticated and more philosophical version of one of Allen's nightclub monologues.

"I thought it was terrible, completely unsalvageable," said Brickman. "It was like the first draft of a novel, like the raw material from which a film could be assembled, from which two or three films could possibly be assembled." This would prove quite literally true. It is a sign of the film's importance that material cut from it would continue to show up in his work for the next twenty years, like fragments of rock from a distant eruption. Much of the Coney Island material would end up, rewritten, in *Radio Days*. A fantasy sequence in which Annie and Alvy take a guided tour of hell in an elevator would reappear twenty years later in *Deconstructing Harry*. And of course the murder mystery would return as *Manhattan Murder Mystery*.

And *Annie*? Watching the rough cut, it was clear to everyone that the film started moving whenever it hit present-tense material involving Allen and Keaton. Brickman said that should be the focus: the love affair. So they began cutting in the direction of the relationship. The opening monologue was cut to just six minutes; sections dealing with Alvy's first and second wives (Carol Kane and Janet Margolin) were reduced to brief flashbacks. Out went Cousin Doris, the Nazis, the interrogation dream, the Maharishi, and the Garden of Eden. "There was a lot of material taken out of the picture that I thought was wonderfully funny," said Allen. "I was sorry to lose just about all of that surrealistic stuff. It was not what I had intended to do. I didn't sit down with Marshall Brickman and say, 'We're going to write a picture about a relationship.' I mean the whole concept of the picture changed as we were cutting it."

The ending went through several iterations. The original script ended with Alvy in jail, desperate to be reunited with Annie in Hollywood. Said Allen, "He was thrown into this context with these terrible-looking people and these lowlifes, and it turned out they were not so bad." At the urging of his editor, Ralph Rosenblum, three new endings were shot in

October, November, and December of 1976. One, showing Alvy and Annie meeting awkwardly outside the movie theater screening *The Sorrow and the Pity*, was "a real downer," said Rosenblum. Another had Alvy in Times Square wondering what to do about Annie, when he looks up at a flashing sign that reads, "What are you doing, Alvy? Go to California. It's OK. She loves you." Allen hated this so much he reportedly threw it in the East River.

The third idea was to return to the denouement of the original murder script: a brief montage showing the course of the affair, accompanied by Alvy's final voiceover. While the two men chewed the idea over, assistant editor Susan Morse quickly flipped through the logbook for candidates and by the time they had decided to go ahead with option three, she had pulled out virtually all of the cuts you see in the final version, edited over Keaton's reprise of "Seems Like Old Times," and ended with a final monologue from Alvy—about needing relationships the way the man whose brother thinks he's a chicken needs eggs—written by Allen in the back of a cab on the way to the editing room one morning.

"I'll never forget," said Brickman of the moment he saw it all cohere for the first time. "Suddenly there was an ending

"A lot of people still think my best films were around the era of Annie Hall and Manhattan, but while those movies might hold a warm place in their hearts—for which I am delighted—they're wrong."

The difficulty of *Annie Hall*'s delivery is significant. You don't expect solipsism as central to a comedy act as it is to Allen's to be overturned without some breaking of eggs, to adopt a metaphor. *Take the Money and Run* and *Bananas* are both essentially picaresques, relaying adventures and misadventures in the life of their hero; seen from the viewpoint of almost any other character, the films don't just fall apart—they are inconceivable. In *Annie Hall*, Allen put an entire film into orbit around another actor's character who was as fully realized, if not more so, than his own. In the chaos of the editing suite, Allen ceded control. He handed the film to Keaton. She is all over the film the same way Anna Karina is in *Vivre Sa Vie*, or Jeanne Moreau is in *Jules et Jim*—like a fragrance. We first hear of Annie during Alvy's opening monologue, in which he puzzles over their breakup ("Annie and I broke up and I-I still can't get my mind around that…"), and then again from his friend Rob (Tony Roberts) as they walk along the street. "Aren't you meeting Annie?" The effect of these mentions is a little like that of all the advance billing Bogie gets before making his entrance in *Casablanca*: little ripples of expectation that give Annie almost a touch of myth.

Finally here she is, late to the Bergman film, because she overslept and missed her therapist. Alvy accuses her of getting her period. "Jesus, every time anything out of the

Part of Annie's charm lay in her unusual dress sense, but Allen had to fight the costume department over some of the more *outré* outfits he wanted Keaton to wear.

there—not only that, but an ending that was cinematic, that was moving. The whole movie could have gone into the toilet if there hadn't been that last beat on it." By the end, pretty much all that remained of the original script was the title: *Anhedonia*. United Artists begged Allen to come up with another. Chairman Arthur Krim jokingly threatened to jump from a window if he didn't. "They won't know what it means," he pleaded. "And if they *do* find out what it means they'll really hate it."

Finally, Allen relented. After several test screenings, each under a different title—*Anhedonia, Anxiety, Annie and Alvy*—he decided, "All right, let's just call it *Annie Hall*."

In one of many departures from the "rules" of the rom-com, the first time we see the central couple together they are bickering in a movie theater ticket line.

ordinary happens, you think that I'm getting my period!" Annie counters. If you came to *Annie Hall* because you heard of its reputation as one of the great cinematic romances, you might be feeling a little nervous by now. In the wake of *Annie Hall*, an entire generation of romantic comedies would spring up, all claiming Allen as their progenitor, but Allen's film is a template for the rom-com in the same way that *Les Demoiselles d'Avignon* is a template for family portraits. Forget boy-meets-girl, boy-loses-girl, and boy-gets-girl. Try this for the course of romance. First boy-and-girl-break-up. Then boy-and-girl-bicker-over-girl-missing-therapy-and-being-late-for-a-Bergman-movie. Then we get boy's-first-marriage. Boy's-second-marriage. Then boy-and-girl-read-in-silence (has the *downtime* of coupledom—that slightly bored, bickering, relaxed companionship—been better represented on screen?). Finally, at around the twenty-two-minute mark, we cut back in time and boy finally meets girl. Keaton plays whack-a-mole tennis at the tennis club and follows up with her memorable speech, in which she backs out of the door and comes on to Alvy at the exact same time, while the ends of her sentences float off like untethered balloons.

The effect of Keaton's arrival in the film is immediate. Away drop all the stylistic pyrotechnics—the direct-to-camera addresses, the breaches of the fourth wall, the fantasy drop-ins, and reality tune-outs—all the tricks by which Allen, as a comedian, seeks to hold the film in his grip as tightly as he once held the mike. His story is now Annie's. The film is now

Keaton's. Her performance is pyrotechnics enough—all the little halts and hesitations, as she futzes out halfway through sentences, or abandons them entirely. "It was remarkable what he did for me," Keaton would later say of Allen's ear for Annie's "Chippewa Falls" language, for the sound of "Annie Hall, flumping around, trying to find a sentence," as she put it. Here was something new—a modern woman, self-conscious, neurotic, insecure, a little jejune in her attempts to sound smarter than she is, but brainy (of course), funny, sometimes caustic, endlessly amused by Alvy, and hungry for all that he can feed her: books, therapy, movies, adult-education classes, confidence, freedom.

"You're the reason I got out of my room, and was able to sing and get in touch with my feelings and all that crap," as she puts it during their third (and final) breakup in the health-food restaurant on Sunset Boulevard, while traffic streams behind her (is there a more ignominious setting for Woody Allen?). "As far as *Annie Hall* goes, the question you raise about it being my first film to be centered on a character not played by me raises a point I've always made about the enormity of Diane Keaton's talent and screen presence," says Allen now. "Like a number of movies that I have done with her, the film was designed to be about me and, while I wouldn't go so far as to say she wipes me off the screen, the movie turned out to be hers. I'm happy to replace myself in films because it opens up more possibilities. If I'm the protagonist it limits the central character to what I look like

and can play and without me there are many good possibilities that open up. To do film after film where the lead character is, for example, a Manhattan intellectual or a neurotic or a little roach like Danny Rose does not allow me to write stories like *Blue Jasmine* or *Match Point* or *Vicky Cristina Barcelona* or *Purple Rose* or numerous others that just don't have a part for me. When I finish a script, if there is a part I can believably play, I do it, but as I get older there are fewer and fewer parts and it's not much fun to play characters that are not the love interest, whether you end up with the girl or not."

The story, as already hinted at in *Sleeper*, is *Pygmalion*—that of the apprentice who outstrips her master—which speaks to Allen's abiding interest in plot reversals but also to a deeper agnosticism in him, borne of experience, toward the gods of romance. *Annie Hall* is remembered as a romantic movie, and in one sense it is, with its sunset walks on the beach, and trysts at the base of the Brooklyn Bridge, where Alvy tells Annie, "Love is too weak a word for what I feel—I luuurve you, you know, I, I *loave* you, I luff you…" These two are destined to break apart on the same ambivalence that lends their overtures to one another such a frisson. The central theme of *Annie Hall* is instead voiced by the Jewish retiree whom Alvy accosts on the street after their breakup. "That's how people are," she tells him with a shrug, "Love fades."

It is the theme of much great literature, particularly poetry—Thomas Moore's "Fare thee well, thou lovely one,"

Shelley's "We meet not as we parted," Yeats's "Never give all the heart"—and drama, particularly from Russia and Scandinavia: Much of Chekhov, Strindberg, and Ibsen is founded on the transitory nature of romantic love. If love has to end, Hollywood has always preferred the idea of some third-party intercession being to blame—a call of duty (*Casablanca*), the Civil War (*Gone with the Wind*), or a stray carcinogen (*Love Story*). That most love affairs simply cool, like once-glowing coals, is one of those facts that makes Hollywood nervous and second-rate dramatists blanch. Don't let the fact that it won the Best Picture Oscar put you off, as it did Allen—*Annie Hall* is better than that, its theme of fading love nestled within an intricate remembrance of things past, the loose-leaf structure which Allen once developed to accommodate a stream of gags now serving as the supplest of spines for a relationship album in which his gifts as comic and dramatist are fused.

"His ear for metropolitan speech has never been finer, his approach to character never so direct, his feeling about hypocrisy never so ringing, his sobriety never so witty," wrote Penelope Gilliatt in the *New Yorker*. "This is a love story told with piercing sweetness and grief, for all its funniness." In *Time*, Richard Schickel called it "a ruefully romantic comedy that is at least as poignant as it is funny and may be the most autobiographical film ever made by a major comic." People who think of the movie and sigh are not misremembering it. The movies, too, are a kind of love affair, going by in a flash—this one is just ninety-three minutes long but lodged deep in the limbic brain of a generation. People had a love affair with *Annie Hall* in 1977. To revisit it is to find an old flame packing the old magic.

"Writing is a complete pleasure for me.
I love it. It's a sensual, pleasurable,
intellectual activity that's fun. Thinking
of it, planning it, plotting it, is agony.
That's hard."

Interiors

1978

One day in the summer of 1977, a copy of Allen's latest script arrived by messenger at the house of his editor, Ralph Rosenblum. He read it over the weekend, and turned to his wife in puzzlement. "I think they sent me the wrong script," he said. This one was "indescribably dreadful." His wife skimmed it and was as perplexed as he was. "How could this happen?" she asked. A few days later Rosenblum met Allen for lunch to discuss the project.

"Don't make it," he advised him.

"Well, I want to," replied Allen.

It would mark the beginning of the end of a ten-year collaboration between the two men, who had worked together since *Take the Money and Run. Interiors* was different.

Even before *Annie Hall* was finished, Allen pitched his new script to United Artists through his agent, Sam Cohn at ICM. The material was not your typical Woody Allen script, Cohn explained, rather, a muted chamber piece very much in the vein of Ingmar Bergman about three sisters whose lives are wrecked by their perfectionist mother. A few days later, UA's Eric Pleskow met with Cohn, Charles Joffe, and Jack Rollins. "I'm sure they were all set for a knock-down, drag-out fight," said Pleskow, but instead they got the go-ahead. It was something "Woody needed to get out of his system," reasoned UA chairman, Arthur Krim, who felt that "in the long run, something good would come of it." Around the corridors of UA, however, executives took to calling the director "Ingmar Allen" behind his back. The green light for *Interiors* was, said UA's Steven Bach, "one of the rare instances in modern American movie history in which an artist has been allowed to make a picture because of what it might mean to his creative development, success or failure."

The movie tells the story of a wealthy New York family ruled by an icy matriarch, an interior decorator named Eve

(Geraldine Page) who is, in Allen's words, "psychotically and intensely devoted to aesthetics," fussing over the exact arrangement of vases, and coordination of beiges and earth tones in her "ice palace" of a house. Her eldest, favored daughter is Renata (Diane Keaton), a successful poet married to Frederick (Richard Jordan), a self-loathing, alcoholic novelist who represents, to Allen, "the failed artist who invariably turns to intellectualism, cerebralism, criticism." The middle daughter is Joey (Mary Beth Hurt), unemployed and unfulfilled, "a character who's full of feelings but has no artistic talent at all." The third sister is Flyn (Kristin Griffith), the only one who seems happy, although her career as an actress in TV movies is disdained by her more artistically inclined family and who "was just supposed to represent kind of an empty sensuality." The movie starts with their father, Arthur (E. G. Marshall), announcing over breakfast that he

Opposite: The three statuesque sisters Renata (Diane Keaton), Flyn (Kristin Griffith), and Joey (Mary Beth Hurt) gaze into the middle distance.

Right: Their icy mother, Eve (Geraldine Page), focuses on something closer to hand.

wants to leave his wife and live alone, and ends with him marrying Pearl (Maureen Stapleton), a cheerful vulgarian from Florida who wears furs and scarlet dresses, who shakes Arthur into vivid life, and offers his daughters the chance of "a second birth from a new mother."

Allen had wanted Ingrid Bergman for the role of the mother, but she was already committed to shoot *Autumn Sonata* in Norway, so, on Keaton's suggestion, the part went instead to Page. Working again with cinematographer Gordon Willis, Allen began shooting on October 24, 1977 in the Hamptons, with Allen behind the camera but, for the first time, not in front of it; he thought his presence would detract from the seriousness of proceedings. He rode his actors harder than usual, telling Page after one take, "That was pure soap opera. You could see this on afternoon television," and had a tough time hiding his anxiety while editing. "He was against the wall," said Rosenblum. "I think he was afraid. He was testy,

he was slightly short-tempered. He was fearful. He thought he had a real bomb."

Preview screenings in December met with stunned silence. Fearing the worst, UA held back release until August 2, 1978, whereupon it made back only $4.6 million of its $10 million budget and was panned by critics. In the *New Republic*, Stanley Kauffmann called it a "tour of the Ingmar Bergman room at the Madame Tussaud's wax museum." "Disaster perpetrated on a gullible public by a man with a Bergman complex," said John Simon. "The people in *Interiors* are destroyed by the repressiveness of good taste, and so is the picture," wrote Pauline Kael in the *New Yorker*, "*Interiors* is a handbook of art-film mannerisms, so amateur and studied it might have been directed by the icy mother herself—from the grave."

Much as one might wish it otherwise, the film is not one of those works, misunderstood at the time, which has improved with age. If anything, its palate of slate grays, stonewashed

> "I was not going to do a little bit of drama or a conventional drama or a commercial drama. I wanted to go for the highest kind of drama. And if I failed, I failed. That's OK."

Opposite: Renata and her self-loathing, alcoholic husband, Frederick (Richard Jordan).

Right: A quiet word with Kristin Griffith. For the first time in his filmmaking career, Allen stayed behind the camera.

Overleaf: Portrait by Brian Hamill, 1979.

blues, and muted beiges, with emotions to match—seems only more distant, like a cross between a Bergman movie and a 1978 Restoration Hardware catalogue. As clenched and tightly controlled as *Annie Hall* had been loose and improvisatory, *Interiors* drew almost exactly the wrong message from the earlier film, falling victim to the very aesthetic neat-freakishness it was attempting to diagnose in its chilly matriarch, whose legacy of unhappiness is handed down to her three daughters. The characters bicker and backbite and undermine one another, speaking only from a place of deepest ink-black bitterness, while gazing out of windows in the pale gray morning light, as if posing for their sculptures. Willis actually suggested calling the picture *Windows*. It was Keaton who suggested *Interiors*, but *Windows* is more accurate—interiors are exactly what these characters lack.

They are all exteriors, brittle surfaces, Bergman-people constructed entirely from the outside, from other people's tart, envious observations of them: "My work once showed promise and I haven't delivered." And: "She has all the anguish and anxiety of the artistic personality without any of the talent." Allen seems lost in a fearful fantasy of artistic bitchery not unlike the schoolboy's vision of sex, which he imagines everyone doing, behind his back, furiously, all the time. Behind the self-taught college dropout's back, everyone is talking in aesthetic abstractions, furiously, all the time. Nobody sounds like this. With hindsight, Allen saw some of the movie's faults. "After *Interiors*, months later, I was sitting at home and suddenly thought to myself, 'Gee, did I make this mistake?' Because of my exposure to foreign films, in my ear for dialogue, was I really writing subtitles to foreign films? When you see, say, a Bergman film, you're reading it because you're following the subtitles. And when you read it, the dialogue has a certain cadence. My ear was picking up on subtitle-style dialogue and I was creating that for my characters. I worried about that. It's something that I never really resolved clearly. I don't know."

In an essay, film critic Richard Schickel once suggested the popular audience left Allen, but the director disagreed. "I left my audience is really what happened, they didn't leave me," he said, as if they were entered into the cinematic equivalent of a marriage. It's certainly the deepest and longest-lasting relationship of most directorial careers, which proceed through a cycle very similar to that of courtship. The young director appears on the scene, eager to please and impress. He catches the audience's eye, makes it laugh, gets its number. He calls and they go out on a date. A big box-office success. They go on a second—they break records—and a third. Finally, he wins an Oscar and they move in together. They get married. But the audience begins to feel suffocated, the very same jokes and quirks that made the filmmaker seem so endearing now grate. Meanwhile, the filmmaker remembers fondly the time when he didn't need to worry about whether he left hair in the sink or the toilet seat up or down. It's pretty clear what *Interiors* represented to Allen—it was a filing for divorce.

"Art is like the intellectual's Catholicism,
it's the promise of an afterlife, but of
course it's fake—you're only doing
it because you want to do it."

Manhattan

1979

Manhattan came out of a conversation Allen had with Gordon Willis while shooting *Interiors* in the Hamptons. Both men used to dine together and one night Allen broached the idea of shooting a movie set in Manhattan, with the city appearing almost as another character, all shot in black and white because that's how he remembered it— which is to say, from old movies. It would be a love letter to the New York of champagne and furs and top hats, of nightclubs and horse-drawn cab rides around Central Park like the one Jimmy Stewart took in *Born to Dance* (1936). Willis suggested shooting in widescreen, with an anamorphic lens, like they used for war movies, only here he'd be using it for this intimate story about love and loss. It would be the irascible cameraman's favorite film with the director. "*Manhattan* is still closest to my heart," he would say. "What we perceived this film to be was 'romantic reality,' the things we both loved about New York. Growing up there, I found it very easy to do."

After initial reservations about allowing him to shoot in black and white, United Artists gave Allen the go-ahead and they commenced filming in various locations in and around Manhattan. "Woody is bypassing a lot of red tape by borrowing on his past experience from the *Candid Camera* days," noted one columnist. "He and the company just arrive and start shooting." The film would mark the high point of Allen's collaboration with Willis, bringing to maturity the simple, elliptical style they had worked on-the-fly for *Annie Hall*—long scenes playing without a cut, without even a close-up or a reverse angle to break up the flow, with actors repeatedly wandering out of frame entirely, still speaking, only to return at a later point in the conversation. "I remember just stringing masters together in *Manhattan*. Gordon and I always used to figure out ways to get the actors off camera and then

Shot in black and white, *Manhattan* was Allen's sixth film collaboration with Diane Keaton.

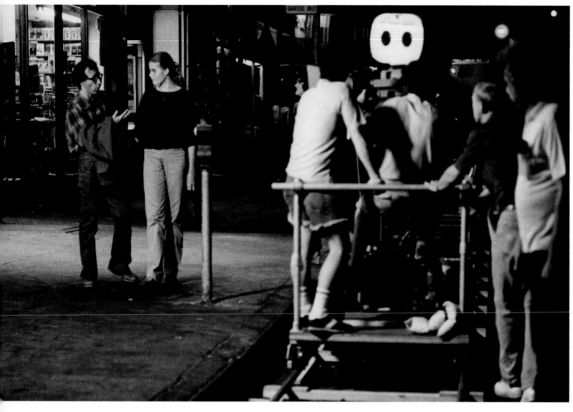

get them back on again, on and off all the time … We used that style in many other films."

Filming at the Hayden Planetarium, Willis convinced Allen to shoot Isaac (Allen) and Mary (Diane Keaton) in the barest of silhouettes. For the shot of the two of them on a bench at the base of the Queensboro Bridge, watching the sun come up, they had to get up at 3 a.m., and bring their own bench. "The bridge has two sets of necklace lights, which the city has on a timer," said Willis. "When the light comes up, the bridge lights go off. Knowing this, we made arrangements with the city to leave the lights on. We said we'd let them know when we had the shot. After that, they could turn them off. Something always tells me to never totally trust these arrangements. Anyway, I turned to the production guy who made the calls to the city, and in my calmest tone, said 'You know I need these bridge lights, right? You know that if they go off when the light breaks, I will kill you.' Ten minutes later, they were on the bench, dawn broke and … one string of lights goes out. What's in the movie is a great shot, but it'll forever be with only one necklace."

For the role of Tracy, Allen cast sixteen-year-old Mariel Hemingway after seeing her in her film debut, *Lipstick*, and a spread in Andy Warhol's *Interview* magazine.

Hemingway barely knew who Woody Allen was, having only seen *Sleeper*, at her local cinema in Idaho, but by the time she read for him at his office in New York, she had done her homework and was so nervous she hid her face behind her script, so he couldn't see her. "I literally was a really naïve girl, so I didn't have much life experience. I never had a boyfriend so Woody being my older boyfriend in this movie and talking about sexual things that I had no clue about was challenging for me." In particular she had never kissed anyone before, and was terrified about their horse-drawn smooch in Central Park, worrying about it for weeks, until she finally asked her mother for advice. "How do I make out? What do I do?"

But her mother was too embarrassed and shushed her. "So I was like, 'Thanks, that really helped.'"

She ended up sitting in front of the mirror kissing her arm trying to see what she would look like. Come the day, she was relieved to find Allen filming the scene in long shot so she didn't have to do that much. He also took her on numerous dates around the city, to museums and art galleries, to build her comfort levels and familiarity around him. "I think he knew that unless he befriended me or became close that I wouldn't get it," she said, "so when it came to that scene at the Soda Fountain and he's breaking up with me there was this natural feeling of breaking apart a family, there was a breaking apart of something that had become very familiar to me because I really cared about him as a friend. I remember looking him in the eye and listening to what he said and listening *very, very* carefully. So when I cried it was real, because I thought about 'this too will end,' you know? This family will be gone. And, I will miss you."

His ending—in which Isaac suddenly realizes that Tracy is the one for him, just as she is about to leave for London—Allen got from Chaplin's *City Lights*, where the blind girl regains her sight and finds out that the Tramp is the one who

has been helping her all along. In particular he treasured the bashful, poignant smile Chaplin flashes. "The very last shots were always the same," he said, "but there was a missing climax where I went to Yale's classroom and confronted him. That was never there." In the original script Isaac dealt with Yale (Michael Murphy) over the phone but co-writer Marshall Brickman's wife saw it and said, "What's missing is some kind of scene where you pay off that problem." Brickman pushed Allen to write a new scene in which Isaac and Yale have it out in person, against a backdrop of human and ape skeletons in a biology lab.

The Gershwin music, too, was a late addition. Originally the music over the opening sequence was going to be Bunny Berigan doing "I Can't Get Started," because that was always the song playing on the jukebox at Elaine's, the restaurant where the first scene took place. But once Allen devised the idea of starting the movie with a montage—showing the Manhattan skyline at dawn, the Empire State Building in silhouette, Radio City Music Hall, neon-lit giant advertisements on Broadway, a Coca-Cola sign, snow-covered and lamp-lit Central Park—his editor, Susan Morse, said, "I just see *Rhapsody in Blue* here." Allen ended up shooting material to fit the music, rather than the other way around, in particular the race over to Tracy's house at the end. The crew scratched their heads, puzzled at the pains he was taking to

collect various shots of the city minus his actors. "When you see this with the music, you'll see what I mean," Allen thought. "I knew I wanted a block of musical indulgence, and a number of times I would stretch things out so I could leave myself a lot of room to do a big dose of Gershwin."

On April 14, 1979, United Artists screened the film for the director's friends and close associates in the old MGM Building on Sixth Avenue. Steven Bach flew in specially from London to see it. If any two hours of his entire time at UA stood out in his memory as "pure unambiguous pleasure, they are the two," he later wrote. When the lights came up, he nodded wordlessly to Rollins and Joffe, then went for a stroll down the nearly deserted Sixth Avenue, grinning in recognition of "all the reasons I had wanted to live in New York, all the reasons I had wanted to be in the movie business."

Allen, however, hated what he saw, and wanted to buy the film back from UA, offering to direct another movie for them free of charge, rather than see it released. "I just thought to myself, 'At this point in my life, if this is the best I can do, they shouldn't give me money to make movies,'" he said. "I wanted to make a film that was more serious than *Annie Hall*. A serious picture that had laughs in it. I felt decent about *Manhattan* at the time I did it, it does go farther than *Annie Hall*. But I think now I could do better. Of course if my film makes one more person feel miserable, I'll feel I've done my job."

"For some reason, the picture had enormous resonance, and success, all over the world. I was as surprised as anyone."

Opposite: When Allen watched the finished film, he hated what he saw and even offered to buy it back from UA rather than see it released.

Right: "This…this, I think, has a kind of wonderful otherness to it, you know—a marvelous negative capability." On this visit to the Museum of Modern Art, Isaac and Mary are able to joke about their difficult first meeting at the Guggenheim.

By the time *Manhattan* opened, on April 25, 1979, the backlash against Allen that started with *Interiors* was in full swing. In a long August 16 piece for the *New York Review of Books* entitled "Letter from Manhattan," Joan Didion wrote:

"The peculiar and hermetic self-regard in *Annie Hall* and *Interiors* and *Manhattan* would seem nothing with which large numbers of people would want to identify. The characters in these pictures are, at best, trying. They are morose. They have bad manners. They seem to take long walks and go to smart restaurants only to ask one another hard questions. 'Are you serious about Tracy?' the Michael Murphy character asks the Woody Allen character in *Manhattan*. 'Are you still hung up on Yale?' the Woody Allen character asks the Diane Keaton character. 'I think I'm still in love with Yale,' she confesses several scenes later. 'You are?' he counters, 'or you think you are?'… The paradigm for the action in these recent Woody Allen movies is high school. The characters in *Manhattan* and *Annie Hall* and *Interiors* are, with one exception, presented as adults, as sentient men and women in the most productive years of their lives, but their concerns and conversations are those of clever children, 'class brains,' acting out a yearbook fantasy of adult life."

The charge of parochialism was easy enough for Allen to rebut: Why ever would his films be so successful in Paris, or Buenos Aires, if this were so?

A more troublesome bar to clear is any misgivings we might have about a forty-two-year-old man romancing a teenager, as Allen does in *Manhattan*. "What man in his forties but Woody Allen," asked Pauline Kael, "could pass off a predilection for teenagers as a quest for true values?" Mores have changed sufficiently in the thirty-five years since the film was released that, were it made today, it is unlikely Allen would have begun one of his spit-balling sessions with Marshall Brickman, "Wouldn't it be funny if I liked this really young girl?" That it worked for audiences in 1979 speaks largely to the unthreatening figure Woody Allen then presented. Dressed in jeans, sneakers, and T-shirt, fixated on girls, knocking around town with his son, Isaac seems barely a notch above adolescent himself; walking down the street together, they are almost the same height. The humor in *Manhattan* is more jaded than it was in *Annie Hall*, the satirical sights a little sharper, the gags at the expense of Diane Keaton's art chatter ("I think it has a wonderful negative capability") his most sustained broadside against intellectualism—or at least the cocktail-chatter version of it that he had himself been attempting to master all these years. But the animus of the film is, as Didion realized, that of the eternal adolescent. One of the first things Isaac does in *Manhattan* is quit his job as a TV comedy writer ("Welcome to *Human Beings: Wow…*"), leaving him free to roam around Manhattan, railing against the phonies of the art, media, and

film worlds like Holden Caulfield all grown up—or not. Only Tracy stands out from the chattering nabobs, her broad-boned face an image of purity against the phonies like Holden Caulfield's younger sister, Phoebe, and perhaps therein lay Allen's dissatisfaction with *Manhattan*: that his version of *The Catcher in the Rye* never came anywhere near close enough to Holden's anguish to count as much more than a beautifully photographed rom-com.

Still, there's beautiful photography and there's beautiful photography and then there's *Manhattan*. The plot is essentially a replay of *Play It Again, Sam*, with Allen again going after his best friend's girl (Keaton), only here she's a mistress, not a wife, which makes her slightly fairer game—just. Fear of people seems to entail a certain sneakiness in the dating habits of Allen's protagonists; locked into their tight inner circles, they have only friends, and the girlfriends of friends, to choose from. Allen never once in his films seems to pick a girl out of the blue and go on a straightforward *date*. Isaac waits until Mary has broken it off with Yale, but their romance is already underway, courtesy of an all-night walk to see the sun come up at the base of the Queensboro Bridge, and a rain-soaked dash for the planetarium, where their static-sparks of attraction and ambivalence play out against a backdrop of Saturn's rings—gorgeous, gigantic, mocking. Gordon Willis's cinematography ingeniously mines the mock-heroic mode. Everyone remembers the film's fabulous bookends—the

Manhattan skyline lit up with fireworks and Gershwin cymbal clashes, reprised again at the end, as the city basks in end-of-day contentment—but more impressive still are the elliptical compositions throughout, by which Willis frames the human figures against blank gallery walls, or against empty corridors, or else cuts them out altogether, as he had first done in *Annie Hall*. *Manhattan* is a murmuring chorus of off-screen dialogue, recorded so intimately you can hear every plosive pop, laid over images of walls and corridors that seem to keep the characters apart as much as bring them together—the city as isolation tank as much as it is romantic catalyst.

The effect is a little spooky, the characters like mice in a maze, their pillow talk hanging in the air like the ghosts of conversations past and future. These walls really *do* talk, and they seem like they will outlast Allen's scurrying quartet as surely as the Yorick-like skull which mocks his final speech to Yale. The dressing-down he receives in the book written by his ex-wife (Meryl Streep) is Allen at his most self-hating: "He was given to fits of rage, Jewish liberal paranoia, male chauvinism, self-righteous misanthropy, and nihilistic moods of despair. He had complaints about life but never any solutions. He longed to be an artist but balked at the necessary sacrifices. In his most private moments, he spoke of his fear of death, which he elevated to tragic heights when in fact it was mere narcissism." Ouch. The movie's drama hinges on the following nubbin of plot: Should Isaac date someone brainy but insecure, like him, or should he go for someone too young to see the difference? In the end, even this dilemma is resolved for him, as Mary dumps him and gets back together with Yale, and Isaac breaks into that famous run of his—it looks like the first run he's ever broken into, complete with stops to huff and puff—to reach Tracy just minutes before she leaves for England. What follows is probably

"I like to think that, a hundred years from now, if people see the picture they will learn something about what life in the city was like in the 1970s."

Woody Allen's finest piece of acting on screen, although the praise should probably be split with Hemingway—so beautifully considered in her reactions, she seems to be operating at her own speed, as if every emotion had first to resonate up through those broad, dense cheekbones. She draws a tenderness from Allen that we haven't seen before or since. Watch Isaac plead with Tracy not to leave, his voice growing ever softer, his face swimming with the realization that, on this occasion, he may not be successful; the prospect of romantic defeat seems to open him up completely, and when Tracy asks him to have "a little faith," the tiny grimace Isaac makes, first glancing down, then around the frame, as if wondering where he might find such a thing, is priceless.

There were lines around the block when the film opened. Andrew Sarris began his *Village Voice* review by calling it "the one truly great American film of the seventies." In the *Chicago Sun-Times*, Roger Ebert wrote that it was "one of the best-photographed movies ever made." *Time* film critic Frank Rich called it "a prismatic portrait of a time and place that may be studied decades hence to see what kind of people we were." *Manhattan* eventually took nearly $40 million at the box office, Woody Allen's biggest hit to that date, but, unhappy with the film, he rode out its release in Paris, taking the first vacation of his career. "You have to understand that Woody is almost always questioning what he's doing," said Willis. "That's who he is." It would be the subject of his next film.

"I not only was totally in love
with Manhattan from the earliest
memory, I loved every single
movie that was set in New York,
every movie that began high
above the New York skyline
and moved in."

At home in his Upper East
Side apartment overlooking
Central Park. Portrait by
Manuel Bidermanas, 1979.

Stardust Memories

1980

"It's about a malaise, the malaise of a man with no spiritual center, no spiritual connection," Allen would say of *Stardust Memories*. "The whole picture occurs subjectively through the mind of a character who is on the verge of a breakdown, who's harassed and in doubt and who has a fainting fit at the end from his imaginings about all these dark things. He has a terrifying sense of his own mortality. He's accomplished things, yet they still don't mean anything to him."

Allen would swear off autobiographical readings of Sandy Bates until blue in the face, but by 1979, he, like Sandy, had experienced enough of wealth and fame to know they did nothing to buy off his demons. He bought two penthouses on Fifth Avenue, filling them with Picassos and German Expressionist paintings. He purchased a Rolls-Royce and season tickets to the Knicks. He stopped carrying cash, relying on friends for pocket change and came to resent autograph hounds. *Stardust Memories* drew on one weekend in particular, in April 1973, when he travelled to Tarrytown, New York, about an hour north of Manhattan, to deliver a talk at a film weekend organized by *New York* magazine critic Judith Crist. Throughout the event Allen was besieged by fans asking for autographs, and requests that he read this or do that. One Yale law student asked if he would come to New Haven and be a karate expert in a mock trial.

"I'm up there doing the best I can as a favor to Judith Crist, who I liked very much, and I thought that would make a funny movie," he said. Through the walls of his room that night he heard a couple arguing about his films, the woman reading his short play *Death Knocks* aloud, in a comically exaggerated Jewish voice. He was offered another room but declined, too curious to hear what they had to say. Some of this would find its way on screen, including Judith Crist, who shows up in one of the film's many Felliniesque fantasy sequences. The two

"We love your work. My wife has seen all your films."
"I especially like your early, funny ones." Harassed director Sandy Bates braves the crowd of fans who have come to greet him at an out-of-town film weekend.

"The backlash really started when I did Stardust Memories. People were outraged. I still think that's one of the best films I've ever made. I was just trying to make what I wanted, not what people wanted me to make."

Opposite, top: The photomural in Sandy's apartment is used as a device to reflect his prevailing state of mind. Here Groucho presides over a flashback to a happy time in his relationship with ex-girlfriend Dorrie (Charlotte Rampling).

Opposite, bottom: During a surreal outdoor gathering, Sandy demonstrates his magic skills on his neurotic groupie Daisy (Jessica Harper).

Above: Sharon Stone made her screen debut in *Stardust Memories*, as a pretty girl in a lively carriage traveling in the opposite direction from the somber one on which Sandy finds himself at the start of the film.

movie execs who criticize Sandy's film would be played by UA exec Andy Albeck and Allen's co-producer Jack Rollins. Charlotte Rampling's character, Dorrie, was believed to have been modeled on Allen's second wife, Louise Lasser. The film's working title, meanwhile, was "Woody Allen No. 4," prompting Allen to self-deprecate, "I am not even half of the Fellini of 8½."

The unusually long production, six months, began in September 1979 in the decaying resort town of Ocean Grove, New Jersey, some of whose mansions, warping with age beneath flaking paint, acted as a halfway house for a local population of psychiatric patients whom the nearby mental hospital had deemed safe enough to release back into the community. They could occasionally be seen wandering around, dazed on medication—the perfect ambiance for Sandy Bates's fictional nervous breakdown.

"At the beginning of *Stardust* I thought we'd never get it right," said production designer Mel Bourne. "He [Allen] would just sit around and say 'I don't think this is going to work.' My spirits would drop down to zero. In the end that sort of thing is bound to get you down." Working again with Gordon Willis, Allen was insistent on the light being right, waiting weeks for the right type of sky, while the cast and crew

played stickball or poker, and by early December they were five weeks behind schedule. "It was an extremely complicated film to do because it was extremely well orchestrated," said Allen. "And there were reshoots on it. Weather problems. It was just a hard film to do."

The finished film threw even the jovial Charles Joffe into a funk. "When I walked out of the first screening I found myself questioning everything," he said. "I wondered if I had contributed over the last twenty years to this man's unhappiness. But I talked about it with my ex-wife, my kids, who grew up with Woody, and I talked with Woody himself for hours. He said to me, 'Does this really seem like the way I feel?'" Even so, the film was excoriated by critics for what they took to be its show of ingratitude—how dare Woody produce this prolonged whine about the various nuisances of fame! In the *Village Voice*, Andrew Sarris thought the film seemed "to have been shaped by a masochistic desire to alienate Allen's admirers once and for all." In the *New Yorker*, Pauline Kael called it "a horrible betrayal … a whiff of nostalgia gone bad. If Woody found success so painful, *Stardust Memories* should help him stop worrying." Allen grew so tired of defending the film that eventually he gave up, "Maybe it worked for no one but me."

Is *Stardust Memories* the closest we will come to knowing what the first cut of *Annie Hall* was like? For here is a stream-of-consciousness picture about a man unable to experience pleasure, a comedian who doesn't want to be funny any more, the remembrance of a failed relationship—this time with Charlotte Rampling—while flashbacks illuminate his Brooklyn childhood. It's the evil twin of the earlier popular picture—its sourpuss doppelgänger. It even ends in a jailhouse, just like Allen wanted *Annie Hall* to. "I don't want to make funny movies anymore," complains Sandy Bates, taking time off from wrangling with studio heads to attend a retrospective of his films in a fading resort town, where Sandy chews over the same $64,000 question that preoccupied Isaac Davis in *Manhattan*: Should he continue to date beautiful wackadoodles or not? By 1979, Allen could pick them out of the crowd by the rattle of their prescriptions. When Sandy dials his shrink from a phone booth on the pier, only to find his neurotic, beautiful groupie Daisy (Jessica Harper) doing the same in the booth opposite him, it's his equivalent of the meet-cute in *Bluebeard's Eighth Wife* where Claudette Colbert and Gary Cooper want to buy different halves of the same set of pajamas.

Or should he go with nurturing, maternal Isobel (Marie-Christine Barrault)? Not even his memories of the bipolar Dorrie (Charlotte Rampling) seem able to divert Sandy from his old habits. The sequence of close-ups of Rampling running the gamut of emotion, from happiness to hysteria and back, are among the film's highlights, but she's a mere ghost of girlfriends past; there's nobody to pull Allen out of himself, or challenge him, as Diane Keaton did in *Annie Hall*,

and the result is one of his most formless pictures, which circles solipsistically back to Sandy, buffeted by the chant of requests that starts up whenever he shows his head in public. "Could I have ten minutes of your time? I'm writing a piece about the shallow indifference of wealthy celebrities," asks one reporter, never seen again. "Could you just say, 'To Phyllis Weinstein, you unfaithful, lying bitch'?" asks one

Charlotte Rampling as Dorrie, the ghost of girlfriends past who haunts Sandy throughout the film.

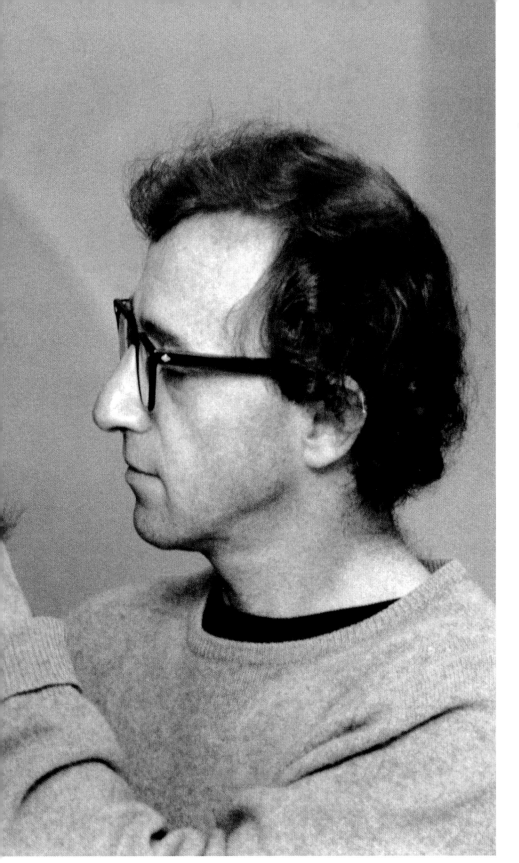

"So beautiful and so sexy and so interesting. She has an interesting neurotic quality."

WA on Charlotte Rampling

did in *Being There*, or Jerry Lewis did in *The King of Comedy*; we are the children of *The Larry Sanders Show*, Larry David, and reality TV. From today's perspective the problem with the picture is not that Allen appears ungrateful about his fame but that he doesn't go far enough—he doesn't have the courage of his own rancor. For alongside Allen's complaints about how oppressive he finds our laughter is a constant contraflow of gags designed to elicit it—"You can't control life. Only art you can control. Art and masturbation. Two areas in which I am an absolute expert." "To you, I'm an atheist; to God, I'm the loyal opposition." Well, should we laugh? Or shouldn't we?

Stardust Memories is a confusing picture, made more so by a knot of self-deception on Allen's part. The studio philistinism that Sandy complains of in the film is, after all, something Allen had rarely encountered, his experience on *What's New Pussycat?* aside. (UA even let him make *Interiors*!) His control over his own filmmaking process was already the stuff of Hollywood legend. The only person forcing Woody Allen toward happy endings at this point in his career was Woody Allen. The argument in *Stardust Memories* is not with his critics, or the audience, it is with himself, the crowd-pleaser and the artist fighting for the upper hand. Once Allen recognized this, the result would be an entirely different and much more successful picture about the indignities and absurdities of fame: *Zelig. Stardust Memories* has a lightness to it but it's not the lightness of comedy, rather it's the kind of veiled, half-joking threat a child issues to its parents which, upon being challenged, results in a sulk.

autograph hunter. These doomed petitioners link up and form a constant background hum throughout the picture, like the squawking of the gulls that circle overhead.

Much of this has a nicely acidic zing. The idea of celebrity deconstruction is far less shocking to us than it was to the original audience of *Stardust Memories*. We are more used to the sight of comedians dropping the mask, as Peter Sellers

A Midsummer Night's Sex Comedy

1982

Mia Farrow and Woody Allen met while he was shooting *Stardust Memories*. They'd come across each other once before, briefly, at a party in California, after which she wrote to tell him how much she enjoyed *Manhattan*; he wrote back, politely thanking her. But it wasn't until 1979 when she was performing in Bernard Slade's play *Romantic Comedy* opposite Anthony Perkins that they got to know each other properly. Thirty-four and divorced for nearly a year from André Previn, Farrow was introduced to the director by her old friend Michael Caine and his wife one evening in Elaine's after the show. Allen was there at his usual table; Caine stopped to say hello and introduced Farrow.

"I could go on about our differences forever," Allen later told the *New York Times*. "She doesn't like the city and I adore it. She loves the country and I don't like it. She doesn't like sports at all and I love sports. She loves to eat in, early—five thirty, six—and I love to eat out, late. She likes simple, unpretentious restaurants; I like fancy places. She can't sleep with an air conditioner on; I can only sleep with an air conditioner on. She loves pets and animals; I hate pets and animals … She likes the West Side of New York; I like the East Side of New York. She has raised nine children now with no trauma and has never owned a thermometer. I take my temperature every two hours in the course of the day."

A Midsummer Night's Sex Comedy was the first creative fruit of their union. Written in two weeks while Allen was waiting for the budget to be worked out for *Zelig*, it was originally intended to be serious and poignant by way of counterbalance—"a kind of serious Chekhovian story in the style of *Interiors* almost." But the more he got into it, the more it emerged as the lacier kind of boudoir farce—a small intermezzo with butterfly nets and badminton courts and a few laughs. "I wanted to do for the country what I'd done for

"I consider myself eminently privileged. I work as an independent, answerable to no one. If an idea strikes me as the seed of an interesting film, I start to work on it without provoking too much curiosity, and if I go wrong in a scene, I can do it over again without too much drama."

"I wanted to do for the country what I'd done for New York in *Manhattan*." Despite being "at two with nature," Allen located his next film in a rural setting in the Hudson Valley.

Seeking refuge behind a mosquito net during the hot, humid summer shoot.

New York in *Manhattan*," he said. "We wanted to film during the most beautiful days in the country that you could think of. We just made it as lovely as we could. And everything was subsumed into that. We made sure that the light was perfect all the time and that the sun was at the exact right place."

Allen hated the countryside, of course—"I am at two with nature," as he once wrote—and the shoot, in the summer of 1981, on the Rockefeller estate, about forty minutes from New York, was hot, sticky, and short-tempered. Farrow, who, shooting for the first time with her new lover, was at times, "overpowered by such a paralysis that I couldn't understand who the characters were supposed to be or what they were doing," she later wrote. "Woody, now my director, was a stranger to me. His icy sternness pushed my apprehension toward raw fear. I was no artist, only the most inept poseur." This is not the only evidence to suggest that Allen was unusually short with his actors. He made José Ferrer deliver the line, "These are not my teeth," fifteen times until finally Ferrer stormed off the set, proclaiming, "Now I can't do it! You've turned me into a mass of terrors!" Halfway through production Farrow had an ulcer and was taking Tagamet four times a day. By the end of the summer they were painting the leaves on the trees green—a fitting symbol for the critical verdict that followed the film's release on July 16, 1982.

"The film is so low-key, so sweet and offhand and slight, there are times when it hardly even seems happy to be a movie," wrote Roger Ebert in the *Chicago Sun-Times*. "You feel there was no pressing reason for Woody Allen to make this picture—not even the pleasure that some directors find in making movies," wrote Pauline Kael in the *New Yorker*, picking up on the same air of diffidence. "If you're not in a frame of mind to see the world in a funny light and you're writing, directing, and starring in a comedy, you're lucky to achieve whimsicality, which is what Woody Allen has got in *A Midsummer Night's Sex Comedy*."

In upstate New York, six principals in various states of romantic and sexual bewilderment converge, by carriage or automobile, at the summer house of a crackpot inventor, Andrew (Allen), and his frigid wife, Adrian (Mary Steenburgen), who has been pleading off sex with a headache for six months. First to arrive are Andrew's best friend, Maxwell (Tony Roberts), a horndog physician, and his current fling, Dulcy (Julie Hagerty), a young nurse with nymphomaniac tendencies. Then we have Adrian's cousin Leopold (José Ferrer), a triumphantly pompous scholar, and his young bride-to-be, the beautiful Ariel (Mia Farrow), who has decided that the only way to curb her sexual rapaciousness is the cold shower of Leopold's pedantry; after their wedding, his plan is to take her to London, on a "rare opportunity to visit Thomas Carlyle's grave." The rules of the roundelay that follows are simple: 1) Every character must, by day's end, fall in love with at least one other person than

Six characters in search of a storyline: Adrian (Mary Steenburgen), Dulcy (Julie Hagerty), Ariel (Mia Farrow), Maxwell (Tony Roberts), Leopold (José Ferrer), and Andrew (Woody Allen).

the person they came with. And 2) the audience must affect to notice the difference.

Allen's first attempt at an ensemble picture suffers from a case of the sames. All the women blur into one taffeta-wrapped blur of wispy-voiced, needle-thin nymphomania, while the men are variations on a single satyr. Farrow looks uncomfortable in a role that is essentially miscast. It was written for Diane Keaton, but she was off filming *Reds*, so Allen turned instead to Farrow but he had yet to find her speech, her rhythms, in the same way that he had found Keaton's by the time of *Annie Hall*. Here coiffed to within an inch of her life to resemble a Pre-Raphaelite wood nymph, and shot from behind in haloes of light, she peers out timidly through Bambi lashes. She's supposed to have slept with the entire infield of the Chicago White Sox but looks like she would have difficulty working her way through a Waldorf salad. "You have to admit I wasn't one of your shrinking, mousy, inhibited little virgins," she tells Andrew, seeming very much as if that is the role she would rather be playing.

If Allen's film has even a whisper of Shakespearean summer madness, it comes from José Ferrer. He gives

the buffoonish Leopold all the plummy orotundity you might want, but the film is a retreat in every sense. If *Interiors* represented Allen's petition for divorce from the mass audience who had flocked to *Annie Hall*, and *Stardust Memories* was the final fight on the steps outside the courtroom, then *A Midsummer Night's Sex Comedy* is the motion-picture equivalent of moving back into separate apartments. The first of four consecutive period drama-comedies—preceding *Zelig*, *Broadway Danny Rose*, and *The Purple Rose of Cairo*—it saw Allen exchange the sharp teeth and wild riffing with which he went after the contemporary world for a soothing visual palette, classical music soundtrack, and echoes of Shakespeare's *A Midsummer Night's Dream*, Ingmar Bergman's *Smiles of a Summer Night*, and Jean Renoir's *La Règle du Jeu*—all of Allen's favorite emollients in one picture. Nothing so rowdy as laughter ripples its placid, beautifully photographed surfaces. Rather, it seeks to raise a series of wry smiles, at best quiet chuckles, with a mixture of frolics and flying bicycles in a summer pageant as soft and insubstantial as a dandelion seed head: One puff and it's gone.

Zelig

1983

Zelig grew out of an idea for a short story. The germ of the idea was to do a character study of a man who agrees with everyone about everything—what films they like, what books they read. "It's that need to be liked which on the most basic level leads you to say you liked a particular film or show, or read *Moby Dick*—when you didn't—just to keep the people around you pacified," said Allen. "I thought that desire not to make waves, carried to an extreme, could have traumatic consequences. It could lead to a conformist mentality and ultimately fascism. That's why I wanted to use the documentary form: One doesn't want to see this character's private life; one's more interested in the phenomenon and how it relates to the culture. Otherwise it would just be the pathetic story of a neurotic."

To put it another way, Leonard Zelig *has* no private life. This made the writing a particularly exacting task. Initially the setting was a contemporary one, with Zelig a worker at WNET, the Public Broadcasting Service television station in New York. Allen's friend Dick Cavett was then hosting a series of historical specials for HBO in which Cavett was inserted, via matte photography, into archival footage. Fascinated by the process, Allen hit upon the idea of making a spoof documentary—as he had done with *Take the Money and Run*—using narration, newsreel footage, still photographs, and interviews, and ordered up hundreds of thousands of feet of stock footage from the 1920s, including the Nazi rallies, Babe Ruth in action, and the only known footage of F. Scott Fitzgerald, most of it from family albums and film archives like the Bettmann. "It was a pain in the neck," said Allen, "but the shooting was a cinch."

Using actual lenses, cameras, lights, and sound equipment from the 1920s, they shot in studio space all over New York. "Of all the films we made, the atmosphere on this set was the most relaxed," said Mia Farrow, playing

The "ultimate conformist" Leonard Zelig in a photo call with heavyweight boxing legend Jack Dempsey.

the psychiatrist Dr. Eudora Fletcher, who ends up falling in love with Zelig during her "White Room Sessions," filmed in the same house they had used for *A Midsummer Night's Sex Comedy*. The rest of the cast were almost all non-professional actors—family, friends, crew members—in order to elicit the faltering naturalism of actual interviewees circa 1920. Allen also wrote to Greta Garbo who didn't respond, but Mae Questel, the original voice of Betty Boop, provided the voice of Helen Kane singing "Chameleon Days." Saul Bellow, invited to offer up a philosophical interpretation of Zelig's existence, did so only after first correcting Allen's grammar—"It's all right if I change this, isn't it? Because this is grammatically incorrect."

The shoot wrapped in just twelve weeks, but postproduction took over a year, as cinematographer Gordon Willis and the visual effects team undertook the arduous task of marrying different types, ages, grains, and qualities of film footage together. "You can't imagine how many crates of film we accumulated," said Willis. The greatest challenge was finding footage with enough space around the subject to accommodate Allen. "Those shots were usually crowded," said editor Susan Morse. "We needed enough room, we needed a reason for him to be standing there, and we needed to be sure that no one walked in front of him." After that, the new footage had to be "aged" to match the old. They put scratches in the negative, crumpled the reels, overexposed them, left them in the sun—anything to make them match the grainy, de-saturated footage of the 1920s and 1930s. Willis even took exposed negatives into the shower and stamped on them. "There was a point when I thought we were never going to finish, a point when I thought I was going to go nuts," he said. "I have never worked so hard at making something difficult look so simple."

"Woody said to me one day, 'Do you think we've gone too far?' At the time, I thought maybe we had. It was very difficult to balance the material visually and emotionally. It had to look right, but it also had to work for the audience, it had to be entertaining. There was always a danger of working so hard on a particular shot that we'd forget about how it should work in the finished movie. But when you feel yourself losing sight of that, you've got to back off for a while and start again. And that's just what happened."

The first cut ran for only forty-five minutes, so Allen shot some additional scenes and cut in some more archive footage. All that remained was to come up with a title. Allen had struggled throughout to come up with a name—possibilities including *The Chameleon Man*, *The Changing Man* (the name of the film within the film), *The Cat's Pajamas*, *The Bee's Knees*, and *Identity Crisis and Its Relationship to Personality Disorder*. In the end he had a "title derby with my friends over dinner," said Allen. "We'd shoot titles down. The only fun was the next person's contribution. That was very unproductive. Finally, I shot several titles and ran them through with the film. The second I saw it with *Zelig*, I knew."

Zelig is one of the gems of Allen's oeuvre: a matchless comic conceit, beautifully developed and executed with a flourish, winding its way to genuine pathos, but too light on its feet

Making *Zelig* was a painstaking process, involving meshing precisely shot footage of the actors with archive 1920s newsreel, including New York street scenes and Charles Lindbergh's ticker-tape parade.

to dwell on its untold subtextual riches. "Woody Allen i poignant here in the way that Chaplin was often poigna noted Pauline Kael, and for the same reasons: Save for t few words we hear Leonard Zelig speak on scratchy tap during his sessions with Dr. Fletcher, he is as voiceless a is faceless. Of all Allen's tributes to and thefts from Cha Chaplin, Buster Keaton and Harold Lloyd, Zelig is the character with the greatest claim to their legacy—a silen ghost, unable to voice complaint or kvetch, only to mim

his persona as a comic. Though it may lack the more obvious autobiographical detailing of a picture like *Radio Days*, it offers up what is, in many ways, his most penetrating self-portrait.

Like Allen's own parents, Zelig's are locked in a state of perpetual warfare, causing their son to grow in the opposite direction—"extremely antisocial" with "bad manners and low self-opinion," he is almost pathologically people-pleasing, desperate to be liked and to feel "safe." His various incarnations—as a Chinaman, a gangster, a Negro—land him in the papers, and then hospital under the care of Dr. Fletcher

(Farrow), where "he undergoes severe mood changes and for several days will not come off the wall"—a reference to another famous ceiling-hugger who ventures "nowhere except up and down the floor, walls, and ceiling of his room." That, of course, is poor Gregor Samsa in Kafka's *Metamorphosis*, his transformation more permanent than Zelig's fleeting impersonations, but giving off much the same allegorical glint. Of all Allen's characters, he has probably attracted the most scholarly readings—see Iris Bruce's marvelous "Mysterious Illnesses of Human Commodities in Woody Allen and Franz

"It took three years to do, an arduous schedule with incessant technical experiment."

Opposite, top, and right: "If I'm not there, they start without me." Holed up in upstate New York as a study subject for Dr. Eudora Fletcher (Mia Farrow), Zelig becomes convinced that he, too, is an academic—and needs to get back to the city to teach his course in advanced masturbation.

Opposite, bottom: Taking on a presidential air with Calvin Coolidge and Herbert Hoover.

Kafka" for a take on Zelig as a figure out of Kafka, also as representative of the Jewish diaspora, eager for assimilation, and the ultimate American, a melting pot of one.

Zelig was always destined for the academy. Allen seems to have known there was something about his fable that would attract academic attention, for budding Zeligologists must take their place behind Saul Bellow, Bruno Bettelheim, and Susan Sontag, all playing themselves in the film, to offer their interpretation of Zelig's condition. "I myself felt that one could really think of him as the ultimate conformist," opines Bettelheim. Indeed, Zelig is a born zeitgeist reflector—he gleams prismatically with reflections of the culture at large—although something in Allen's decision to frame his story thus should serve as fair warning that he didn't want his film throwing its lot behind any one interpretation, instead offering something of a buffet selection while Zelig himself scuttles free, elusive as ever. What is most striking today is how unimpressed the movie is by its own cleverness, instead pressing ahead to chase yet further gags and mine genuine pathos from the love story. "Perhaps it is his very helplessness that moves me," says Dr. Fletcher, warm, anxious, and maternal in a part that *was* written for Farrow and fits her like a glove. "She doesn't challenge him (as Diane Keaton did in her pictures from him)," wrote Kael, "she frees him from

stress, and he comes up with fresh delicate scenes like the one in which under hypnosis, he murmurs, '*I love you*,' and then in a whimper, '*You're the worst cook…those pancakes…I love you, I want to take care of you…No more pancakes*'…"

Zelig is the most prescient of all Allen's screenplays. Leonard Zelig is the fall guy for the entire twentieth century, like T. S. Eliot's Prufrock and John Lennon's nowhere man—without him, there would almost certainly have been no Forrest Gump. Allen's feel for the shape of American public lives is spot-on, as Zelig is first hoisted aloft as a Jazz Age celebrity, then vilified and "sued for bigamy, adultery, automobile accidents, plagiarism, household damages, negligence, property damages, and performing unnecessary dental extractions," before finding redemption with some Lindberghian derring-do, piloting a plane to beat the Nazis. To say that Zelig is Allen is too neat, but the portrayal draws deep of the chameleon nature lurking in all dramatists—that wily opportunism, just an inch away from empathy, which allows them to finagle their way into the hearts and heads of others. For those who care to see it, *Zelig* contains an uncannily accurate forecast of the arc of Allen's own career. In the years to come he, too, would be vilified as an adulterer, and worse, before finding redemption with a return to the crowd-pleasing entertainments with which he first found favor.

"I make films for literate people. I have to assume there are many millions of people in the world who are educated and literate and want sophisticated entertainment that does not cater to the lowest common denominator and is not all about car crashes and bathroom jokes."

Billed as the "human chameleon," Zelig starts off as a freak show hawked around fairgrounds by his sister, and soon becomes the focus of a nationwide craze.

Broadway Danny Rose

1984

The story of hapless talent agent Danny Rose (Allen, right) is told in flashback by a group of Broadway comedians and managers (including Allen's own co-manager Jack Rollins, far right) over lunch at the Carnegie Deli.

One of the favorite diversions of couples in New York is finding oddball, memorable characters in the city milling around them. At one of Woody Allen and Mia Farrow's dining spots in New York, Rao's, a tiny Italian restaurant at 114th Street in East Harlem, the couple found a figure that amused them no end: the owner's daughter-in-law Annie, with her towering bouffant hairdo, stiletto heels, dark glasses, wry sense of humor, and teetering cigarette wedged into the corner of her mouth. "Gee, I would like to play a woman like that once," confided Farrow one evening.

Such was the germ of the idea that would become *Broadway Danny Rose*, Allen's twelfth film, about an ever hopeful manager of no-hoper nightclub acts. As narrated by a group of comics, Borscht Belt Scheherazades trading tales

at the Carnegie Deli, the story took Allen back to his roots on the outskirts of show business in the 1950s, when he and Jack Rollins and Charles Joffe used to migrate, post-show, to one of the delis around Broadway and Seventh Avenue—the Carnegie, the Stage, Lindy's—at a time when they were barely making enough to cover their meals. One table would be occupied by comics, another by their agents, and a third by the managers, all swapping stories for hour after hour. The confidence booster which Danny Rose gives his acts—the "three S's: Star, Smile, Strong!"—is something Allen heard a comedian share at the Carnegie one night, while the venue where Danny tries to book some of his acts, Weinstein's Majestic Bungalow Colony in the Catskill Mountains, was the first place Allen performed as a teenage magician.

"I just knew that milieu very well," he said. "The impetus to do it was really twofold. One, that Mia wanted to play Mrs. Rao, Annie Rao, who we knew and would see up at the restaurant all the time. And I wanted to play a different kind of character, not a neurotic, literate New Yorker. And one of the characters I can play is a lowlife. The truth is I come from the streets of Brooklyn. I'm not educated—I mean I was thrown out of college in my freshman year... I'm not a gangster but I'm more in that world. I'm more the guy that's home with the beer in his undershirt watching the television set, watching the ball game on television, than I am, you know, poring over the Russian Novelists. I mean, I've read those things over the years to keep up with my dates but the truth of the matter is my heart has always been at the ballpark."

Again approaching Gordon Willis, he told the D.P. "I see this in black and white."

"I couldn't agree more," said Willis.

They saw scores of candidates for their singer, considering Danny Aiello, even Robert De Niro and Sylvester Stallone at one point. Getting a little desperate, Allen's casting director, Juliet Taylor, took to cruising Colony Records on Broadway, scooping up schmaltz by the armful, when one day she happened to pick up an album entitled *Can I Depend on You* by someone named Nick Apollo Forte. A beefy, dimpled crooner in his mid-forties, the Italian-American also worked as a part-time cocktail pianist and fisherman. "It was as though he had been waiting for this big break," said Taylor. "He was a guy from Connecticut who worked these little clubs,

ninth or fiftieth choice," as she tartly noted. She found that even with a ton of makeup, her Bambi-ish eyes gave her away, so she decided to wear sunglasses for the entire movie but for one scene where you glimpse her in a bathroom mirror for a few seconds. "That was a very, very brave thing for her to do," said Allen, "because she had to act the whole picture without ever using her eyes, and that's really hard to do."

"Woody Allen hasn't found a way to lyricize Mia Farrow on screen the way he lyricized Diane Keaton," wrote critic James Wolcott in *Vanity Fair*. "There's something muffled about his adoration, something withheld. He seems to dote on her from a distance, approaching her on tiptoe. It's revealing, I think, that in both *Zelig* and *Broadway Danny Rose*, the union of Allen and Farrow is established at the end, with a discreet long shot. He keeps us at a distance, too." It's a perceptive observation on the changing nature of Allen's on-screen and off-screen romances. If Keaton had been the challenger, highly strung but standing her ground—"I say what's on my mind and, if you can't take it, well then fuck off," she told Isaac Davis in *Manhattan*—then Farrow was a warm, soothing presence, the doctor piecing together Leonard Zelig's scattered soul. In *Broadway Danny Rose*, Allen pays her the compliment he paid Keaton in *Sleeper* and would do again in *Manhattan Murder Mystery*. It's the first thing he does with all his most treasured leading *inamorata*: He hits the road with them, like Bing Crosby and Bob Hope in their "Road" pictures—Allen's ultimate version of romantic togetherness.

"If you take my advice, you'll become one of the great balloon-folding acts of all time!" Danny Rose (Allen), tells one

and he did a nice audition. Then I had a cluster of finalists, a number of whom were very famous—Jerry Vale was in there. So I showed the audition tapes to Diane Keaton, who is one of my north stars for these things, and she said, 'This guy is the best,' and I had to agree with her."

Once production started, in the fall of 1982, however, Forte's talents found their limit and Allen had to give acting lessons to the singer to get him through even very simple actions like crossing the street. Farrow, meanwhile, had gone to town with Tina Vitale. She found her attitude in a mixture of Annie Rao, and Honey, the former wife of Frank Sinatra's buddy Jilly Rizzo, drinking milk shakes all day to gain ten pounds, working to lower her voice, watching *Raging Bull* on a loop and taping hours of conversation with Brooklyn women to get the accent right. "Maybe it's my physical look that confused people. I was very thin. I know people think of me that way," said Farrow who was "not Mr. Rollins's first,

Above and right: Danny's faked relationship with Tina is convincing enough to land him in trouble with the Mob.

Overleaf: Working on his penultimate Woody Allen film, cinematographer Gordon Willis perfectly captured this tender moment in the back of a taxicab.

of his acts when we first meet him, a perennially optimistic but hopeless talent agent plugging away for peanuts. "You're gonna fold balloons at universities and colleges!" His only hope of hitting the big time rests with an alcoholic lounge tenor, Lou Canova (Nick Apollo Forte), who was a star in the fifties and is scheduled to make his comeback on Milton Berle's "Nostalgia Special." Lou can't perform without his mistress, Tina (Farrow), in the audience, but Tina, an Italian spitfire in leopard print and a haystack of teased blond hair, is furious with him for "cheating on me with his wife." Moreover, her Mafioso family thinks Danny is the new man in her life. His task therefore becomes twofold—he has not only to get her to the show, but escape the goons sent to whack him along the way.

In figure-hugging pants and dark glasses, cigarette dangling from her mouth, Farrow wiggles into the role as if into a tight pair of jeans. In the bathroom scene, her fine-boned face

registers almost like a glimpse of a nude. "Stripped of her brassiness…she's tender, pure—newborn," wrote Wolcott, who like many spotted a light bead of sweat to Allen's performance: Talking fast, his every other word "sweetheart" or "darling," his arms flailing like an air-traffic controller guiding a 747 in for landing, Allen is wearing a pair of outsized shoes, to be sure, but the loose fit of the role doesn't detract from his fun, or the audience's—our sense of these two meek mice playing ritzy, motor-mouthed extroverts, like a couple dressing up in old clothes at the weekend. Allen's overacting is all of a piece with Danny Rose himself, that ultimate ham, and the rhythm he and Farrow establish is so ticklish that they carry the film. It skips along, making no apologies for its slightness—just another showbiz tall tale recounted by the old diehards at the Carnegie Deli, a piece of Damon Runyon, sliced pastrami thin, but no less zesty and flavorful for that.

"You know what my philosophy of life is?"
That it's important to have some laughs,
but you've got to suffer a little, too.
Because otherwise you miss the whole
point to life."

Danny Rose

The Purple Rose of Cairo

1985

Above: Allen channeled his love of 1930s and 1940s movies into *The Purple Rose of Cairo*.

Opposite: Gil Shepherd (Jeff Daniels) runs into Cecilia (Mia Farrow), his biggest fan and the one person who knows where to find his fugitive alter ego.

Of all Allen's films *The Purple Rose of Cairo* is the one he claimed came closest to his original conception. "Ninety-nine per cent of the time the film I end up with bears little relation to the brilliant idea I had in the bedroom. The film may be a success with the public, but I feel that if only they knew what I had conceived in the bedroom they could really see something great. If only I could've given them *that*."

The script drew in spirit on the long afternoons spent with his cousin and fellow movie fanatic Rita, in whose bedroom, papered with pictures of stars cut out from *Modern Screen* and other fanzines, Allen whiled away so much of his childhood. By the time he was eleven, he could recite the names of pretty much every actor from comedies of the 1930s and 1940s—a silvery, vaulted realm where everyone always wore tuxes and lived in Park Avenue penthouses and drank champagne in

glitzy nightclubs, swapping witty repartee. His first thought was: Wouldn't it be fun if a character were to come down from the screen? "I wrote it and halfway through it didn't go anywhere and I put it aside. I toyed around with other ideas. Only when the idea hit me, a long time later, that the real actor comes to town and she has to choose between the [screen] actor and the real actor and she chooses the real actor and he dumps her, that was the time it became a real movie."

The role of Tom Baxter/Gil Shepherd originally went to Michael Keaton, whom Allen had loved in *Night Shift*, but when he looked at dailies, he found he got no sense of a 1930s movie star from Keaton—he was too contemporary, "too cool"—so after ten days of shooting, Allen bought him out and after convincing Orion that the film oughtn't to be rewritten as a vehicle for him, he cast twenty-nine-year-old Jeff Daniels, then coming off *Terms of Endearment*. "No discussions about characters, motivations, and backgrounds," noted Daniels. "It's as if he's got a feather in his hand and he blows it and it goes in a dozen directions."

Shooting in Piermont, New York, a small town on the Hudson River that still bore some resemblance to a 1930s factory town, Allen dressed an entire block and built the exterior of a movie house. For the interiors, he shot inside one of the iconic movie houses of his youth, the Kent in Midwood—"one of the great, meaningful places of my boyhood"—home of the twelve-cent movie, so close to a railway line that you could hear the freight trains going by every five minutes. He even found a role for Van Johnson, the Golden Era matinee idol who had starred in *A Guy Named Joe* and *The Caine Mutiny*. Allen was so shy he could barely talk to him. "I mean, I'm standing three feet away from Van Johnson! This is the guy who, when I was a kid, I could walk out of a life of tedium and drabness, and there was Van

"My perception is that you are forced to
choose reality over fantasy and reality hurts
you in the end, and fantasy is just madness."

"There's nothing exotic in this film. It takes place during the Depression and deals with poor people who are out of work and, to kill time while waiting for something to turn up, keep going to the cinema."

Tired of his on-screen existence amid cocktail-drinking Manhattanites (right), pith-helmeted explorer Tom Baxter steps through the fourth wall and whisks Cecilia away to a fancy restaurant (left).

Johnson in the cockpit of a plane, or down in Argentina with Esther Williams, who was quite a dish. So maybe that total identification of an actor with the role he plays is one of the things that *Purple Rose of Cairo* is about."

As with *Zelig*, there were a few purely technical problems. The black-and-white film within a film was easy enough but getting the eyeline of the actors to correspond to the people in the audience they were talking to "took a lot of work, a lot of looking at it on paper," said Allen. "It was mathematically tricky." Also problematic was the downbeat ending, at least for the executives at Orion, one of whom called Allen and asked him if he was committed to it. A happy ending would be worth many millions more, he pointed out. "The ending was the reason I made the film," insisted Allen, who had been going for something of the "nostalgic, melancholy feeling" of Fellini's 1973 *Amarcord*. He later reiterated the point to an

interviewer for *Esquire* magazine. Why hadn't he gone with a happy ending, he was asked?

"That *was* the happy ending," came the reply.

You hesitate to call *The Purple Rose of Cairo* a minor work exactly, for like most of Allen's best films from this period— *Zelig, Broadway Danny Rose, Radio Days*—it aspires to the level of beautifully crafted miniature, nostalgic in tone, the product neither of excessive ambition nor of aggressive raids on reality, heeding the gentle diktats of an imagination whose flight patterns were set many years before, in childhood and in the culture he then soaked up like a sponge. "The greatest kind of tranquilizer and embalmment you could think of," Allen once called his youthful moviegoing. That's how Mia Farrow looks watching movies in *The Purple Rose of Cairo*— tranquilized and embalmed. Of all his characters Allen has

called Cecilia the one with whom he most identifies. Drinking in movies at the local cinema, waifish Cecilia (Farrow) wears exactly the same look of milky-eyed transfixion—hand on slow auto-glide from popcorn bag to mouth—that Allen himself wore in the opening credits of *Play It Again, Sam*. In that film, Bogart came down off the screen to dispense dating tips. In *Purple Rose*, Allen goes one better: What about a fully fledged romance between the fictional and the real? Taking in her favorite white-telephone comedy for the umpteenth time one night, Cecilia's eyes widen still further when the hero of the film, a square-jawed, pith-helmeted explorer named Tom Baxter (Jeff Daniels), steps off the screen, leaving his cast of cocktail-drinking Manhattanites lounging around the screen in various states of boredom and panic. "All they do is sit around and talk!" complains one of the theater's patrons, as if at a Woody Allen movie.

What follows is palookaville Pirandello—sweet, multilayered, lyrical, bearing the unmistakably inky thumbprint of Allen's prose writing, in particular "The Kugelmass Episode," his short story about a professor of humanities who slips inside the pages of *Madame Bovary* to enjoy a torrid affair with its heroine, disrupting its plotline for generations. He reverses the procedure and brings Emma to New York, only to find himself paying her enormous hotel bills, and putting up with her pouting and despondence. Kugelmass swears he'll never cheat on his wife again, but three weeks later he seeks to be projected into *Portnoy's Complaint*, only to end up in a Spanish grammar where he is pursued by the verb "to have." The parallels with *The Purple Rose of Cairo* are clear enough, but so too should be the differences between the playful palimpsests of Allen's literary work and the full-bodied

imaginative effort fanning his screenplays into life. The
magician had finally worked out how to make himself
disappear. "It is the first Woody Allen film in which a whole
batch of actors really interact and spark off one another,"
noted Pauline Kael. "Though it doesn't have the sexual
friskiness and roughhousing of some of his other comedies,
and doesn't speak to the audience with the journalist
immediacy of his movies in contemporary settings, it
may be the fullest expression yet of his style of humor."

It is certainly the fullest expression of the central collision
in his work between Allen's glandular urge toward fantasy and
the irksome pinch of reality. "I just met a wonderful new man,"
says Cecilia. "He's fictional but you can't have everything."

The conceit ramifies with wonderful briskness, Daniels's
"real-life" character, Gil Shepherd, pulled out of a publicity
tour as the studio panics over the thought of a rogue double
running around town, while Tom romances Cecilia, bounding
over her protestations like a Labrador. "Right now the whole
country is out of work," she points out. "Then we'll live on
love." Daniels has always had an air of Ralph Bellamy to him—
one of cinema's dimpled dependables—and the role of Tom
Baxter plays to his mixture of gallantry and strangely innocent
egotism. He expands on the latter for the role of Gil Shepherd,
the gloriously self-involved Hollywood star who arrives in
town to confront his double but dissolves into a puddle at the
slightest flattery from Cecilia.

> "That to me has always been a favorite, because I had an idea,
> and I got that idea on the screen as I wanted it. When it was finished,
> I said, 'Yes I had a script and an idea—and there it is!'"

"As might a true Surrealist, she accepts the illogical as the natural order of things." *New York Times*'s film critic Vincent Canby singled out Mia Farrow's performance in his review.

His face as it responds to praise is one of the finest things in the picture: a delighted grin, quickly half-suppressed into a show of mock humility, a glance into the middle distance to suggest the Hopes and Dreams of *un homme sérieux*, followed by a beady-eyed drill for more. Daniels's image of a feather blown from Allen's hand is perfect, for if ever a film existed to show that art has a life beyond the imagination of the artist it is this one; a rambunctious comic colloquy on the nature of creation, *The Purple Rose of Cairo* is the product of a creative mind inured from the world but in full, invigorating dialogue with itself. Perhaps more than any other film Allen made since *Annie Hall*, it reveals the true grain of his talent—its nature, its essence, its inner disposition—and reveals the creative imagination as, in many ways, his greatest subject. His work returns again and again to Pygmalion-ish creators given the runaround by their disobedient creations. In his one-act play *Old Saybrook*, an author gives up on a half-finished script and throws it in the drawer only to have the characters rebel, push the drawer open and take over his Connecticut house. "It worked very well when I directed it for the Atlantic Theater," recalls Allen. "Years ago Larry Gelbart told me he was writing a show and the characters got away from him and I recognized that problem as it has happened to me and usually leads to chaos. I think it's important to keep control of your invented characters and *Purple Rose* is a good example of what happens when you don't."

Hannah and Her Sisters

1986

Above, left to right:
Hannah (Mia Farrow) and
her sisters—Lee (Barbara
Hershey) and Holly
(Dianne Wiest).

The title came first. Then the idea: A man falls in love with
his wife's sister. Allen had always been fascinated by sisters.
While shooting *Take the Money and Run*, he had been close to
his co-star Janet Margolin and her two sisters; Diane Keaton
and her two sisters had formed the original inspiration for
Annie Hall. *Interiors*, too, had been about three sisters. "I have
a tremendous attraction to movies or plays or books that
explore the psyches of women, particularly intelligent ones,"
he said. "I very rarely think in terms of male characters. I
was the only male in a family of many, many women. I had a
sister, female cousins, a mother with seven sisters. I was always
surrounded by women."

He had just recently reread Tolstoy's *Anna Karenina* and
liked the idea of a narrative that roamed through a group
of characters, telling first one person's story, then the next.

"People have been telling me, 'The film is so positive,
so up,' and I think, 'Where did I go wrong?'"

Opposite: Family portrait. Mia Farrow with her real-life children and mother (Maureen O'Sullivan), who assumed the same roles in *Hannah and Her Sisters*.

Right: A winter walk through Central Park during production, early 1986. Having not appeared in *Purple Rose*, Allen returned to the screen as Hannah's ex-husband, Mickey.

The sisters acquired parents, a husband, an ex-husband, and assorted friends and relatives, all mixed into the course of two years and three Thanksgivings, during which time relationships begin and end, things change, and life goes on. "While we walked, worked, ate, slept, and lived our lives, the story of Hannah was fleshed out, detail by familiar detail," said Mia Farrow, whose relationships with her two sisters, the younger of whom, Tina, had already taken a small part in *Manhattan*, gave Allen much of his inspiration. However, when she was handed the completed script to read, Farrow was unusually critical.

"The characters seemed self-indulgent and dissolute," she later wrote. "At the same time he was my partner. I loved him. I could trust him with my life. And he was a writer: This is what writers do. All is grist for the mill. Relatives have always grumbled. He had taken the ordinary stuff of our lives and lifted it into art. We were honored and outraged."

Allen told Farrow she could choose any part but hoped she would pick Hannah, the most complex and enigmatic of the sisters, whose silent strength he likened to that of Al Pacino's Michael in *The Godfather*. This comparison contained all the ambivalence he felt about the character, whose exact degree of virtue he had been undecided on, while writing. For Hannah's husband, Elliot, he wanted Jack Nicholson, but Nicholson had a commitment to make *Prizzi's Honor* with John Huston, so Allen turned to Michael Caine, Farrow's friend of over twenty

years who had first introduced the couple. "The atmosphere on Woody's set was a bit like working in church," said Caine. "He was a very quiet and sensitive man who liked to work in a very quiet atmosphere, so even the crew on his pictures—who for the most part have worked with him many times—were the quietest crew with whom I have ever worked."

Collaborating for the first time with Antonioni's cinematographer Carlo Di Palma, Allen began shooting in the fall of 1984 in New York City, using Farrow's real-life apartment at the Langham, on Central Park West, as Hannah's home in the film, and her own children for the big family Thanksgiving scenes that bookend the film. They would go in at eight thirty in the morning, block out the moves, and sometimes only got around to shooting at eight at night because it took so long to light. "The place was pandemonium," said Farrow who some nights couldn't find her own bed. "The rooms were clogged with equipment. Forty people arrived at dawn crowding into any available space, our personal treasures were spirited away to who-knew-where. The kitchen was an active set for weeks…It was strange to be shooting scenes in my own rooms—my kitchen, my pots, my own kids saying lines, Michael Caine in my bathroom, wearing a robe, rummaging through my medicine cabinet. Or me lying in my own bed kissing Michael, with Woody watching…The commotion, and not being able to find anything, sometimes got me a little crazy. But the kids loved it."

"I don't know if you remember me, but we had the worst night of my life together." A chance meeting in a record store enables Mickey and Holly to put their disastrous first date behind them.

"The film had a simple plot about a man who falls in love with his wife's sister…but I reread Anna Karenina, and I thought, it's interesting how this guy gets the various stories going, cutting from one story to another. I loved the idea of experimenting with that."

As usual, Allen's only real direction to his actors was to change the wording of the script until they felt comfortable with it. "The first thing he says is, if you're not comfortable, change it," said Dianne Wiest. "Little nudgy things like changing the verb and the noun or adding on a 'you know.' You know?" He also encouraged everyone to talk at the same time, interrupting and reacting to each other's lines. "Woody would come out and say, 'Don't just listen passively. You should be responding audibly,'" said Farrow. "Other directors dislike overlap, because it disrupts their ability to cut into the film in a conventional way, with close-ups and over-the-shoulder scenes. But Woody's pace is to keep the camera going in long master shots, covering the scene all in one fluid motion, and that means making atmospheric dialogue sometimes rather than really relevant stuff. One cameraman calls it 'putting a little fluff in there.'"

Only if he heard phoniness did he pounce. Once catching Carrie Fisher fall into an imitation of Diane Keaton's halting delivery, he told her, "Don't do that, say the whole sentence in one clump," and when she arrived at a party scene gesticulating wildly, he told her, "You're coming in like my

Aunt Velma." He also personally picked the wardrobe and hairdo for each actress, checking the makeup and rechecking, even reshooting a scene if he felt a minor detail of their appearance was wrong. One time, Barbara Hershey wore one of her favorite blue sweaters to the set on the off-chance of wearing it in the movie. "He told me, 'Never wear that color as long as you live.' I've had a hard time putting it on ever since."

Only about twenty percent of the original script ended up in the film. Many completed scenes were discarded, such as an art gallery sequence with Tony Roberts and a sex scene between Hershey and Caine; and there were the usual reshoots, including the ending, which originally showed Elliot still hopelessly in love with Lee but stuck in his marriage to Hannah. "But when I looked at it, it was like the picture dropped off the table. It was negative, a downer. So I guided the thing instinctively to an ending where all the characters came out happy, and the picture was very successful. But I never felt positive about it. I felt I had a very poignant idea but finally couldn't bring it home."

From this splinter he would fashion the wedge that would allow him to divorce the film entirely ("*Hannah and Her Sisters* is a film I feel I screwed up very badly")—as he did any movie of his that became a popular success—but many disagreed, including Barbara Hershey. "The overview is how silly and sad and funny and endearing we are for being so involved in all these relationships when really we're going to die. And yet, what else are we going to do? It's this wonderful view of how life is important, and in the little time we have what better thing can we do with it except make total fools of ourselves in trying to live. That kind of sweet ending really moved me."

Upon the film's release, critics lifted it to the roof beams. "Woody's greatest triumph," declared Rex Reed in the *New York Observer*. "Allen's writing and directing style is so

strong and assured in this film that the actual filmmaking itself becomes a narrative voice," wrote Roger Ebert in the *Chicago Sun-Times*. Even Pauline Kael was charmed, calling it "an agreeably skillful movie." The film broke records in London's West End and was the toast of Cannes, where it was accompanied by a specially filmed interview with Allen directed by Jean-Luc Godard. It went on to win three Oscars, for Best Original Screenplay, Best Supporting Actor for Caine, and Best Supporting Actress for Wiest, none of which deterred Allen from his glum opinion of the picture. "I don't think *Hannah* is as good as *Blue Velvet*," he said. "The best picture of the year was *Blue Velvet*, in my opinion. I just liked everything about it." When David Lynch received an Oscar nomination he quipped to the press, "I'd like to thank Woody Allen."

The problem for creative talents as allergic to reality as Allen is: material. As his old joke has it, he may hate reality but it's still the only place where you can get a good steak. Life must be lived, experience endured, material gathered if the writer is not to exist in a state of wan, hermetically sealed self-delight. Now, Allen's powers of self-delight are formidable. After the trauma of popular success in the late 1970s, he spent most of the 1980s in retreat, holed up in a nostalgic imaginative idyll that spanned from Babe Ruth's first home run to the last Marx Brothers movie, fashioning works like *Zelig* and *The Purple Rose of Cairo*—films as intricate and delightful and self-contained as Fabergé eggs. But, by the by, he'd also been learning from Farrow, the same way he learned from Keaton, picking her up like lint: her habits, her rhythms,

her interactions with her family. From its very first scene, a Thanksgiving dinner brimming with chatter between Hannah (Farrow), and sisters Holly (Dianne Wiest) and Lee (Barbara Hershey), during which we are privy to the lustful thoughts of Hannah's husband, Elliot (Michael Caine), toward Lee, and Lee's thoughts on the cab ride home ("Is it my imagination or does Elliot have a little crush on me?"), *Hannah and Her Sisters* reveals itself with the density of a novel while availing itself of the full freedoms of a movie. It's Allen's richest script since *Annie Hall*, and would remain the high-water mark of what happens when he is fully engaged and in the world, his senses awake, his wits about him.

He never did work out whether Hannah was a sympathetic character or not and the result is Farrow's most nuanced performance. He gets at something withheld in the actress; for all her warmth, Hannah's very perfection ("disgustingly perfect") lends her an enameled finish, as if refusing the flaws by which others get to know one another, even as she anchors the story and raises her small army of children with her financial-analyst husband. "There's something very lovely and real about Hannah. She gives me a very deep feeling of being part of something," thinks Elliot on the night he has first slept with Lee, guiltily resolving to finish the affair, only to receive Lee's midnight call, lighting up at the sound of her voice. Caine's performance is a remarkable balancing act of intoxication ("I'm walking on air!") and agony, as he wriggles like a worm stuck on his own hook. Allen's range of male alter egos tends to suffer terribly from Woody Allen-itis, as gifted actors struggle to impersonate his mannerisms and halting delivery, but Caine's soft English prevarications prove a perfect vessel for all of Allen's romantic ambivalence—his buccaneering and opportunism and dashed moral sobriety are all there in Caine's face, flashing and faltering like a loose lightbulb.

Lunch descends into an argument between Holly and Hannah, while Lee is preoccupied with guilt over her affair with Elliot.

All of Allen's intellectual pride and misanthropy, on the other hand, is poured into Max von Sydow as Lee's artist lover, Frederick, a somber highbrow sitting in his Soho loft watching Holocaust documentaries, only to have his critique of the twentieth century cut short by the revelation of Lee's infidelity. Rapping his knuckles against his head as if cursing his own intellect, Frederick's anguish lends genuine moral gravity to this portrait of an affair—a full-blown anatomy, from first blush to breakup, scored to Bach not the big-band jazz that bustles the rest of the picture along. "The heart is a resilient little muscle," says Allen himself, providing comic relief as Hannah's ex-husband, Mickey, a hypochondriac whose near-miss with a brain tumor causes him to quit his job as TV writer, like Isaac Davis in *Manhattan*, and take up Allen's favorite orbital position, lobbing smart bombs at fat joggers, punk rockers, and Hare Krishnas. Another first: his first ensemble with him in a supporting role in which he doesn't steal the show. Everyone is their own sun here, with the audience privy not just to Allen's character's thoughts, via voiceover, but those of Caine's and Hershey's and Wiest's

and Farrow's, too, as if tuning through radio stations, while cinematographer Carlo Di Palma tracks and pans his camera from room to room, and face to face, as the three sisters converge for brunch in a diner.

Time has only served to underline how much Dianne Wiest is one of Allen's true leading ladies—alongside Keaton and Farrow. As Holly, she jangles with neuroses and bad choices, but so forgivingly observed that her face, which seems always to photograph in soft focus, may be all you want to look at—she's Allen's most appealing flake since *Annie Hall*. For once, the critical plaudits were accurate: *Hannah and Her Sisters* may well be Allen's greatest accomplishment as a writer-director. At 107 minutes, it was his longest picture to date but deft and brisk and bustling, with riches around every corner, and a cast of characters caught between their foolish hearts and rueful heads, all observed by a filmmaker who could almost be their father—a benevolent paterfamilias who treats each of his characters with the tenderness and bluntness one reserves for a blood relative. The film is, in every respect, family.

Radio Days

1987

Above: Joe (Seth Green, second from right) and his friends go on the lookout for Nazi aircraft, but are soon distracted by another kind of siren.

Opposite: Joe's crowded, noisy household was an exaggerated version of Allen's own childhood home.

"A big colorful cartoon, almost a musical but not quite," said Allen of *Radio Days*. It evolved from the music. He started by picking out a group of recordings that were meaningful to him growing up—Artie Shaw's version of "Begin the Beguine," Bing Crosby and the Andrews Sisters' "Pistol Packin' Mama," the Merry Macs' "Mairzy Doats"—and let each one suggest a memory, embroidering or exaggerating as need be. "Some things are very close and some things are not," he said. "My relationship to the teachers was like that. My relationship to radio was like that. The same with the Hebrew school. And we used to go to the beach and look for German aircraft and German boats. And I did have an aunt who was forever getting into the wrong relationships and unable to get married. She never did get married. And we did have those neighbors who were communists. Much of that was true. I was taken to New York to the Automat and to radio programs. My cousin lived

with me. We did have a telephone line where we could listen in on the neighbors. All these things occurred."

The film was shot in Rockaway, a run-down Long Island resort, in the winter of 1985, with Carlo Di Palma's characteristic deeply saturated colors against the slate-gray backdrop of Rockaway Beach. Allen thought nothing of leaving seventy extras standing—or scrapping shot material—because the light was not right. "Whenever I'm shooting around a beach I wait for the flat days," he said. "Of course, many people make the country look incredibly beautiful. In some of these English pictures and Stanley Kubrick's, it's to die for, it's so beautiful. But my personal taste and favorite is to shoot at the beach on gray days."

Originally Allen's idea was to tie each song to the exact time and place his alter ego, Joe (Seth Green), is when he first hears it, but that soon grew monotonous so Allen started braiding his story with those of the other listeners and radio personalities. Jeff Daniels played a 1940s radio star named Biff Baxter. Danny Aiello, Diane Keaton, Wallace Shawn, Mia Farrow, Julie Kavner, and Tony Roberts all turn up in roles, the only time Farrow and Keaton have ever appeared in the same Woody Allen film. Allen had a hard time writing Keaton into the all-Jewish setting of the movie, but eventually had her sing the Cole Porter classic "You'd Be So Nice to Come Home To" on New Year's Eve. Farrow's character, Sally, was only revealed after thirty-five different takes, using thirty-five different voices. They didn't pick the one they were going to use until they had started editing.

As was now becoming usual, there were extensive reshoots. A cast of more than 200 speaking parts—"the biggest we've ever had"—was cut down to 150. An initial decision to contrast the warm domestic interiors with the cool art deco of the broadcasting studios was abandoned and material reshot.

"I think of Radio Days basically as a cartoon. And I picked out the actors for their cartoon quality."

"A purely pleasurable, self-indulgent thing."

Opposite: Covering all the angles with Mia Farrow as Sally, a cigarette girl who has ambitions to break into radio.

Right: Diane Keaton in an unusually minor role as an unnamed New Year singer. *Radio Days* is the only Woody Allen film in which Keaton and Farrow both appear.

Below: "Ceil, I'm home! Ceil, I got fish! I got great fish today." Uncle Abe (Josh Mostel) brings home another catch.

With Dianne Wiest attending her father's funeral, Allen came up with some extra scenes involving Sally and a gangster who is supposed to whack her, instead taking her home to meet his mother. Thanks to the low cost of shooting a Woody Allen picture—even with reshoots *Radio Days* cost only $16 million—he could quite literally sketch out his movie then fill in detail, or come up with whole subplots, later in production. No writer-director in the history of motion pictures—not Chaplin, not Preston Sturges—has ever made use of the flexibility inherent in their hyphenate status with anything quite like this suppleness.

That *Radio Days* works as well as it does is largely down to this unique working method. Allen himself called it a "purely personal, self-indulgent" exercise in nostalgia—a "cartoon." The film could easily have been a succession of sketches, loosely linked by the music alone. It shows you how deeply music infiltrates his filmmaking, and how intricately he found his memories honeycombed with those old songs, that such a conceit instead yields an entire world, full of incident and

Above: "Boy, that was fast. Probably helped I had the hiccups." Sally assesses her rooftop tryst with the lecherous Roger (David Warrilow).

Right: On location at Rockaway Beach in Queens.

vivid characterization, the nearest he has come to an account of his childhood, with its attendant bustle of noisy aunts and uncles, and a ne'er-do-well father bursting with cockamamie schemes to get rich before finally being unveiled in his job as a cab driver. In this regard, the most important scene of all may well be the one in which young Joe makes his way through the gilded art deco corridors of the Radio City Music Hall to see James Stewart and Katharine Hepburn embrace in *The Philadelphia Story*. "It was like entering heaven," narrates Allen of this primal bliss, his version of Bergman's first encounter

with a magic lantern. "I'd never seen anything so beautiful in my life."

Any novelist would be familiar with the liberties Allen takes with his own story as well as the fun he has with the distortions of memory in *Radio Days*. It is not quite enough to call the film "nostalgic," if that term is meant to damn with faint praise. Along with those other gems of his 1980s writing career—*Zelig, The Purple Rose of Cairo*, and *Broadway Danny Rose*, with which it shares its sense of oral history, of tall tales stretched in the retelling—the stretch marks of *Radio Days*

are the story. Hence the three different endings he gives us to the story of Sally trapped on the roof of the St. Regis with the lecherous Roger (David Warrilow), each version more crowded than the last, until finally it seems like an All-Star Woody Allen reunion party up there, with Farrow joined by Jeff Daniels, Wallace Shawn, and Tony Roberts, all seeing in the 1944 New Year with champagne as a giant lightbulb-illuminated top hat is hoisted aloft over Broadway. We may have no better re-creation of the inside of Woody Allen's head, on any given hour in any given day.

September

1987

September was a muddle from the start. The idea had been to shoot something at Mia Farrow's house at Frog Hollow, Connecticut, where the isolated acres and weeping willow–shrouded lake once prompted the thought, in an idle, lounging Allen, that it was no wonder people kill themselves. The germ of something Chekhovian about unrequited familial love and past traumas presented itself. Delayed by the reshoots for *Radio Days*, Allen finished his screenplay in October 1986, by which time the coming winter had obliterated any semblance of late summer/early fall, so the entire movie was shot on a single soundstage at the Kaufman Astoria Studios in New York. With his agoraphobic inclinations, this suited Allen down to the ground—"I wanted all those rigors of a play structure," he said, "the more internalized we got, the happier I was"—although one has to wonder about a piece of cinema whose initial inspiration was a landscape foregoing

that inspiration so blithely, no matter how inwardly driven the filmmaker at the time.

If *Hannah and Her Sisters* and *Radio Days* had shown what Allen's remarkable method of shooting could achieve when playing to his strengths, *September* highlighted exactly what can go wrong when a film plays to the fussily perfectionistic instincts of a filmmaker not in command of his material. "We reshot every single scene as we went along—sometimes four or five times," noted Farrow, who played the central character, Lane. "Woody rewrote major scenes overnight or at lunch while the cast scrambled to learn the rewrites and to make the long speeches and sometimes ponderous dialogue sound credible and fresh. Fine actors fell by the wayside, including my mother. Parts were recast. There was a shaky feeling in the air."

Initially cast as the terminally passive Peter, Christopher Walken was deemed too sexy in the role and replaced with Sam Shepard, whom Allen scarcely liked better, blowing a fuse when the actor launched into an improvised monologue about the glories of Montana ("Montana?" he huffed in private, "*Montana?*"). As soon as he saw Denholm Elliott in the role of Lane's physicist stepfather, he thought he would be better as the widower neighbor Howard, played by Charles Durning, whose performance he was also unhappy with, along with that of Farrow's real-life mother, Maureen O'Sullivan, as her fictional mother. Watching his first edit, Allen hated it.

"The first time I saw *September*, I knew I had to do it over," he said, "So I said to myself, 'Well, as long as I'm going to do four weeks of reshooting, why not reshoot the whole thing and do it right?'" Orion executive Eric Pleskow was "numb" when he heard the news, which sent shockwaves through the studio's executive suites. Reshoots were one thing but discarding a picture that had completed principal photography was almost unheard of. But "we weren't going

Take two. Allen stunned his studio by completely reshooting the film with a new script and a radically reworked cast. Here on set with new recruits Elaine Stritch and Sam Waterston.

to destroy a relationship over that one thing," said Pleskow, so with Shepard committed to one of his plays in California, and O'Sullivan ill with pneumonia, Allen rewrote the whole script, recast almost every major part, and filmed the entire thing a second time, this time with Sam Waterston in Shepard's role and Elaine Stritch in O'Sullivan's, Denholm Elliott switched over to Durning's role—"same performance, more money" quipped Elliott—and Jack Warden was brought in to play the stepfather. For the first time, Allen more than doubled his production costs and came in well behind schedule. "I knew full well it wouldn't make a dime," he said, "Not a dime."

Taking only $486,000 at the box office, *September* remains Allen's lowest-grossing movie. It's not hard to see why. The film is constructed as a series of dialogues which are actually alternating monologues by characters doing private battle with their ambivalence. Everyone operates at the highest possible level of indecision, hovering and blurring like hummingbirds. Traumatized by her brassy, overbearing mother, Lane (Farrow) frets ineffectually about her lack of career direction, holding herself quiet as a mouse, as if she would otherwise implode. As her mother, Stritch walks into each room as if holding her own at a cocktail party with people she has just met. The recasting can hardly have helped the actors mesh as an ensemble. During a storm, Peter, Howard, Lane, and her friend Stephanie (Dianne Wiest) reveal unrequited crushes on one

another that are instantly rebuffed. Lane's mother has more luck communicating with her dead lovers via a Ouija board. Indeed, the whole film has the funereal hush of communication with the spirit world. It's so faded and finessed and fussed-over it passes right through you—a ghost of a movie.

This was the seventh movie he had made with Farrow and their collaboration was beginning to curdle, the characterizations he gave her fraying at the edges with resentment, the actress seeming to shrink further into herself with each role. The first of three films in which Farrow wrestled with a boozy, failed actress mother, *September* seems to come less from a desire on Allen's part to craft an involving drama than to psychoanalyze his partner. The film is introspective but numb, like *Interiors*. Indeed, a pattern seemed to have been established, wherein Allen responded to the trauma of popular acclaim with a picture as shut-down as the characters it claims to diagnose—after *Annie Hall*, *Interiors*. After *Hannah and Her Sisters*, *September*. Allen's misreading of the ending of *Hannah* is, in this instance, informative. If you see the optimism of the final Thanksgiving dinner in *Hannah*'s apartment as an ambrosial sop to the masses, as he did, rather than as a crucial leavening of charity that fills out the worldview of any major artist, then you come up with a picture as glum and monotonous as *September* to even things up.

"It's not what I sat down to write, exactly. It's called 'floundering.'"

Another Woman

1988

Another Woman started life as "a Chaplinesque sort of comedy" about a man who overhears a woman talking to her analyst. When he discovers she is beautiful, he uses the information he gleans from her sessions to transform himself into her dream man. Allen was not in a mood for such romantic chicanery—the eavesdropping seemed to hang heavy with Hitchcockian overtones—but still the idea nagged at him, before it finally morphed into another of his studies in repression: a woman, emotionally shut down, but now in her fifties and no longer able to wall her emotions out. "What the movie is about is a woman who is cold and intellectual and bright, and doesn't want to know the truth about her life, is not interested in the truth and has blocked it out," he said. "Her husband cheating on her. She's blocked that out. She's cold. She's cold to her brother. She's not had a close relationship with her father. All of this she doesn't want to know and doesn't want to face. And finally… she gets to be middle-aged, and the truth encroaches upon her."

It was his first time shooting with cinematographer Sven Nykvist, who had developed an intimate, close-up–driven style of shooting with Ingmar Bergman which he called "two faces and a tea cup." Allen was less enamored of close-ups than Bergman, and preferred a darker palette that took some getting used to. "It's hard to do a picture entirely in mud," quipped costume designer Jeff Kurland. "But their faces look like tomatoes," complained Nykvist. "He got to like it," said Allen. "But even now the lab doesn't believe how dark I want the film."

The casting was something of a roundelay, as *September* had been. Mia Farrow was supposed to have played the main

character, Marion, but her pregnancy prevented that, so he gave the role to Gena Rowlands, originally opposite Ben Gazzara as Marion's husband, Ken, but Allen recast Ian Holm in the role. Dianne Wiest was set to play Hope but had to back out due to illness so he gave the role to Jane Alexander, but when she didn't work out he wound up back with Farrow, whose pregnancy could now be written into the part. Producer Robert Greenhut and production manager Joe Hartwick were driven to distraction by Allen's rewrites during shooting. The film was originally to have opened with a single tracking shot following Marion walking down the street carrying groceries for her new apartment. After crews spent two hours setting up track, Allen changed his mind. "No," he said simply. The crew set about dismantling the shot. Another scene which

Opposite: Headed in the same direction with Gena Rowlands (Marion).

Right: *Another Woman* contains a ten-minute dream sequence from Marion's subconscious, during which her husband, Ken (Ian Holm), and her friend Claire (Sandy Dennis) rehearse a play.

Allen insisted on rewriting and reshooting, on the last day of production, never even made it into the finished film.

A more engrossing film than *September*, it was nonetheless only half the breakthrough Allen thought it was. More specifically, the first half, which thrums with an unfamiliar feeling in his oeuvre: suspense. Alone in the apartment she has rented for writing, the sternly beautiful Marion (Rowlands) overhears a suicidal woman (Farrow) unburdening herself of her fears about her marriage to her psychiatrist. "Self-deception," she diagnoses. "Bit general isn't it?" says the shrink. So is the film, which suffers from a crucial lack of development. The overheard conversations prompt reflections from Marion on her own life—her first marriage, her unfulfilling second marriage to a successful cardiologist (Ian Holm), the memory of a man (Gene Hackman) who once loved her passionately— all of them deftly sketched, but right at the point where you're expecting the plot to thicken, Allen hits us with a stultifying ten-minute dream sequence, à la Bergman, in which Marion seeks closure with her various ghosts in stiff, literary language, while Eric Satie's third *Gymnopédie* tinkles tastefully in the background. Ads for bathroom freshener should be so tasteful.

"I guess we all imagine what might have been but that was long ago," says Hope, after a chance meeting brings her and Marion together. That, too, flares briefly with dramatic possibilities and then fizzles out in a damp exchange of regrets.

If the film had been a comedy, Allen would almost certainly have asked himself the old Danny Simon question, "And *then* what?" But his films from this period—particularly *September*, *Another Woman*, and *Shadows and Fog*—seem slack and easily exhausted, exploring lives stuck in ruts whose fitful, fruitless energies they unintentionally mimic. Highbrow aspirations seem to bring on Allen's perfectionist impulses like a rash, banishing the very energies that whip his comedies into life and wrapping his dramas in layer upon layer of technique that muffle the emotions at their center. They are obsessive but woolly, like someone driven mad by an itch they cannot reach through seven sweaters. Given all these floating intimations of doom, not to mention plots involving infidelity, one can't but wonder at the oncoming train crash in Allen's domestic life, already detectable as faint vibrations on the tracks—not so much art imitating life as art pregnant with life's plots before they even hatch.

"I see this as the culmination of a journey
that I thought might take ten years but
has taken about twenty-five."

Cliff (Woody Allen)
discovers that he has lost
Halley (Mia Farrow) to his
despised brother-in-law
Lester (Alan Alda).

Crimes and Misdemeanors

1989

Allen wrote *Crimes and Misdemeanors* in a series of hotels
while vacationing in Europe in the summer of 1988, banging
out the drafts on the stationery of whichever hotel he
happened to find himself—the long, thin sheets of the Villa
d'Este on Lake Como; the wide, pure white, gold-embossed
letterhead of the Gritti Palace in Venice; the elegant blue of
Claridge's in London. By the time he reached London, his
coat pockets, where he stored the drafts, bulged as if they held
loaves of bread, and his assistant, Jane Martin, convinced him
to stash the work in the hotel safe, if only to avoid spilling
soup on it in a restaurant. Each day Allen would accumulate
more scraps of paper, fold them in half, and lock them away
before going out to wander the West End.

Returning to New York he had the first draft of what was
tentatively titled *Brothers*, about two siblings, one of whom,
a distinguished surgeon who is being blackmailed by his
mistress, asks the other to commit murder on his behalf.
"And he gets away with it! And leads a wonderful life after,
presumably. If he doesn't choose to punish himself then
he's gotten away with it," noted Allen. "Someone else doing
Crimes and Misdemeanors could have a brilliant murder
scene. Alfred Hitchcock or Martin Scorsese—a guy knocks
on the door holding flowers and she answers it and what
ensues is a minute and a half of brilliant cinema. The only
explanation I can give is that for me, because I'm more writer
than anything, all that stuff becomes material for me to make
my points on, to talk about, to philosophize over. I'm not
interested in the killing itself. The killing takes place so guys
can talk about guilt and God."

Called in to audition for the role of Judah, Martin Landau
was keen to do the part but worried about whether he would
lose the audience. "Why on earth would people want to
spend time watching this asshole?" he asked, but Allen hired

159

him on the spot and agreed to make a few revisions to the script, particularly to his scenes with the mistress, played by Anjelica Huston, who received only the portion of the script dealing with her character. Similarly, the actors playing Judah's family knew nothing of Huston's part, only that Landau's character kept disappearing to make guilty phone calls. Originally, Allen had no plans to appear in the movie himself but at Touchstone's request he wrote a small part for himself as a documentary maker named Cliff Stern shooting a film about old vaudevillians, who falls in love with Mia Farrow's nurse. "Well," said Allen after seeing the first cut, "the good news is it's better than I thought, apart from some obvious necessary cuts and trims. The bad news is, Mia's and my story doesn't work."

Over the next few weeks he threw out fully one third of the story, including the vaudeville documentary, and revamped the plot, ending up reshooting eighty of the film's 139 scenes. A radical overhaul even by Allen's standards, this

made it, bar *September*, his most reshot film. As production progressed, the boxes of film with scenes of characters who were no longer in the picture piled up in the screening room: Sean Young's scenes were cut; Daryl Hannah's involvement reduced to a brief, uncredited cameo. Meanwhile, the role of Alan Alda as Cliff's blowhard brother-in-law Lester, originally a bit part improvised in rehearsal for a single scene where he was supposed to appear at a party with Daryl Hannah on his arm, was greatly enlarged. Allen realized he had come up with a worthy antagonist. "In the first version, Channel 13 was making a film on him and I [Cliff] resented that all these legitimate sources fell prey to his charm," said Allen. "And so I had the idea of, 'Why don't I make the film and integrate the story more?' And then it came to life."

Allen gives his most dolorous performance as Cliff, the frustrated documentary filmmaker who tags around resentfully after Alan Alda's showboat TV producer in *Crimes*

Opposite: A flashback to a run on the beach for Judah (Martin Landau) and his troublesome mistress Dolores (Anjelica Huston). The actors playing Judah's family knew nothing of Huston's part while they were shooting the film.

Right: "Let me ask you something. Am I a phony?" Lester confides in his sister Wendy (Joanna Gleason), Cliff's wife.

and Misdemeanors. Allen's face has succumbed to the droop of middle age, acquiring a hangdog air of utmost softness—a saintly loser doomed by his integrity. He gets plenty of bits of comic mischief to perform—notably a silent flurry of sarcastic laughter behind Alda's back —but the film is his most overt thesis statement on the false grail of American success: In both plots, winners thrust muscularly and aggressively to the fore, while the virtuous plummet. Such was the theme, too, of *September*, in which Mia Farrow got chewed up by her deafeningly strident mother. In Allen's world, mid-period, the meek do not inherit the earth. They get shoved aside and trodden underfoot by rhino-skinned victors.

Allen was rightly mesmerized by Landau's performance as Judah, his face graven with guilt, his low, mellifluous voice giving cello-timbre resonance to Allen's ruminations about guilt and God. "We went from a small infidelity to the meaning of existence!" notes his rabbi, played by Sam Waterston. But Landau's performance is actually in

contravention of Allen's central thesis—he's the very picture of stricken conscience—and at its weakest when having to chew over the moral and philosophical implications of his actions, notably in a scene in which Judah interacts with a childhood memory of his family discussing the evil of the Nazis. "History is written by the winners," says one aunt. Well, yes. But the Nazis lost. Hitler died in a bunker as Berlin fell. The right people won there, surely.

Alda, too, is terrific as the oleaginous smoothie Lester, his arms snaking around every woman's waist, pontificating loudly on all of Allen's pet subjects from the city of New York to politics to comedy ("Comedy is tragedy plus time") while Cliff rolls his eyes, incredulously. That the successful are also horribly shallow is one of the more consoling illusions of the *New York Review of Books*–reading public, although one might reasonably ask what aspects of success Allen found to be so meretricious, exactly at this point in his career? Lionized at home and abroad, the winner of every award a filmmaker

Right: The two main plot strands intertwine in the end scene when Judah and Cliff finally meet.

Opposite: "It'll give me a little distance." "About 3,000 miles, to be exact." Cliff is taken aback by Halley's announcement that she is going away to London.

can hope to win, Allen had more in common with the Lesters of this world than the woebegone Cliff. Lester is Allen in a distorting mirror—liberated from self-doubt, lapping up the applause, enjoying his success as Allen never could.

"When I put out a film that enjoys any acceptance that isn't the most mild or grudging, I immediately become suspicious of it," he said. "A certain amount of positive response makes me feel comfortable and proud. Then beyond that, I start to feel convinced that a work of any real finesse and subtlety and depth couldn't be as popular as it is." As if to prove him right, *Crimes and Misdemeanors was* overpraised upon its release, in part because critics were so relieved to see Allen back on screen again, kvetching like it was 1977, John Simon calling it "Allen's first successful blending of drama and comedy plot

and subplot" in the *New York Times*—an obvious nonsense. In fact, the two halves of the film swing almost wholly free of one another, linked only by theme until the final scene in which Cliff and Judah finally meet—the sinner, scrubbed of guilt, and the saintly but self-flagellating loser, sitting side by side on a piano stool, pondering the world's iniquities. In the script, the scene was supposed to be between Judah and Ben, the rabbi, but Waterston was unavailable for shooting, so Allen stepped in, and now, of course, it's hard to imagine it any other way. The scene is so gentle, Allen's face etched in Nykvist's delicate charcoal shadows, that he could almost be talking to himself, as indeed he was after a fashion, strapping superego and furtive subconscious brought into hushed, intent dialogue with one another.

"There are certain movies of mine that I call 'novels on film,' and Crimes and Misdemeanors is one of them, wherein a number of characters are being dissected and a number of stories are going on at the same time...The trick is then to keep all the stories up in the air at the same time, so that you can follow them all and get involved in them all without getting bored."

Alice

1990

The idea for *Alice* came to Allen when he sought an alternative treatment for a stye in his eye. "I remember at that time friends were going to a quack doctor in Chinatown, sucking up these herbs and paying a fortune for them. So I was having an eye problem of some sort and I couldn't get rid of it. It just went on and on and I took all sorts of medicine. Finally my friend said, 'I'll buy you a session with this doctor and I guarantee he will get rid of it.' I said, 'I'm not going to Chinatown.' And she said, 'He'll come over to your house and he will cure you. What do you have to lose? Give him one session and if he doesn't cure you, then no harm.' So I said okay and the guy comes over to my house and he's got a pussycat whisker. And he puts it in my tear duct and he leaves—and of course it had zero effect. When I told my eye doctor, he said, 'Don't ever let anybody put anything in there! You could get an infection! God knows what could happen!'"

The story about the cat's whisker had already popped up in *Crimes and Misdemeanors*—where it is retold by one of Judah's dinner guests—but the story for *Alice*, working title *The Magical Herbs of Dr. Yang*, was more directly a refashioning of Allen's last film but one. "*Alice* is a comedy version of *Another Woman*," he said. "In *Another Woman*, Marion, the main character, hears voices through the wall and these voices provoke her to change her life. And in this story it's the comic approach. The same kind of woman comes to reexamine her life in a different way, but still with a similar purpose." The story of a hypochondriac upper-class housewife, Alice Tate (Mia Farrow), who is ignored by her wealthy husband, Doug (William Hurt), and partakes of various prescriptions written by a Chinese herbalist, *Alice* allowed Allen to turn the tables on his own skepticism. The twist is that the potions work, making Alice invisible and allowing her to spy on her husband being unfaithful, conjure up an old lover, have an affair with

another man, and nurture her aspirations to be a writer. The quack works.

"*Alice* had a little style to it," said Allen, "a nice cartoon quality, to some degree like *Radio Days*." The shooting also saw a resurgence of the director's perfectionism, now in high season. After filming for just six days in the November of 1989, he felt he had no usable footage and started reshooting, maddened by a wrong camera angle, or the sudden glimpse of Farrow's white dress under her red coat as she walked across Central Park. "All this obsession, it isn't perfectionism," he insisted, "It's compulsion—and all of that is no guarantee that the film is going to be any good."

A distinction without a difference, maybe—but the film *was* good, an enchanting fantasia of mid-life regeneration. Praised by critics only as a trifle following the more heavily themed *Crimes and Misdemeanors*, *Alice* finds the director playing for magic realism what *Another Woman* and *September* had

Opposite: Mia Farrow as Alice Tate, a hypochondriac upper-class housewife, in this enchanting fantasia of mid-life regeneration.

Right: Seeing eye to eye with Farrow and Alec Baldwin (Ed).

Above and opposite: "Tell me I don't look so bad considering I'm dead." "Oh no, considering you're dead you look *great*." The acupuncturist's prescription summons up the spirit of Alice's ex-boyfriend Ed.

Right: Alice's magical experiences help to reveal the failings of her husband, Doug (William Hurt).

treated as somnolent tragedy. The conceit is perhaps a little baggy, pushing the film's running time out to an unusually prolix 102 minutes, as Alice uses the acupuncturist's herbal teas to disappear and spy, invisibly, on her saxophonist crush, Joe (Joe Mantegna); to summon the ghost of the Boyfriend Who Got Away, Ed (Alec Baldwin); take a magical flyby of Manhattan's skyscrapers; before heeding the advice of an unusually streetwise muse (Bernadette Peters) and confronting her mother and sister about the lies cobwebbing their family. Magic, too diffusely defined, can seem a thin proxy for the dramatist's own devices and desires.

But the film works, chiefly as a vehicle for Farrow, the whole movie seemingly pitched to her astonished, house-mouse whisper. You lean in to watch it. Her greatest gift has always been her credulity—she's one of the screen's great

believers—as Roman Polanski realized when he first opened those eyes to demonic goings-on in *Rosemary's Baby*. That guilelessness is of particular use to a comic fabulist like Allen, whose plots feature such magical elements as movie actors who come off the screen, and human chameleons who can change shape at will. Farrow's reactions—a marvelous blend of doubt and wonder, though never disbelief—kept the central conceits of *The Purple Rose of Cairo* and *Zelig* afloat. In *Alice*, she stretches those wide eyes wider still until they seem willing to swallow the world whole, while her seduction scene with Mantegna, in which she throws her voice down low to grill him about saxophone reeds ("… *reeds*, Joe, between the lips …"), may be the funniest thing she has ever filmed. She is the perfect assistant to Allen in full magician mode. Think of *Alice* as his parting gift to her before making himself disappear.

Shadows and Fog

1991

Based on Allen's one-act play *Death*, a comic pastiche of Franz Kafka's *The Trial*, *Shadows and Fog* was an exercise in pure cinematography—a chance for Allen's director of photography Carlo Di Palma, together with the production designer Santo Loquasto, to evoke the grey shadowland of German Expressionism with use of fog and low-key lighting effects to summon striking silhouettes from the good-looking loom. "A tribute to Carlo," Allen called it. "Part of the metaphor of the film [is] that once you get out in the night, there is a sense that civilization is gone...the city is just a superimposed manmade convention, a function of one's own inner state. And the real thing that you're living on is a planet. It's a wild thing in nature. And all the civilization that protects you and enables you to lie to yourself about life is all manmade and superimposed."

One of his most expensive films to that point, *Shadows and Fog* was originally to have been shot with models, but when that proved unworkable, Allen instructed his crew to build a full-scale 26,000-square-feet set at the Kaufman Astoria Studios in Queens. Drawing on images of vintage Paris by Eugène Atget, and such classic Weimar-era films as F. W. Murnau's *Nosferatu* (1922), G. W. Pabst's *The Joyless Street* (1925), and Fritz Lang's *M* (1931), they re-created a portion of an old Eastern European city, complete with sinister dead-end alleys and a church that looked like a prison,

Opposite: An exercise in pure cinematography, *Shadows and Fog* was an homage to the classic works of German Expressionist cinema.

Right: Paul (John Malkovich), a circus clown, and Marie (Madonna), a tightrope walker, in a passionate embrace.

and damp cobblestone streets filled with fog—in fact a soy concoction that billowed from hidden oil drums, putting the hypochondriac Allen in fear of cancer. It was the biggest set ever built in New York, and even then he worried it was not big enough. "When the set was finished, we had no idea if after a week of shooting we would have used up the whole set and think, 'Oh God, we need ten sets like this.'"

It was his last film for Orion, which in May 1991 reported a loss of $48 million, contributing to a debt that by November would reach $690 million and cause the company to file for Chapter 11 bankruptcy. Any hope Orion president Eric

169

"To get the right atmosphere it would have been incredibly hard to film in modern-day New York. Also, I didn't want to spend from seven at night to seven the next morning out in the winter, and perhaps get a cold."

Pleskow had that Allen was going to bail them out of their hole with a big hit was dashed when he saw the finished film. "He looked like he'd been hit with a mallet after he saw it," said Allen who watched the executive struggle for nice things to say about it. "I've got to say, whenever I come to see one of your films I'm really surprised that they're all so different," he finally managed in a voice from which not all traces of tremolo had been eliminated. "He was groping for something to say," recalled Allen. "But again, it was something I wanted to do and I hoped there would be enough people who saw it that studio people didn't bother me."

The film's domestic release was delayed until March 1992 because of Orion's financial problems, whereupon it took less than $2.75 million. It's a strange creature, all right: a queasy blend of high-flown allusion and porridgy atmospherics played straight. Allen plays a schnook named Kleinman who is suspected of being a serial strangler, a version of Kafka's K. as Allenesque schlemiel, rubbing his hands sweatily and hyperventilating as he tiptoes down tenebrous, winding streets. The only comic thing in sight, he seems almost to

have wandered into someone else's movie. He runs into a circus girl (Mia Farrow), a clown (John Malkovich), a mad scientist (Donald Pleasence), a metaphysical magician (Kenneth Mars), and a harem of philosophical hookers (Jodie Foster, Lily Tomlin, and Kathy Bates), before being pursued by a group of inept vigilantes seemingly on leave from a Fritz Lang film.

Not even the serial killer plot ties it all together. For sheer density of allusion, the film *Shadows and Fog* most closely resembles is *Love and Death*, but the Woody Allen who made that film would have almost certainly bounced some gags off the doomy atmospherics: All that fog seems to cry out for slapstick, but Allen plays the German Expressionist elements straight; the high-end cinematography works actively against the humor.

Shadows and Fog lives up to its title. It's all sets and lighting and great-looking camerawork—a $14 million doodle, not boring exactly but the work of a bored filmmaker, and the culmination of a period of fussy perfectionism that was about to come to an abrupt end.

Husbands and Wives

1992

"*Husbands and Wives* was just a fun experiment," said Allen. "I wanted to make a picture with no relation to beauty or any rules. I wanted just to do whatever I needed to do, like cut in the middle of scenes. It was one of those pictures that worked like a charm because I decided before I made the picture that it would be crude-looking and anything goes. I wouldn't care about cutting, I wouldn't care about angles, I wouldn't care about matching. And so we just shot it and if I was playing a scene with someone or someone was playing a scene and the scene was very good and then it got boring and then got very good again, we just cut the middle out and stuck them together."

He wanted a documentary rawness to his tale of warring couples, played by himself, Mia Farrow, Sydney Pollack, and Judy Davis, initially intending to shoot the whole thing on 16 mm, but his new benefactor, TriStar, wanted it shot in more traditional 35 mm. Even so, he gave his actors great freedom within the frame, asking Carlo Di Palma to light whole areas of the set, so that they could move wherever they wanted, telling them, "'Go where you want, just walk wherever you want. Walk into darkness, walk into the light, just play the scene as you feel it.' Everybody—from a physical point of view, from a technical point of view—had more fun on this movie than anything else."

The recurrence of that distinctly un-Allen-like word "fun" should be warning enough, if those provisos ("from a physical point of view, from a technical point of view") don't give the game away: *Husbands and Wives* was the film Allen was making when news of his relationship with Farrow's

adopted daughter Soon-Yi Previn detonated his domestic life and turned his private life into a tabloid gawk-box. Even before the news broke, the ten-to-twelve-week shoot, on the campus of Columbia University's Barnard College, had taken its toll. It was "a very nervous film" to shoot, said Di Palma, "an emotional experience." In the script, the scene in which Sydney Pollack drags Lysette Anthony out of a party and tries to shove her into his car was meant to be played for laughs, but once the scene was filmed, Allen didn't like it. "He said, 'We're going to have to reshoot this and just make her really obnoxious,'" said Anthony.

"I said, 'Woody, I don't know what the fuck I'm supposed to be talking about. You have to help me here.' So he just said, 'Crystals, tofu, this, this, this.' I don't know what the hell I said, but I went back and did it."

175

"If the content of the film—as in Husbands and Wives—is highly jagged, neurotic, fast-paced, a nervous New York film, it just calls for that kind of shooting, editing, and performance."

The beginnings of Jack and Sally's reconciliation (left), while Gabe and Judy realize that their marriage is over (opposite).

The realism and ugliness of the resulting clash were undeniable. "It got incredibly violent. I couldn't sleep for three days after—I'm not exaggerating," said Anthony. "Afterward there were people with their mouths open, going, 'My God, we've never seen this much violence in a Woody Allen film.'"

The darkening clouds finally broke on January 13, 1992, when, just two or three days before production wrapped, Allen received a phone call from Farrow, who hadn't been shooting that day. "I remember him answering the phone," said producer Robert Greenhut. "We were waiting for him to shoot the sequence. I could tell something disturbing was happening on the other end of this phone call." Farrow had discovered evidence of Allen's relationship with Soon-Yi. It took her ten days to return to the shoot. Allen's behavior

was "gentle, apologetic, and caring," she noted, but the scenes themselves were torture. "I don't know how I went back and filmed them." During the scene in which her character, Judy, tells his, Gabe, that their marriage is over ("It's over, and we both know it"), Farrow looks ghostly and haggard.

Anticipating a *succès de scandale*, TriStar moved the film's release date up five days to September 18 and increased its distribution from just eight cities to 865 screens nationwide, the widest ever for a Woody Allen film. They also spent $6 million on publicity, three times more than for Allen's previous few movies. "Whatever it would have done, it will do two to three times better," said one admiring rival studio chief. Journalists crashed the usually strictly controlled advance screenings. "Jesus, it's easier to get into Yale than

into this screening!" cried one in the Los Angeles queue, braving quadruple checkpoints with publicists. A print on its way to Dallas to be screened for one of the film's other stars, Liam Neeson, was hijacked en route, drawing the attention of the FBI. Bootleg copies of the movie appeared, selling for $200. By the time the film itself finally saw day, TriStar was rewarded with an opening weekend of $3.5 million, setting a new record for a Woody Allen film, although audiences quickly tailed off thereafter.

The handheld camera shaking and darting around the room. Actors wearing no makeup beneath harsh lighting. Language coarse enough to strip paint. Jump cuts to match the characters' frazzled nerves. This is not the Woody Allen who

was once adopted as a cuddly feminist mascot—the "thinking woman's huggy-bear" to use James Wolcott's phrase. In many ways Allen's answer to Bergman's *Scenes from a Marriage*, *Husbands and Wives* has a flayed, punch-drunk candor that lifts it head and shoulders above the more somnolent explorations of midlife crisis—*September, Another Woman*—which Allen seemed stuck making, over and over, with an ever mousier Farrow. She seemed to shrink into herself in those films, as if sensing herself under attack, the peevishness of her characterization hemming her closer and closer in. In *Husbands and Wives*, she and everyone else lets loose. The air of silent, passive-aggressive attrition gives way to open hostility and barked profanity. Allen's fangs finally find flesh.

It's his loosest, most stylistically innovative picture since *Annie Hall*, using the faux-documentary form—a narrator, handheld camera, interviews to camera—to convey journalistic immediacy: We could as easily be watching a documentary about primates in the wild as the mating habits and midlife crises of these affluent Manhattanites. Beneath the ragged form lies a sturdy dramatic conceit. When Jack and Sally (Sydney Pollack and Judy Davis) announce to their friends Gabe and Judy (Allen and Farrow) that they are divorcing, the response is shock, grief, disbelief. "Have you met other people?" inquires Gabe. "I just feel shattered," declares Judy, almost as if one couple were breaking up with the other. This is the film's startling central question: What if breakups are contagious, the promise of chaos spreading like a disease, or a forest fire, to those standing nearby?

And so it turns out, as Sally's newly single experience, particularly her dates with a handsome editor, Michael (Liam Neeson), proves unexpectedly appealing to the censorious Judy. Jack, meanwhile, becomes involved with his dim-bulb aerobics instructor, Sam (Lysette Anthony), prompting Gabe to flirt with the idea of an affair with one of his students, the twenty-year-old Rain (Juliette Lewis), which gives Allen another crack at the perennial appeal of the "kamikaze" woman. "Maybe because I'm a writer there's some aesthetic or dramatic component to it," reasons Gabe. "There's a certain dramatic ambience, almost as if I fall in love with the person and in love with the situation." The idea of a dramatist caught up in the excitement of his own dramas is a compelling self-diagnosis and may be as close to a genuine self-insight as Allen has ever come in one of his films. As he says, with a shrug, of the night he kisses Rain during an electrical storm, "The scene demanded to be played."

The film's febrile air of emotional opportunism is, needless to say, a gift to his cast. Farrow glints with passive-aggressive steel; Juliette Lewis continues her performance in *Cape Fear* as an attention-hungry colt; but it's Judy Davis who flourishes most. Whether pouring screeds of hatred down the phone at her ex-husband while on a date—"*They should have cut his fucking balls off!*" she snaps, of Don Giovanni—or breaking away from a kiss with the excuse "metabolically, it's not my rhythm," she plays a violin concerto on this woman's highly strung nerves. By the end, she is reconciled with Jack, the fire of destruction moving on to gut Gabe and Judy's relationship instead. Usually, the bleaker he gets, the more lethargic Allen's dramas, as if he had mistaken lack of vitality for emotional subtlety, or a morbid preoccupation with life's imperfections with genuine tragedy, but *Husbands and Wives* crackles and hums with black electricity, with an ashen gravity that is no put-on or aesthetic pose. It's lightning-struck—Allen at his darkest and most convincing.

Left: Juliette Lewis as Rain, a gifted creative writing student who is a catalyst in the disintegration of Gabe's marriage.

Opposite: Allen's relationship with Mia Farrow came to an abrupt halt shortly before the end of shooting for *Husbands and Wives*.

"When I finished the script for Husbands and Wives
it was strictly an act of imagination. I finished the
script long before anything happened that you read
in the newspapers. It had nothing to do with that."

Manhattan Murder Mystery

1993

Allen had long toyed with the idea of picking up the *Annie Hall* characters to see what had become of them—"I've saved some footage from the original, so I could show them young and old," he once mused—but *Manhattan Murder Mystery* was as close as he ever came. The film was adapted from one of the spare parts of the story that didn't get used back in 1977: the part involving Annie and Alvy putting on their sleuthing hats to solve a murder in her apartment building hallway. Back then, he told his writing partner Marshall Brickman he could have the story, to do with as he wished, but nothing ever came of it and fifteen years later, fishing around for new ideas, Allen called up Brickman and asked him, "Why don't we try to whip this into shape?"

That Allen should return to the scene of his greatest box-office and critical triumph in the wake of his breakup with Mia Farrow is not surprising, although the film was initially written with Farrow in mind to play the part of Carol. With a court case over the custody of their children beginning in August 1992, he called Diane Keaton that fall and asked her to take it on instead; she immediately accepted and flew to New York. "She took a million calls from me and let me kvetch on her shoulder," said Allen, "It was fun to work with her. It was great therapy for me, a great palliative."

With Keaton in the role, the tenor and direction of the film changed. "She is such a strong comedienne, such a vibrant comedienne, that the whole emphasis shifted. She became the comic center of it. Mia could play comedy and had a delightful comic sense. But I was a stronger comic than her. Keaton is a stronger comic than me; she just has the more magnetic and funny screen personality. I could labor all year and give myself a thousand funny lines, but when the camera hits her, that's what you want to see. I think that next to Judy Holliday, she's the greatest screen comedienne we've had."

Woody Allen and Diane Keaton as husband-and-wife gumshoes Carol and Larry Lipton in this recycled offcut from *Annie Hall*.

Above: Anjelica Huston in her second Woody Allen film, but this time she did not play the murder victim.

Opposite: Carol and Larry give us a glimpse of what Annie and Alvy might have become if they had stayed together.

Keaton had to overcome some initial panic in her first scene with Alan Alda, who played a recently divorced friend called Ted. A week into filming, Allen "just said it was no good," recalled Keaton, steeling herself to return to the set. "Of course, I was completely terrified. But Woody is very clear. He says, 'You'll shoot it again.' That's the great thing about him, he's totally honest, non-sentimental. He responds to me the way he always responded to me, which is like I'm a complete idiot. It's like an old marriage or like I'm a kid sister."

Anjelica Huston, who played the sexy author in black leather who helps the Keaton-Allen husband-and-wife team, Carol and Larry Lipton, solve the mystery, called the set "oddly free of anxiety, introspection, and pain," at least when compared to the shoot for *Crimes and Misdemeanors*, during which Allen had been quiet and distant. "On this movie, he showed up in the hair and makeup trailer to tease Diane about her hair and her big photography books, all diligently marked with yellow stick-'em paper. Around Diane, he was open and accessible."

The ending was problematic for a long time. The murderer was originally a stamp dealer until Allen changed it to a movie house owner, which gave him the setting of a broken-down cinema, complete with *Lady from Shanghai* mirrors. The joke that ended the picture originally came in the middle—Allen thought it was "a nice joke but not that great. After I first cut the movie I realized it would work there, so we went out and shot it." With the murder solved and Carol and Larry out of harm's way, the two walk down the avenue talking about all that has happened. It turns out there was no romantic spark between Carol and Ted. Larry says dismissively of him, "Take away his elevator shoes and his fake suntan and capped teeth and what do you have?" And Carol, without skipping a beat, answers, "You." The screen cuts to black.

If Annie Hall and Alvy Singer had married, grown middle aged together, and bought exercise bikes, they might well have resembled Carol and Larry Lipton, the central couple in *Manhattan Murder Mystery*. "You don't think we're turning into a comfortable old pair of shoes do you?" asks Carol after an evening spent with two of their neighbors down the hall, Paul and Lillian House (Jerry Adler and Lynn Cohen). The Houses seem sweet enough, if a little boring, with their stamp collections and plan for twin cemetery plots: the Ghosts of Marriage Future. The next day, Mrs. House is carried out of her apartment feet first: heart failure. Except Mr. House doesn't seem very upset. It can mean only one thing, concludes Carol: The sweet old guy murdered his wife and is going to run off with his bit of fluff on the side. The old pair of shoes are about to play gumshoe.

Such is the setup for Allen's comedy of marital renaissance—a kind of *Rear Window* for retirees, dizzy

"I just felt I had done—I don't know—
twenty-two, twenty-three pictures and
I just wanted to take part of a year and do
this little thing for fun. Like a little dessert
or something. Not a real meal."

Carol becomes obsessed by the mysterious death of their elderly neighbor.

and mellow at the same time, spritzed along by performers who cannot hide their delight at finding the old chemistry still fizzing. The idea for the film, much like its central couple, seems only to have improved with age. Neither Brickman nor Allen could make the murder-mystery plot stick to Alvy Singer and Annie Hall when their love affair was in full bloom, because that was mystery enough. But to drop an opportunity to play Miss Marple into the laps of a middle-aged couple for whom the biggest rush of adrenaline comes with a pair of season tickets to the Met makes a lovely, generous-spirited sense. Both Carol and Larry get romantic rivals: Ted (Alan Alda), an old friend who's not shy about his attraction to Carol and indulges her conspiracy theories about her neighbor, and Marcia (Anjelica Huston), an author at Larry's publishing firm who is soon afire with theories and strategies of her own. The tiny nuances of this quartet keep Carlo Di Palma's camera busy as it bobs and weaves, even sky-rocketing dizzyingly across the Manhattan Bridge at one point. Nothing could more effectively signal Allen's message: I'm back.

Clearly enlivened by Keaton's presence, he delivers what may be his last truly focused comic performance. It's like a time-lapse digest of his entire career, only in reverse. We start with the fuddy-duddy, grouch, and professional naysayer, trying to put his foot down as the man of the household, "*I'm your husband; I command you to sleep. Sleep! I command it. I command it. Sleep!*" As the plot progresses, however, Larry's skepticism melts, and Allen's comedy rejuvenates: He gets some great bits of physical shtick with a pack of cards and a fistful of unspooled tape, and there is even a brief glimpse, during a bedroom scene, of that rarest of sea mammals: the Allen smile. Finally, impersonating police officers ("They lowered the height requirement"), he and Keaton approach the delightful skittering rhythm of their work together on *Sleeper* and *Love and Death*: They could be infiltrating Napoleon's palace all over again. The final gag is great but even better is Allen's tiger growl to camera the moment Keaton delivers her punch line, as if to say: *Can you believe that I get to go home with this?* He looks all of twelve years old.

Upon the film's release, there was a tendency among critics to pat it on the head and send it gently on its way. "Successful lightweight Woody—no more, no less," concluded Owen Gleiberman in *Entertainment Weekly*; a "mild, middle-aged, atypically blithe comedy," wrote Janet Maslin in the *New York Times*, "gratifyingly gentle and uncomplicated." It was as if distraction by the Farrow brouhaha had made everyone of the same mind as Allen himself, who gently deprecated the picture as having "no hidden meaning, or even meaning." By that measure, neither do the Marx Brothers. It's also nonsense. That he painted so warm a portrait of a marriage so soon after *Husbands and Wives*, a work seemingly made by someone in whom the state of matrimony inspires much the

Chaplinesque brilliance from Allen, as Marcia (Huston) gives Larry a poker lesson.

Overleaf: Portrait by Michael O'Neill, 1994.

same feelings as the Spanish Inquisition, was the surest sign that Allen was in the throes of a fully fledged renaissance. The first fruit of his creative bachelorhood, it initiated a period of artistic *glasnost*, as, creatively single for the first time in over a decade, Allen found himself slaking a renewed thirst for collaboration, at first with old and trusted friends such as Brickman, Keaton, and Alda, and then with a new generation of actors—Sean Penn, Julia Roberts, Leonardo DiCaprio—who came of age during Allen's adventures in High Seriousness.

"Liberating," he told me in 1999 when I asked him to describe the effect the breakup had had on his work. "Because I don't feel when I sit down to create a project that I automatically have one character in mind. It's a liberating thing. I feel like I can write and then cast, rather than have to think of a role for them. Now, I didn't mind doing that with Diane Keaton so much, but with Mia, who is a wonderful actress, it went on too long. There were just too many movies starring her. She never disappointed me, but you've done twelve, thirteen movies and want a different chemistry."

"There are people that think in a narrative linear mode all the time, and make wonderful movies that way. And there are people that think in a way that is less linear, more digressive. I tend to do that more. I tend to move around at times. Not deliberately, just instinctively."

Bullets over Broadway

1994

Written during the tumultuous year of Allen's custody battle, *Bullets over Broadway* marked the single biggest test of his ability to find refuge and salvation in his work. He and co-writer Douglas McGrath started meeting at Allen's apartment each day in January 1993. They sat on opposite, matching couches and pitched the movie to one another. One day, pacing back and forth while recounting the plot, waving his arms like Zorba the Greek, Allen came to a sudden halt, snapping his fingers to signal start of show. "It's the Roaring Twenties, and there's this playwright who thinks of himself as a great artist…"

Then, according to an account by McGrath, the phone rang. Allen lifted one finger—wait a second—and took the call, speaking in low tones. "*A long history of mental problems …*" McGrath overheard, "*… tried every drug known to man… private detectives…*"

Allen hung up, caught his breath, turned back to his collaborator, smiled, lifted his arms, and snapped his fingers again. "Okay… roaring twenties… playwright… great artist, and he goes to a producer seeking a production of his play but he wants to direct it himself to protect its artistic integ—"

The phone rang again. Allen answered it. "*Intensely claustrophobic…*" McGrath overheard him say quietly into the phone, "*two red eyes at the window… sent her child to the Post… hairs in a glassine envelope.*"

Finally, after a third call interrupting their labors, he hung up and smiled sheepishly.

"Okay," he said, hoisting his eyebrows. "Let's get back to work on our little comic bauble…'"

The period following the Farrow scandal was one of rapid reorganization in Allen's normally quiet world. As he found a trusted collaborator in McGrath, others slipped quietly away, including TriStar, who, after both *Husbands*

and Wives and *Manhattan Murder Mystery* underperformed at the box office, pulled out from their three-picture deal. Horrified at the treatment of her friend, producer Jean Doumanian offered Allen a deal with her new company Sweetland that gave him a twenty-five-percent larger production budget, a generous director's fee in the low seven figures, and a cut of the profits after Sweetland recouped its investment. Doumanian received four bids to distribute what was, in effect, Allen's first independent film and settled on Miramax, who bid sight unseen.

Despite Doumanian having pared back much of the production team that Allen had built around him since *Annie Hall*, *Bullets over Broadway* wound up being his most expensive movie to date, costing $20 million, thanks to the period setting, requiring such locations as the old ballroom at the New Yorker Hotel, an art deco co-op on the twenty-second floor of a Tudor Place duplex in Manhattan, the Cort Theatre on Forty-Eighth Street. "New York is inexhaustible," commented Allen, for whom the film's sepia-tinted world of speakeasies and newsstands was another tribute to the work of Damon Runyon. "I've had the idea for years of the gangster who turned out to be the real playwriting talent but I would not have pursued it had not Doug McGrath been so high on it," he says now. "The real epiphany in *Bullets* was when the gangster decided to kill the girl to save his play. Before that it was just a funny notion that went part of the distance but not all the way, and that decision to kill her made the whole idea."

He considered taking on the lead role himself, but felt his neophyte dramatist, David Shayne, would be better played by a younger actor and chose John Cusack, who had impressed him on *Shadows and Fog*. He picked Chazz Palminteri after casting director Juliet Taylor showed him Robert De

On set during shooting of this behind-the-scenes portrait of a 1920s Broadway production. Allen later adapted the film into a stage musical, which opened at the St. James Theatre, New York in April 2014.

189

Above: *"Don't speak!"*

Opposite: "Who am I? Some vain Broadway *legend!*" Dianne Wiest delivered an Oscar-winning performance as Helen Sinclair, one of Allen's great narcissists.

"It was just a great, colorful time. Everything was very glamorous. Everyone smoked cigarettes and dressed for dinner and went out to nightclubs. It was really highly sophisticated. So I like to set some of my films in those years, because it's fun."

Niro's *A Bronx Tale*, in which he played a bus driver from the Bronx. As Olive, the gangster's moll, Jennifer Tilly was encouraged to improvise freely, and step all over everyone's else's ad-libs. "After the first five minutes on set I realized that Woody not only wants you to improvise, it became apparent to me he wanted Olive to never stop talking," she noted. "He had this idea about Olive. He said, 'She's in her own little world and it just revolves around her and she just talks and talks and talks.'"

It took Allen several conversations to convince Dianne Wiest of her ability to pull off the role of the Norma Desmond-ish diva Helen Sinclair. She was initially skeptical, as was McGrath. "Dianne Wiest for that vain, hammy actress?" he said. "It seems so not like Dianne Wiest. She's so sweet and vulnerable." Allen was insistent. "No, she has to do it," he said. "She can do anything." McGrath let it go, thinking: *Sink your own picture, what do I know?* After the first day of shooting, Allen phoned Wiest and invited her to dailies to see what they had shot. She sat there, horrified at what she called "this painful, painful attempt for me to do this role—pathetic, pathetic."

"You know, it's terrible," said Allen.

"I told you so!"

"What are you going to do?"

"Well, you've got to pick up the phone and find someone who can do this," replied Wiest. "It's not me. You've got to replace me."

"No, I think it's something to do with your voice. We'll reshoot it."

Wiest, who has a high-pitched speaking voice, lowered it almost an octave, and after the scene was reshot Allen said, "That's it." Wiest says, "That was the character. I'd be in the middle of a take and he'd go, 'Voice! Voice!'" The lower she dropped it, the funnier it became. Come Oscar time, *Bullets over Broadway* garnered seven nominations, the most for any Allen film since *Hannah and Her Sisters*, including film, director, original screenplay—Allen's eleventh nomination for this award, putting him on a par with Billy Wilder—also Wiest, Tilly, and Palminteri for supporting actress and actor. As she had with *Hannah*, Wiest won.

Dianne Wiest is the gift that keeps on giving in *Bullets over Broadway*: Crooning lines of purest purple while shrewdly assessing Shayne's ability to keep her supplied with praise, she is one of Allen's great narcissists, pausing only to let others admire her exquisite rendition of herself, milking every pause for full reverb. "Let the birds have their song and let ours remain unsung…" she insists in her husky baritone, before putting her finger to Shayne's lips—*"Don't speak!"* When lines like that achieve liftoff—it became an instant classic—it's invariably because they traverse invisible power lines. It packs all of Helen Sinclair's vanity into two syllables, a snatch of self-absorbed haiku, but also stands at the center of a drama crisscrossed with competing egos and conflicting agendas—a giddy, vivacious farce lightly satirizing the artistic temperament whose layered writing places it alongside *The Purple Rose of Cairo* at the

apex of Allen's achievement as a fabulist-farceur. If not his best movie, it has a good claim on being his most richly and repeatedly enjoyable.

The characters are all lined up like skittles and then sent spinning into one another. There's Wiest's velveteen diva, lightly pickled in dry martinis, sweeping into every room to loose gloriously overdone pauses ("Mrs. Alving [*chk*]… Uncle Vanya… there's Cordelia, there's Ophelia… Clytemnestra!"). There's Tilly's helium-voiced moll, as woefully out of her depth as she is ignorant of the fact ("charmed, charmed…"); also Jim Broadbent's plummy thesp, swelling with cake and chicken drumsticks as production progresses; Tracey Ullman's giddy ingénue, who comes to closely resemble her own Chihuahua. Finally, we have the calmest and quietest of the bunch, standing out in a film full of plush, plumed verbiage: Chazz Palminteri's Cheech, the bodyguard who sits in the back, listening to Shayne's turgidly sub-O'Neill script, *God of Our Fathers*, before finally declaring, "It stinks on fuckin' hot ice!"

Cheech is the ultimate Allen combo-fantasy, "the aesthete who packs heat," in the words of the *New Yorker*'s Anthony Lane, "as frightening in his defense of artistic autonomy as he was in the footsteps of his boss. Allen respects that point of view, I think, more than he would admit." Allen's lily-livered screen persona has always been a front for the most muscular of artistic wills, so many of his dramas relying for their strength on his ability to step outside of himself, and give voice to opinions and viewpoints in direct contravention of his own. Is he David Shayne, the uptight playwright played by Cusack, loftily using his characters as mouthpieces for his own precious *pensées*? Or is he Palminteri's hoodlum, the very embodiment of that advice, rewriting Shayne's play ("You don't write how people talk") with a jolt of electricity from the streets? In truth Allen is both men, sophisticate and Runyonesque thug, which is perhaps why he allows their conversation in the pool hall to run long, each man obscurely fascinated by the other, as if sensing some secret

Planning a rehearsal scene
with Cusack, Tilly, Tracey
Ullman (Eden Brent), and
Chihuahua (Mr. Woofles).

kinship. His later films are littered with such pairings: between the real Gil Shepherd and fictional Tom Baxter in *The Purple Rose of Cairo*, between Alan Alda's Lester and his own Cliff in *Crimes and Misdemeanors*, between Cheech and Shayne in *Bullets over Broadway*. You don't get many villains in Allen's oeuvre, which fights shy of outright demonization, but there are plenty of doppelgängers, doubles, and twinned souls, particularly in the plots tending to reversal, in which one character emerges as a version of the other, thus satisfying both Allen's comic instincts—his delight, inherited from Kaufman, Perelman, and Thurber in a topsy-turvy universe in which up is down, and every man his opposite—and also his dramatic itch for a good fight, with himself if need be, if no one else is forthcoming.

"A comedy with a serious point to make" is how Allen described *Bullets over Broadway*, the point being the unfairness with which the creative gene is handed out. It's nothing Allen hadn't told us before—as Isaac Davis declared all those years ago in *Manhattan*, "talent is luck"—but it is a theme to which he would return in the 1990s with renewed vigor, in *Sweet and Lowdown* and *Deconstructing Harry*, as if media vilification had only sharpened his desire to beat everyone to the observation of his own clay feet. So much of David Shayne's play sounds like bad Woody Allen ("The days blend together like melted celluloid, like a film whose images become distorted and meaningless…"). He's turning himself inside out in *Bullets over Broadway*, emptying his own pockets. "*I'm not an artist!*" cries Cusack's playwright at the end and it could easily be Allen's own liberated *cri de coeur*.

Bullets over Broadway grossed $13 million in the United States upon its release on January 18, 1995, then bettered its domestic returns in seven countries, including France, where Allen went on TV to promote the film with the help of Charlotte Rampling, and where it grossed $2.5 million in Paris alone. "We thought Woody Allen had lost touch with the entire world, not to mention his audience," wrote Lane. "Instead, he seems to be leveling with us, to be contenting himself with our pleasure, more keenly than ever before. Make 'em laugh."

"What I really like
to do best is
whatever I'm not
doing at the
moment."

Portrait by Brian Hamill
during the shooting of
Bullets over Broadway, 1994.

Mighty Aphrodite

1995

Allen had often wondered about the origins of his adopted daughter Dylan Farrow. To be so intelligent and charming, he decided, Dylan must have inherited "good genes." He got to wondering about her biological mother and father and saw the glimmer of a story about an adopted kid whose adoptive parents love the kid so much they seek out the mother and fall in love with her. Or, they find her mother but her mother's a prostitute. The more they find out about the child's provenance, the worse the situation seems. It reminded him of Oedipus. He'd always wanted to make a movie with a Greek chorus, bouncing gags off it the same way he did with the documentary form in *Take the Money and Run*. "A lot of things that are taken for granted as very serious, like the documentary style of filming, or a Greek chorus, can also be used comically and very effectively because of their inherent solemnity," said Allen. "I felt, 'My God, it's got a kind of Grecian irony to it.' Then I thought, 'This film is one to do as Greek fable.'"

It's an idea he'd been toying with for years. The Greek scenes were shot at an open-air theater, the Teatro Greco, the site of the Taormina Film Festival, which he had visited in 1971 while promoting *Bananas*—the first time Allen had shot outside of America for twenty years. He cast the film while promoting *Manhattan Murder Mystery* in London, giving Helena Bonham Carter the role of his wife and only reluctantly admitting that an American, F. Murray Abraham, had the right Shakespearean plumminess for the leader of the Greek chorus. Allen also believed he could find his hooker, Linda Ash, in England, and at first passed on Mira Sorvino, who had auditioned in New York, until Sorvino turned up at Allen's hotel suite in London wearing boots and short skirt, speaking in a high-pitched voice. "The minute she walked in I thought she was perfect," said Allen. "Frankly, I couldn't figure out how she got past the house detective."

Opposite: Mira Sorvino's standout performance as simple-minded sex worker Linda Ash earned her an Academy Award for Best Supporting Actress.

Right: Family time for Lenny (Woody Allen), his wife, Amanda (Helena Bonham Carter), and their adopted son, Max (Jimmy McQuaid).

He told the Harvard-educated actress, "I don't want a glimmer of intelligence to show through." She researched the role by walking around Philadelphia for three days in character, talking to strippers and a porno actress. The voice she based on a friend of her mother's. At first Allen was unsure about it. Four weeks into the production, he began to worry and asked her if she had another she could use. "I thought, 'My God, if they don't buy in to the voice, I'm really in trouble.' But I bought it and I went by my instincts and it turned out I—or, should I say, she—was right."

Mira Sorvino strides through *Mighty Aphrodite* with the nonchalance of Judy Holliday and the imperturbability of Boadicea, her long legs connecting distantly with the ground via teetering heels, a giraffe-like miracle of balance. Her performance, like her accent, is to be found somewhere in

the ozone layer, enunciating perfectly empty thought bubbles in an adenoidal voice somewhere between Minnie Mouse and Miss Piggy. "I once did a film called *Beaver Patrol* about these boy scouts who find drunk girl scouts in the woods and they take them into a cabin and they reach into their packs and they pull out these dildos…" Upper East Side sports writer Lenny Weinrib (Allen) sits there, open mouthed, his face swimming with lust and horror that *this* beautiful moron is the mother of his adopted child. Lenny doesn't know where to look: the phallic knickknacks of her apartment or her Vargas-Blonde body.

"Curiosity, that's what kills us," says the Greek chorus leader (F. Murray Abraham), but it wasn't curiosity that drew Lenny to look up Linda. It was a row with his wife (Helena Bonham Carter), which left him hankering for that old honeymoon feeling. And it's not curiosity that drives Lenny's Henry Higgins-ish desire to reform this gaudy broad and set her on the track to becoming a hairdresser. "Hubris!" shouts the Greek chorus. "He's playing God!" But it's not hubris, either. It's thwarted romantic fixation—or, if you like, lust, and Allen's failure to face this fact lends *Mighty Aphrodite*

a strangely furtive, evasive air, and sends its plot scuttling into some very odd corners indeed. "At my age if I made love to you they'd have to put me on a respirator" says Lenny, instead becoming a matchmaker-uncle figure, fixing her up with a young boxer, hilariously played by Michael Rapaport, who is keen to return to his brother's upstate onion farm. "Can I say two words to you?" Lenny asks, touting Linda's wholesomeness. "Butter churn."

The scenes with Rapaport are some of the best in the movie but this subplot, too, must end in disaster, as the comic Gods dictate, leaving Allen with something of a mess on his hands, as romance, outsourced to younger proxies, swings by Lenny's way again, for a night of passion that will lead to its own even stranger resolution. Was it the ungainliness of the material—the sense of not being able to get characters to do what he wanted—that first suggested the Greek chorus to Allen? How funny you find the film depends largely on how much heft you grant the intellectual superiority of a middle-aged sportswriter who clearly lusts after the object of his condescension. Intellectual asymmetry is built into all of Allen's on-screen romances, of course—intellectual

Opposite: Allen cast
Bonham Carter while he
was in London promoting
Manhattan Murder Mystery.

Right: When he traces Max's
natural mother, Lenny is
overcome with a mixture of
lust and horror.

Below: F. Murray Abraham
as the leader of the Greek
chorus that provides a
commentary on events in
the film.

"Obsession is
dangerous, but
a real staple of
comedy."

insecurity in a woman is what gives the Allen man his advantage, his "in" as her lover-tutor—but in *Sleeper, Annie Hall*, and *Hannah and Her Sisters*, the women quickly surpass the men, their usefulness outlived. An introduction to Kierkegaard does not a lasting union make.

There's no threat of turned tables in *Mighty Aphrodite*, which patronizes Sorvino's character relentlessly—the film makes repeated play with the titles of her porno flicks *Beaver Patrol, The Enchanted Pussy*—although the great thing about Sorvino's performance is her bold refusal to acknowledge that her character is being in the least bit patronized. She plays

ignorant about playing ignorant. "What is remarkable about Sorvino is her refusal to let the character lie still and purr as a creature of fantasy," wrote Anthony Lane in the *New Yorker*. "Sorvino's command of the movie is almost embarrassing; she makes everyone else look listless and indifferent to life." When the Oscars were announced that year, Sorvino won for Best Supporting Actress, against a competitive field that included Kate Winslet's Marianne Dashwood in *Sense and Sensibility* and Joan Allen's Pat Nixon in *Nixon*, making it the fourth time an actress had struck gold at the Academy Awards in a Woody Allen movie.

Everyone Says
I Love You

1996

Allen had always dreamed of one day making his own musical, and while making *Annie Hall* had suggested to co-writer Marshall Brickman that one of the scenes be entirely sung. Doubling down on the audience goodwill he had reestablished with *Bullets over Broadway*, and the embrace from the Hollywood community signaled by Mira Sorvino's Oscar for *Mighty Aphrodite*, *Everyone Says I Love You* was Allen's all-star version of the all-singing, all-dancing "champagne comedies" he had soaked up in his youth, "where no one's ever at a loss for the right phrase and everything comes out right at the end. After the double feature, you'd walk out again at four o'clock in the afternoon and suddenly the horns would be honking and the sun would be shining and it would be ninety degrees, and it wouldn't be Fredric March and Douglas Fairbanks, Jr. I personally felt I wanted to grow up, move into Manhattan, and live like that. I wanted to pop champagne corks and have a white telephone and trade ever-ready quips."

His major innovation was to include an element of that quotidian reality: He wanted all of his actors to use the voices they might use when singing in the shower. He refused to tell any of them they were appearing in a musical until after they had signed. "If that person could sing, fine, and if that person couldn't sing, that was fine, too," he said. "The important thing was not the technique, because what I wanted was an untrained quality to the voices." Only Drew Barrymore was dubbed, after she convinced Allen that her singing was simply too awful even for the realistic singing he was after; both Goldie Hawn and Edward Norton actually sang too well—he had to tell them to roughen their voices up a little to make them sound like normal people just breaking into song.

The dance numbers, choreographed by Graciela Daniele, who had choreographed the Greek dances in *Mighty*

Exploring Venice with Soon-Yi while making *Everyone Says I Love You.*

Alan Alda and Goldie
Hawn as wealthy Upper
East Side couple Bob and
Steffi Dandridge.

Aphrodite, were shot in single long takes, using very few close-ups, the way Fred Astaire used to insist his numbers be shot, with the dancers fully visible. "That's all I wanted, straight on, simple, proscenium and no cuts," said Allen who, unusually, "had a very good time making that film, but when I showed it to Harvey Weinstein, who had paid a lot of money for it sight unseen, he hated it. He's usually very good with my films. Whenever I show him a film, he loves it. But with that film, he fell into that group of people who feel in a musical people have to be able to sing. But in the end he was very nice about it. And I was such a grouch. He wanted me to take out the one dirty thing, where they said 'motherfucker,' because then he could open the picture at Radio City Music Hall. And I just would not take it out. It's not how I make my pictures. So in the end he was a good sport and put out the picture nicely."

As if to show how reconciled with crowd-pleasing Allen was at this point in his career, *Everyone Says I Love You* takes a leaf or two from his most successful film up until that point, *Hannah and Her Sisters*. It's a family album, centered on the wealthy Upper East Side household of lawyer Bob

Dandridge (Alan Alda) and his limousine-liberal wife, Steffi (Goldie Hawn). As with *Hannah*, we have a brood of sisters, four this time, Lane and Laura (Gaby Hoffmann and Natalie Portman), Skylar (Drew Barrymore), a creamy debutante engaged to Edward Norton's Holden, and D. J. (Natasha Lyonne), the film's worldly-wise thirteen-year-old narrator. "Now, I'm gonna level with you," she begins. "We are not the typical kind of family you'd find in a musical comedy. For one thing, we got dough. And we live right here on Park Avenue in a big apartment—a penthouse." Except for one thing: They are *exactly* the kind of family you'd expect to find in a musical comedy, certainly in the kind Allen had in mind, and the luxury of the Dandridges' existence in part accounts for the slight frictionlessness that envelops the film, less a musical perhaps than his dream of one, his comfort-blanket version of the feelings those films evoked in him as a child. The film is all grace notes, an ineffably gentle fantasia that seems to have been directed with a feather duster.

That it is only half-successful may tell you much about how braced with reality his comedies are, in fact. The old musicals of the 1930s may have brushed the clouds but

Above: "That's what you get, folks, for makin' whoopee."

Top: Viewing footage with Natasha Lyonne, who played the film's worldly-wise teenage narrator.

there was nothing precious about their vision of penthouse sophistication. They belted out their vision of happiness on behalf of audiences who needed uplift like they needed a meal in their belly. Allen caught this dichotomy perfectly in *Radio Days*, his almost-musical of 1987 whose silvery flights of fancy came rooted in the reality of rainy, suburban Rockaway. What are the Park Avenue princes and princesses of *Everyone Says I Love You* escaping from, exactly? What drives them to song? Any time the gilded world of the Dandridges rubs up against some crumb of outside reality the film bustles into life. There is a great version of "Makin' Whoopee," sung in a hospital by all the nurses and patients, using their gurneys and wheelchairs the way Astaire used his hat and cane, which hints at the kind of joyous vulgarity Mel Brooks might have brought to proceedings. Then, too, there is Tim Roth's hilarious performance as the ex-con Steffi invites into the Dandridge home as part of her push for prison reform and who soon is using Skylar's sports car as an escape vehicle for more holdups. "Can you drop me off on the corner of Park and Ninety-Third?" Skylar asks, as they spin around a bend in the road, pursued by cops.

"When I see a movie, I want to see the dancers in front of me, full length. I hate it when they cut to their feet, I hate it when they cut to their faces. I don't like angle shots. I want to see it the way I see it if I pay ten dollars and I go to City Center and the dancers are in front of me."

Joe (Allen) attempts to win the heart of Von (Julia Roberts) in Venice.

As with *Hannah*, Allen plays a semi-orbital role as Steffi's ex-husband, Joe, trying to finagle his way into the heart of the unhappily married Von (Julia Roberts) in Venice, using a tip-sheet gleaned from D. J.'s eavesdropping on Von's shrink—a plot that had been looking for a home ever since Allen wrote *Another Woman* in 1988 and a reprise of the romantic-schemer routine he had perfected in the 1970s. Using his ill-gotten knowledge he discourses on her favorite painter (Titian), flower (daisy), holiday destination (Bora Bora), each time rolling his eyes to the camera the way he did in *Play It Again, Sam*: *She bought it!* Back then he had Diane Keaton to play off, and would fine-tune their chemistry over the course

of a decade. Now he was in a position to use the Hollywood A-list as his own personal repertory company, but doing so a little blindly. Despite Roberts's best attempts at Farrow-like timidity, she is no neurotic: She gives off confidence like the Colgate glow, and spends much of her screen time doing an impression of a lioness gamely agreeing not to eat the gazelle that is huffing and puffing in jogging shorts in front of her.

The film is most successful when it draws closest to a mood of wry, twinkly regret. "I'm Thru With Love" sings Joe on a balcony at the Paris Ritz in a whispery croak so frail it seems the slightest breeze would whisk it into the night air. At the film's climax, ducking out from a Groucho Marx costume party—Woody Allen heaven!—Steffi reprises the number beside the Seine, spinning and pirouetting on invisible wires in a piece of choreography so exquisite as to bring a tear to the eye. All the film's faults melt away, as it achieves quite literal liftoff. Allen shot the scene on the very stretch of the river where, more than thirty years earlier, he had sought to buck up a suicidal Peter Sellers in *What's New Pussycat?* In many ways it marked a career come full circle. "Just write something where we can all go to Paris and chase girls" had been producer Charles Feldman's recipe for success in that film, much pilloried by Allen at the time, but as his audience in the United States continued to dwindle, he would increasingly turn to Europe for creative sustenance, support, and inspiration. If the Greek scenes of *Mighty Aphrodite* had been his first shot overseas since *Love and Death*, *Everyone Says I Love You* showed the way that would eventually lead to the globe-trotting travelogues of *Match Point*, *Vicky Cristina Barcelona*, and *Midnight in Paris*. Allen may have been through with love, at least as far as his status as a romantic lead went, but his work would increasingly be illuminated by a different kind of love affair: with places, not people.

Above: A memorable song-and-dance routine featuring a chorus of Groucho Marxes singing a French version of "Hooray for Captain Spaulding," the theme of the Marx Brothers' 1930 movie *Animal Crackers*.

Left: Joe and his ex-wife Steffi in the film's rousing finale on the banks of the Seine.

Deconstructing Harry

1997

suffer, he lives in a state of permanent excess, he's addicted to barbiturates, he's a sex addict. That's what happens to the character when he can't keep on transforming reality according to his desire."

Allen tried many actors—Elliott Gould, Dennis Hopper, Robert De Niro, Dustin Hoffman, Albert Brooks—before casting himself as Harry Block, misanthrope, womanizer, scoundrel, and celebrated novelist, who spreads his misery between three wives, six psychiatrists, and numerous girlfriends, harvesting their lives for his fiction all the while. "With you it's all nihilism, cynicism, sarcasm, and orgasm," says his sister Doris (Caroline Aaron). "In France I could run for office with that slogan, and win," replies Harry. The plot, involving an awards ceremony at his alma mater to which Harry can find nobody to accompany him except a hooker (Hazelle Goodman), is really

Originally called *The Worst Man in the World* until Allen realized that title was taken, *Deconstructing Harry* took the theme of the immorality of the artist first explored in *Bullets over Broadway*, and ran with it. "As long as the protagonist evolves within his own reality, the one he manipulates, everything's fine," he said. "As soon as he leaves it—when he has to confront the real world where people don't sing and dance on the street—you can see his life is a total disaster: He's self-destructive, he makes everyone who's close to him

a hanger to carry a series of sketches fetched from Allen's discard drawer, in which Harry's fictions are shown coming to life. The best of these involves an actor (Robin Williams) who finds himself going permanently out of focus; there's another about death coming for the wrong guy, and another, about an elevator trip to hell ("Floor seven, the media. Sorry, that floor is all filled up"), was a leftover from *Annie Hall*.

There's a liberated feeling to the film's raggedy construction and potty-mouthed script, as if Allen, punch-drunk from the

Opposite: On set with Robin Williams, who played an actor who finds himself going permanently out of focus.

Above: Allen gave up trying to tell people that his resemblance to the "nasty, shallow, superficial, sexually obsessed" Harry Block ended with the typewriter.

media vilification he was subjected to in the years following his break with Farrow, were dealing with it the same way you deal with snake bites: by sucking out the poison and spitting it back. But it also repeats a pattern begun many years before, wherein Allen, following a period of popular success, recoils from his role as crowd-pleaser to let off a stink bomb of a picture designed to test the faithful and weed out fair-weather fans. He seems unable to tolerate audience fondness for long. Back in 1980, the crowd-pleaser was *Manhattan* and the stink bomb *Stardust Memories*. Now it was *Everyone Says I Love You* and *Deconstructing Harry*, which might just as easily have been called *Everyone Says I Hate You*. Elisabeth Shue, Judy Davis, Demi Moore and Kirstie Alley all take their turns spit-roasting Harry. The old standard heard over the credits is "Twisted." There's even a cameo for Mariel Hemingway as a purse-lipped matron, which, in terms of Allen oeuvre, is a

bit like Botticelli going back to Venus and painting on devil's horns—an act of vivid self-graffiti.

Initially happy to stress the film's autobiographical elements ("This is a character I feel within myself"), Allen changed tack once it was released and met with hostile reviews. "I thought when the picture was over that I would say, 'Oh, yes, this is definitely me,' and not go through the usual dance where I'm saying, 'It's not me, it's not the way I work, I've never been blocked, I've never kidnapped my kid, I wouldn't have the nerve to act like that, I don't sit home and drink and have hookers coming over to the house all night.' If I was being honored by an old school—which I wouldn't be—I probably wouldn't show up. Apart from the ability to write anytime, there was nothing in the movie at all that was me, but the path of least resistance was to say yes. I've given up trying to say no."

Celebrity

1998

"It has always seemed to me that the culture we live in celebrates the oddest people," said Allen of *Celebrity*. "Whether it's a member of the clergy or a plastic surgeon or the prostitute as played by Bebe Neuwirth, someone rises to the status of celebrity in their area and becomes the specialist doctor you must go to or the priest you see on TV or the famous actor as played by Leonardo [DiCaprio]. All this seems interesting and amusing to me—all the attention we've given to people like Joey Buttafuoco, who now has his own TV show."

Allen was initially unsure whether Kenneth Branagh could bring off an American accent playing the lead role of Lee Simon, a journalist briefly brought into the A-list circle, but after Robert Altman screened portions of *The Gingerbread Man* for him, Branagh got the part. He asked Allen whether he should wear glasses, as John Cusack had done in *Bullets over Broadway*, but they decided against it.

Despite featuring an all-star cast that included Kenneth Branagh and Winona Ryder (above), as well as Charlize Theron as a gazelle-like catwalk model (right), *Celebrity* foundered at the box office.

"I was, however, influenced by him because I have loved his films since forever," said Branagh, who told himself, "If I ever started to do a bad version of Woody Allen he would stop me." Along with Judy Davis, Branagh was the only actor given a complete script, as usual. Everyone else was given only their scenes, including Leonardo DiCaprio as a hedonistic young star, cosseted by his entourage, and Charlize Theron playing a supermodel, something she vowed never to do on screen until Allen wrote her a letter specifically designed to persuade her otherwise.

Shot in black and white by Sven Nykvist, Allen's last film with the cinematographer, the movie also marked the end of

his long collaboration with editor Susan Morse, who had edited all of Allen's films from *Manhattan*. Not so much a narrative as a string of loosely linked scenes on a theme, lightly coated with lubriciousness, *Celebrity* represents the culmination of the coarser streak that had begun to infuse his dramas, first with *Mighty Aphrodite*, then with *Deconstructing Harry*—what some have called his hookers-and-fellatio trilogy.

"His men and women may have gotten on each other's nerves," wrote James Wolcott in *Vanity Fair*, "but their anxieties were equally matched; they clung to the same psychiatrist's couch—the Jewish lifeboat. Since *Mighty Aphrodite*, the balance of sexual power has shifted. Now when

a woman opens her mouth in a Woody Allen movie it isn't because speech is required. As Allen's movies have gotten pornier, oral sex has become the favored way to keep women quiet and occupied."

A late blue period is typical of many male artists—one thinks of Picasso's satyrs, even Scorsese, in *The Departed* and *The Wolf of Wall Street*—but in the case of *Celebrity*, it was more noticeable, and ultimately more detrimental, because the ostensible subject of the film was fame. Allen takes people to task for the shallow objectification of fame while indulging in horndog fantasy about the sex lives of the famous in what aspires to lusty Felliniesque satire—in

many ways the picture is a companion piece to *Stardust Memories*—but you can't satirize with steamed-up spectacles. It blocks the view. Indeed, much of *Celebrity* seems to spring less from A-list reality than Allen's own somewhat seamy fantasy of it.

In the first thirty minutes, Branagh's media gadfly flirts with an actress played by Winona Ryder, gets a blow job from an A-list star played by Melanie Griffith, receives a tongue to the ear from Charlize Theron's gazelle-like model, and accompanies a drug-crazed star (Leonardo DiCaprio) to Atlantic City, where he reluctantly participates in an orgy, hemming and hawing as limbs flail around him.

"I had no tremendous insight into it, only to record that it was a phenomenon that permeated my culture at that point, that everybody had such a reverence for celebrity and that it meant so much. This was what I was trying to do. To what degree I succeeded I don't know, but I tried."

Above: Flanked by his acolyte (Sam Rockwell) and journalist Lee Simon (Branagh), dissolute star Brandon Darrow (Leonardo DiCaprio) hits Atlantic City.

Opposite: Branagh's performance was widely criticized for excessive mirroring of Allen's mannerisms.

Almost every critic rounded on Branagh's Woody Allen impersonation. "Branagh stammers, bobs his head and runs the gamut of other established Woody tics and mannerisms—delivering nervous shtick where a performance would have sufficed," wrote Edward Guthmann in the *San Francisco Chronicle*. "His novelty act belongs in the same bin with his hammy histrionics in *Mary Shelley's Frankenstein*." Despite Branagh's assurances to the contrary, Allen appears strangely incapable of spotting, or correcting, his performers when they start imitating him. Even worse, though, is Judy Davis as Simon's ex-wife, who in one notorious scene is taught how to fellate a banana by Bebe Neuwirth. "Davis picks and pecks at herself, her sulky head protruding from a teeming anthill of mannerisms," wrote Wolcott. "Simmering in *Husbands and Wives*, boiling in *Deconstructing Harry*, she is a veritable triathlete of angst in *Celebrity*, projecting a neediness that could warp gravitational fields."

Celebrity was marketed by Miramax as an all-star vehicle, with Allen's name appearing only in small type in ads. "They're probably ashamed of me," he said, but it did no good: The film tanked. "I make the first DiCaprio film after *Titanic* and it doesn't make a dime," said Allen, wearing it like a badge of honor. His cantankerousness was back in high season, but his passive-aggressive pattern with the audience was running through its cycle much faster this time around. If *Celebrity* had been the *Stardust Memories* to *Everyone Says I Loves You*'s *Annie Hall*, his next picture would be the *Zelig*: as honest a self-reckoning as he had yet put to film.

Sweet and Lowdown

1999

Sweet and Lowdown was a much modified version of *The Jazz Baby*, the script written almost thirty years before, which Allen had elected not to film for UA after he saw their reaction. "I always knew it was a good idea," he said. "I always wanted to do something about a self-centered, egotistical, highly neurotic, genius guitar player." The structure was the same—anecdotal hearsay about a jazz guitarist named Emmet Ray in the faux-documentary manner—and most of the characters were the same, including Hattie, Emmet's mute, mistreated girlfriend, but *The Jazz Baby* was "much less amusing" said Allen. "The impression you get from the original was that the musician was so self-destructive and it's so sad. You've got a big ladle of masochism, of Germanic Emil Jannings masochism. It needed some spirit to it. We had to go find a guy who looked like Django Reinhardt. Not so easy."

He thought of Johnny Depp for the part. Nicolas Cage's name also came up. He thought of playing it himself, but decided against it. When finally casting director Juliet Taylor suggested Sean Penn, Allen was dubious. He knew of his temperamental reputation but after asking around some of the people who had worked with him most recently was reassured enough to meet the thirty-eight-year-old actor and was immediately taken with him. Samantha Morton he had seen in *Under the Skin* and knew instantly she'd be perfect for the mute girl.

"I would like you to play this like Harpo Marx," he told her.

"Who's Harpo Marx?"

"Harpo Marx, the Marx Brother that doesn't speak."

"Who are the Marx Brothers?"

"It shows how old I'm getting," remarked the sixty-two-year-old director. "I couldn't believe it. And I said, well you should take a look at him some time, you'll enjoy it! And she did. Then the first couple of days she was so much like Harpo

Marx, all the moves, that I had to take her down from it! But I saw her face and thought she would be perfect. I never heard of her, I didn't know anything about her. I was completely introduced to Samantha on tape. And I said, get this one. She's got the right face."

The most pleasurable part of the movie was coming up with the soundtrack. Normally, Allen cuts his films and when they're done he goes into a room with his own records—he still has all old LPs—and picks out the music; if something

Right: Samantha Morton as Emmet's mute girlfriend, Hattie.

Opposite: Self-proclaimed "second-best guitar player in the world" Emmet Ray (Sean Penn) attempts a dramatic stage entrance.

Right: Samantha Morton as Emmet's mute girlfriend, Hattie.

Penn excelled in the role of the obnoxious Emmet, whose only displays of sensitivity are directed toward his guitar.

doesn't work, he pulls out another record. "Because this movie was about music, it was an even greater pleasure to use my favorite records throughout the movie," said Allen, who took his title from a George Gershwin song. "The first one I thought of was 'Sweet and Hot,' which is a jazz phrase, and one that I felt matched the characters. But I felt 'Sweet and Lowdown' was even better. You know, that she was sweet, and he was lowdown."

In some ways marked by the cursoriness that is the hallmark of Allen's work from the late 1990s, its documentary frame a poor replacement for proper dramatic structure, *Sweet and Lowdown* nevertheless boasts Allen's most vivid Portrait of the Artist as a Pathological Turd—a theme he had been warming to since *Bullets over Broadway*. What we have is a string-beading of anecdotes in the shape of a biopic about a little-known 1930s jazz guitarist named Emmet Ray (Sean Penn), considered by critics and musicians—including Emmet himself—as second only to Django Reinhardt, whom he calls "that gypsy over in France," but who is in every other respect a louse of a human being. The sensitivity he puts into his playing stands in bald contrast to the mulishness of his relationships with other people, notably his sweet girlfriend

Hattie (Samantha Morton), who soaks up his ill-treatment with the same avidity with which she consumes chocolate sundaes. "I always pick the winners," he self-commiserates, typically, upon finding out that she is mute. "Did someone hit you on the head or what?"

Penn is never far from caricature—a peacock in a three-piece white suit who struts and scuttles beneath delusions of grandeur balanced on teetering insecurities—but his eyes, upon picking up a guitar, close in bliss, eyebrows arching as he hits one perfect note after another, an image of beatific transfiguration. The plot development that would prize him open or turn him upside down never quite arrives. A silent screen career beckons for Hattie, and for a second you think we might be in for another of Allen's soul-swap comedies, with Emmet forced to play second fiddle to Hattie's burgeoning fame, but he sees the threat and shuts it down. Uma Thurman's slumming socialite slinks into frame and steals Emmet away, imploring him to "astonish" her in purring faux-bohemian tones. Cut to the two of them shooting rats in the railway yard: a favorite pastime.

That cut may be the picture's single funniest joke, but Thurman's presence is reiterative: She underlines what we already know about Emmet, whose selfishness essentially

consumes the picture. Coiled inside that structural
monotony, however, is an astonishing performance from
Penn who, like Cate Blanchett in *Blue Jasmine* some fourteen
years later, drills down to plumb one of Allen's truly lost
souls. The film boasts a black pearl of an ending, as Emmet,
deciding he has made a mistake with Hattie, tracks her down
to find her married. "Happily?" he asks, for once lost for
words. The final image we have of him—trying to impress
Gretchen Mol by the train tracks with his rendition of "Sweet
Sue" before smashing his guitar to pieces—is overlaid with
the information that Emmet subsequently disappeared from
public view, but recorded his loveliest work. "Something
opened up in him," says Allen himself, popping up to play
one of the talking heads. "Fortunately, we do have those
recordings he made. They're absolutely beautiful."

That sounds a lot like a self-crafted epitaph. Allen is a
surprisingly fleeting, evanescent presence for someone
who has spent most of his career on-screen, his trail even
harder to follow thanks to the flurry of disavowals and red
herrings he likes to throw in the face of over-presumptuous
interviewers. But every now and again, he shines a light on
himself that is as startling and unmistakable as a glimpse
of the Yeti. Suddenly, there he is. *Sweet and Lowdown* is just
such a work, the bittersweet ache of the final cut to black is
almost unmatched in Allen's work, the enormous care he has
taken to balance his tone between admiration for the art and
disappointment in the artist suggesting a candor only made
possible by dramatic proxies. Like God, he is present in his
absence, Allen's agnosticism owing less to theological belief
than it does to professional rivalry.

Small Time Crooks

2000

Small Time Crooks was the first of four ideas fished from Allen's bedside drawer for DreamWorks. "I thought I ought to start making some of these ideas because I'm getting older, and who knows what could happen to me? I don't want to have them lying around as unrealized, unattempted great comic ideas that I never got to." In truth, it suggests more of Allen's eagerness to please his new masters, who, impressed by the box office of *Antz*, to which he contributed voice work, signed him for a quartet of films, but only comedies—his serious films he was free to shop elsewhere. So there was a certain amount of cynicism on both sides. In many ways, the movies he made for DreamWorks—*Small Time Crooks*,

The Curse of the Jade Scorpion, *Hollywood Ending*, and *Anything Else*—mark, if not the low point of Allen's comic-writing career, then a period of enforced jollity from a dramatist whose comic muse was beginning to fade.

Small Time Crooks is the best of the bunch—a brisk screwball caper about idiot criminals that in some ways harkens back to *Take the Money and Run*. It germinated from a thought Allen had after reading about a gang of thieves who had tunneled into a jewelry shop from a store they'd rented next door. What if the robbery didn't work, but they made a killing from the fake store they'd set up? "I still felt I only had half a story," he said. "So I started pondering, where do they go from there? They become millionaires. But they miss going to the dog track and watching TV. What they really want is a simple life, and the joy of having each other, which is exactly what they lose when they become rich, so all this sudden wealth makes them very unhappy."

Allen is in full Danny Rose mode as petty ex-con turned dishwasher Ray Winkler, who cooks up a plan to rob a bank from a property two buildings away that fronts as a cookie shop. Tracey Ullman plays his wife, Frenchy, a New Jersey ex-stripper who bakes the cookies with the help of her daft cousin May (Elaine May). Throw in Jon Lovitz and Michael Rapaport as Ray's dim-witted gang members and you have enough top-quality shtick artists under one roof to power a fleet of wind turbines—Ullman's tones alone could strip paint. Each scene bulges like a bag of ferrets with insult and invective, as Allen sets his fools loose on one another, while

"You never hear people say about a writer or a painter or a sculptor, 'You know, it's amazing, he has complete control over his work.'"

the plot trips over itself in a series of perpendicular twists of gradually diminishing effectiveness. Frenchy's cookies begin to sell like crazy, and within a year the gang has turned the cookie shop into a multi-million-dollar franchise. Cue Hugh Grant as an art dealer tasked with molding Frenchy into a cultured woman while Ray embarks on a second career as a jewel thief and you have not so much a plot as a running flush of good ideas looking for a comic home, although May just about steals the picture with a prolonged yammer about the weather designed to divert attention from Ray's theft—a small aria of airheadedness. In fact, her head barely comes into it. "I just said what came into my mouth," she says.

May is so funny, and her rapport with Allen so snug, that you may find yourself cursing that this was their first and only on-screen collaboration. "She shows up on time, she knows her lines, she can ad-lib creatively and is willing to," said Allen of finally working with the legendary comedienne. "If you don't want her to, she won't. She's a dream. She puts herself in your hands. She's a genius, and I don't use that word casually. It's in her voice." If *Small Time Crooks* bustles with life whenever the two of them are together, the rest of Allen's movies for DreamWorks would demonstrate how hard it is to summon such chemistry into being.

The Curse of the Jade Scorpion

2001

"I have great regrets and embarrassment," said Allen of *The Curse of the Jade Scorpion*; his most overt valentine to the screwball comedies and detective mysteries of the Jazz Age, the film is his purest attempt at pastiche since *Shadows and Fog*—and with similar results. "I let down an exceptionally gifted cast. I had Helen Hunt, who is a superb actress and comedienne. I had Dan Aykroyd, who I always thought was just hilarious. I had David Ogden Stiers, whom I've used many times and he always comes through. Elizabeth Berkley was wonderful. And it was successful abroad, not so successful here. But I, from my personal point of view, feel that maybe—and there are many candidates for this—but it may be the worst film I've made."

An exaggeration. The idea had come to him some forty years earlier, when he was writing for TV. Allen plays a wisecracking insurance company investigator who, under the spell of a nefarious hypnotist, conducts a series of robberies of which he has no memory and thus no realization that he is the thief he seeks. The hypnosis plot conceit is ingeniously worked out, and contains a delicious turn from Charlize Theron as a platinum-blonde vamp right out of *The Big Sleep*, but the film founders on a single piece of miscasting: that of Allen himself as the protagonist, C. W. Briggs. Briggs was originally a private detective, but upon realizing he would be playing the lead Allen changed him to an insurance company investigator, although even that wasn't enough. Allen's performance, which is asked to carry the picture, drifts uncomfortably between traditional Allen goofing and an attempt at doing hard-boiled—*Play It Again, Sam* with Allen in the Bogart role.

Helen Hunt plays the Vassar-educated efficiency expert Betty Ann Fitzgerald, who has been brought into the company to streamline operations. She and Briggs are supposed to

hate each other in the time-honored screwball fashion that leads to true love, but there's never much joy between Allen and women who play smarter than him and Betty's lack of amusement at the ratfink she sees in front of her proves infectious. Viewing the first cut of the film, Allen wanted to reshoot it entirely, as he had done with *September*, but the expensive period sets had already been destroyed. Instead DreamWorks, encouraged by the success of *Small Time Crooks*, opened the film on 900 screens, the widest release ever for a Woody Allen film, whereupon it took only $2.5 million on its first weekend. "To have Woody Allen play a person whose unconscious is split off from the rest of him is to go against nature itself," noted Peter Rainer in *New York* magazine. Allen was inclined to agree. "I looked but I couldn't find anyone else who was available who had any kind of comic flair," he said. "But I was not right."

Opposite, top: "I find it strangely exciting standing here—in a grungy hovel with a myopic insurance clerk." Audiences found it equally strange that C. W. Briggs (Allen) should excite Charlize Theron's femme fatale.

Opposite, bottom: Having been hypnotized into committing a string of robberies of which he has no recollection, Briggs is mystified to find himself under arrest.

Right: Often the harshest critic of his work, Allen felt that *The Curse of the Jade Scorpion* may have been the worst film he had made.

Hollywood Ending

2002

Hollywood Ending was something Allen had first cooked up with Marshall Brickman a few years earlier as a possible vehicle for Gérard Depardieu. What if he played Houdini and the great escapologist suffered from claustrophobia? What if he also, psychosomatically, lost his sight, and got sent to Dr. Freud in Vienna to straighten himself out? The script was never written, but the idea of a great man struck blind resurfaced in this 2002 film about a once-prominent director, Val Waxman (Allen), who is given a chance to resurrect his career when his ex-wife, Ellie (Téa Leoni), persuades a studio executive—who is also her fiancé—to let him direct a New York melodrama. Just before shooting begins, Val goes blind from hysteria and has to fake his way through the picture.

It's a good joke—"Have you seen the pictures out there?" asks Val's agent, played by the excellent Mark Rydell. Whether it merits a full-length movie, particularly one nudging the two-hour mark, is another matter. One of the first casualties of Allen's move to DreamWorks was his longtime editor Susan Morse, and it's a rare Woody Allen movie from this point on that doesn't feel a trifle sluggish. The speed of the young comic was giving way to an older man's more sedentary rhythms, and in *Hollywood Ending* the wheels of his comedy spin without ever quite connecting with anything besides Allen's Rip Van Winkle-ish sense of having been left behind. His last experience of studio interference, let's remember—indeed his only experience of studio interference—had come more than thirty years earlier, with *What's New Pussycat?* Like many of the films fetched from his bedside drawer to please his new studio masters, *Hollywood Ending* feels like thirty-year-old hat, its satirical targets—money-grabbing producers, bimbo bit players, punk rock, videotape—distant specks in his rearview mirror.

In what would be one of his last lead performances, Allen amps himself up to full-on frantic mode, waving his arms as if flagging down New York taxi cabs and chewing his one-liners to a fine cud—"It's a job I would kill for," Val says of his new directing gig, "unfortunately the people I want to kill are the people giving me the job"—but the performance seems effortful, strangely solitary, the blindness conceit only walling Allen off from the one thing he needs more than anything: his fellow performers. He and Téa Leoni could almost be in different pictures, Leoni too poised for Allen's frantic rhythms and Allen too infantile for Leoni's brisk power broker. "When Woody Allen's newest movie, *Hollywood Ending*, is spitting one-liners, the picture has the gone-delirious feel of Thelonious Monk crunching notes, a wired, jazzy rhythm specific to this comic," wrote Elvis Mitchell in the *New York Times*. "Once the energy from the jokes dies down, we're left with a project so stale you feel like opening a window to let some air in."

The first film of his not to be released in cinemas in the United Kingdom, where it received a direct-to-DVD burial, the picture was, within a month of coming out in the United States, playing in a $4.95-a-ticket discount house in Times Square. Accompanying the movie to France, where it opened Cannes, the director was mystified by its mixed critical reception. "It was the biggest surprise for me of all the films I've done," he told Eric Lax, "because I generally don't love my own finished product, but this one I did."

This overestimation of his own work is not just rare for Allen, it's almost unheard of, at least when it comes to his comedies, the public verdict on which he is usually able to accept without demurral. That he was unable to in this instance suggests both his changed attitude to the public, who maybe mattered more to him now than at any point in his career, and his panic at finding his third film for DreamWorks continuing the tailspin in which he seemed caught. It would get worse before it got better.

Above: Washed-up film director Val Waxman (Allen) wins back his ex-wife Ellie (Téa Leoni).

Left: In an earlier scene, Val introduces his girlfriend (Debra Messing) to Ellie and her new partner (Treat Williams).

"Every now and then, something happens that's funny. And that's refreshing. But then you move back into the real world, which is not funny. You only have to pick up the newspaper in the morning and read about the real world and you see that it's rotten, just bad."

Back to reality. Portrait by
Arnault Joubin, c. 2000.

Anything Else

2003

"There were many funny things in the book but it wasn't really good enough," said Allen of his one attempt at a novel, written after he had stopped doing *New Yorker* pieces, about a young man who falls for a beautiful but mercurial flake and takes counsel from an older guy who teaches him about life, comedy, philosophy, before being institutionalized. Loosely based on Allen's experience as an apprentice writer who married young, the book was given to Roger Angell, Allen's editor at the *New Yorker*, for his opinion in 2001, along with a couple of other friends. "They were very kind to me, and very helpful, but I could see that I just didn't pull it off."

Allen instead recycled much of the material for *Anything Else*, the last of his ill-fated comedies for DreamWorks,

about a young comedy writer, Jerry (Jason Biggs), driven to distraction by his capricious girlfriend, Amanda (Christina Ricci), who seeks solace in his friendship with an older comedy writer, David Dobel (Allen) who was once institutionalized for attacking his shrink and takes a crowbar to thieves who have just nabbed his parking space. It's a good opportunity for Allen to flip his screen persona on its back, loosing paranoiac tirades against many of his old touchstones, from Freud and therapy to art and women, invariably bringing his rants to a close with a piece of dud wisdom sending up the sentientiousness of unsolicited advice ("If you take very good care of your styptic pencil and dry it after every shave, it will last longer than most relationships

"Somebody said it summed up everything that I always say in movies—they were saying this positively—and maybe it did and that was a negative for me. I don't know. I had screenings of it and people seemed to love it. Again, it was one of those pictures that nobody came to."

Opposite: Comedy writer Jerry (Jason Biggs) and his capricious girlfriend Amanda (Christina Ricci).

Right: A sidewalk pep talk for Biggs.

that you're in … Think about that."). If Alvy Singer had gone on hearing the word "Jew" muttered in restaurants but lost anybody to help talk him down from the ledge, he might well have turned out like Dobel—the schlemiel-as-Unabomber.

The younger actors fare less well. Shot by Iranian-born cinematographer Darius Khondji, the film exults in the kind of extended takes that had long become an Allen staple, with Amanda and Jerry walking in and out of shot, chattering about "nihilistic pessimism," name-dropping Eugene O'Neill, Jean-Paul Sartre, Tennessee Williams, but they come off a little like the versions of Alvy and Annie we see impersonating the real thing in Alvy's play at the end of *Annie Hall*—young puppets going through the puppet master's routines. As a writer, Allen is too sensitive to idiom for you not to notice the gulf that frequently opens up in his later comedies between script and player. When he made *Hannah and Her Sisters* he could count on Dianne Wiest, Mia Farrow, and Barbara Hershey to correct small mistakes. A younger generation, overwhelmed to be in a Woody Allen film, could not be relied upon to do the same. Jason Biggs, the star of *American Pie* and *American Pie 2*, is not going to be the one to tell the Oscar-winner that kids don't frequent the Village Vanguard, or "make love," or "go together," any more.

"I rehearse the cameraman all morning and do the complicated lighting and then break for lunch and come back and do the scene and we're finished with seven pages in five minutes," said Allen, who was proud enough of the end result to accompany the film to Italy, where it opened the sixtieth Venice Film Festival, but despite the presence of two young stars and a 1,035-screen opening, *Anything Else* was Allen's lowest-grossing film since *Shadows and Fog*. "None of this adds up to much of a movie; it's more like a filmed hodgepodge of not-fully-thought-out ideas and one-liners

and small shards of jaundiced polemic" wrote Peter Rainer for *New York* magazine. "The real problem with the recent pictures is not that they're bad," wrote Peter Biskind in *Vanity Fair*, with more accuracy, "they're not—it's that they're slight." His fifth successive film recycled from old material, *Anything Else* was a sign not only of Allen's willingness to hustle in a changed film marketplace but also of his increasingly fitful comic muse. Interestingly, his next film would be about that very subject.

227

Melinda and Melinda

2004

Allen had long thought it would be a good idea to shoot the same story two ways—one comic, one tragic. He mentioned the idea to Fox Searchlight's Peter Rice, during one of several phone conversations with the executive. "They didn't like the idea of working the way I work—that is, not seeing the script, not knowing the plot, not knowing anything about it," said Allen. "But he was willing to do it, much to his credit, I think."

Like *Broadway Danny Rose*, *Melinda and Melinda* is framed by table talk. Lingering over dinner at Pastis in the West Village, two playwrights (Wallace Shawn and Larry

Pine) cross swords about the nature of comedy and tragedy. A story is told twice to see which one it is. In the "comedy" section, ragtime jazz tootles lightly as Melinda (Radha Mitchell), the neighbor of married couple Susan and Hobie (Amanda Peet and Will Ferrell), crashes one of their dinner parties, entrances Hobie, and precipitates a game of marital musical chairs that will end with their union. In the "tragedy" section, a string quartet attacks Bartók as Melinda, a recent divorcée trailing bad news like cigarette smoke, arrives at the loft of an old friend and her husband, played by Chloë Sevigny and Jonny Lee Miller. In this version of the story, the husband is bored by this obvious train wreck of a woman, who instead competes with Sevigny for the affections of a gallant pianist (Chiwetel Ejiofor). Another roundelay ensues, this time culminating in a suicide attempt.

Whether a story was a comedy or a tragedy was invariably one of the first questions Allen asked himself, but it often switched as he worked on it. *A Midsummer Night's Sex Comedy* was originally a Chekhovian chamber piece, which is how *Another Woman* ended up until it got retold in comic form in *Alice*. His imagination, one might say, is upward bound—buoying him toward comedy, as much as he tugs it earthward. Certainly, the comic section of the film is the less successful, with Ferrell vying with Kenneth Branagh for the title of Worst Woody Allen Impersonator, made more noticeable by the fact that he is such a distinctive comic performer in his own right. Briefly, when getting his bathrobe

228

Opposite: Shooting an exterior scene in New York with veteran cinematographer Vilmos Zsigmond issuing the instructions.

Above: Melinda (Radha Mitchell) spirals downward in the "tragic" half of the film. Allen wrote the part for Winona Ryder, but had to replace her because the budget would not cover the cost of her insurance.

caught in Melinda's door, while eavesdropping on her lovemaking, Ferrell comes alive, but for the most part this big bear of a physical comedian is squeezed into a much smaller man's self-deprecating routine.

Mitchell's is the more mesmerizing performance, fragile and ditzy by turns, chain-smoking and gulping red wine in the "tragic" section, as she circles back to her self-destructive romantic patterns.

It might be objected that Allen doesn't quite stick to his rules: that he doesn't tell the same story two different ways, so much as tell two more-or-less different stories, linked by their lead actress and a patterning of easily arranged dramatic leitmotifs—a dentist, a leap from a window ledge, a lamp rubbed to grant wishes in one story, and deny them in the other. In the end, the film speaks less to the inextricable intertwining of comic and tragic elements in life, and more to Allen's declining interest in the former and increasing pull toward the latter. He had the same reaction to *Melinda and Melinda* upon finishing it that he had had to *Crimes and Misdemeanors*. "I would have liked to make a picture just of the serious part," he said. "But the comic half never interested me as a writer as much as the other half of it. The other half of it was where my heart was."

The glance back to *Crimes and Misdemeanors* is telling. Of his serious dramas, only a small subset fully succeed and they all have a single subject in common. *Crimes and Misdemeanors* had been his first to deal with it head on. *September* had touched on it, as had *Melinda and Melinda*, but with his next film Allen was to give the theme his fullest treatment in fifteen years. Finally, he was ready for more murder.

"To be even as bad as I am, you do have to practice every day. I'm a strict hobby musician. I don't have a particularly good ear for music. I'm a very poor musician, like a Sunday tennis player."

Stranger on the shore.
Portrait by Brian Hamill,
early 2000s.

Match Point

2005

I just happened to have the right characters in the right place at the right time," said Allen. "Like in *Macbeth* or *Crime and Punishment* or *The Brothers Karamazov*, there's murder but it's used philosophically and not as a whodunit. I was trying to give a little substance to the story so it wasn't just a genre piece."

Originally, it was set in America—in the Hamptons—but since *Deconstructing Harry*, which earned $10.6 million, Allen's US grosses had dipped to about $5 million a picture, against budgets that averaged about $20 million. Fox Searchlight did not even bother to bid on distributing *Match Point* because of *Melinda and Melinda*'s $3.8 million domestic gross. Instead, a lifeline came his way from BBC Films, in England, who agreed to partly fund the film if he made it in the UK with a largely local cast and crew. "*Match Point* was great, absolutely great to do," said Allen of the seven-week shoot in the summer of 2004. The weather was perfect, with lots of gray skies of the type he loved, and there was a deep talent pool of actors to draw on. He initially wanted Kate Winslet in the lead but the actress felt she had been neglecting her family by working too hard, and passed.

Someone commits a murder and then kills the next-door neighbor as a decoy to throw off the police. Starting with that, *Match Point* evolved. Allen thought, Who would the guy be? And then he thought, He'd be involved with some woman that he wanted to kill. And she'd be wealthy and so a good job for him would be a tennis pro who is brought into contact with wealthy people. "*Match Point* just flowed organically.

Juliet Taylor suggested Scarlett Johansson, found out she was available, and Allen sent her the script on a Friday afternoon. By Sunday night, she had committed. The first scene he shot with her, she had flown in the night before, arriving in London in the morning. She came straight to the pub where they were shooting and, with no rehearsals, played drunk to perfection in a scene opposite Jonathan Rhys

Above: Coaching at Queen's Club, Chris comes into contact with wealthy members like Tom Hewett (Matthew Goode).

Opposite, top: Having accessed the privileged world of the Hewett family, Chris strengthens his position by dating Tom's sister Chloe (Emily Mortimer).

Opposite, bottom: But he risks falling off the social ladder by starting an affair with Tom's fiancée.

Meyers. "The first takes were great," said Allen of his new star, with whom he was soon smitten as he had not been for quite a while by an actress. "Everything comes together: Her personality, her voice, her look, her eyes, her weight, her lips, everything comes together in a way that the whole is greater in some way than the sum of the parts."

The usually remote filmmaker spent much of the shoot joking with his stars between takes, so much so that they struggled to recapture the more somber tone of some of the scenes they were filming. "I think with *Match Point* I was maybe the most successful I've been with dark material," said Allen. "You know, I try to make them all good, but some come out and some don't. With this one everything seemed to come out right. The actors fell in, the photography fell in, and the story clicked. I caught a lot of breaks. It turned out to be one of the luckiest experiences I've ever had. Every little break that we needed at every little turning point went right."

Match Point purrs along like an old Jaguar, the filmmaking equivalent of one of the vintage sports cars in which Allen's films from this period take such unalloyed pleasure: self-consciously "classy," in some sense an antique, but fast, shapely, and great on the curves. Allen's direction is a marvel

of suave ellipses. A low-born Irishman, Chris Wilton (Jonathan Rhys Meyers), works at the exclusive Queen's Club in London, where he helps rich members like Tom Hewett (Matthew Goode), the amiable, unserious heir to a business fortune, with their ground strokes. Invitations to the opera follow, and to Tom's house in the country, where his jolly-hockey-sticks sister Chloe (Emily Mortimer) soon takes a shine to the new arrival. Allen makes Chris's rise seem effortless, a daisy-chaining of opportunities leading upward, orchestrated like a kind of ballet, and scored to the vintage arias on the soundtrack. The key to good social climbing, like delivering a good magic trick or joke, is to make it look effortless.

Despite, in fact, being Irish, Rhys Meyers may not be what most people have in mind when they picture "Irishman," but the sense of imposture only aids the unease prickling the edges of his sullenly opaque performance. As he hovers on the edge of conversations, his contributions are perfect little drops of politesse, delivered just a fraction of a beat too soon, sometimes stepping on other people's lines in a way that hints at the rush to follow some private agenda—there's a lot of him lying in wait. He is soon smitten with Tom's fiancée, a silken-voiced voluptuary named Nola Rice (Scarlett Johansson), whom we hear before we see, crowing over a ping-pong opponent—"Who's my next victim?" It's a molten, star-making turn from Johansson, whose scenes with Rhys Meyers have an erotic tension unmatched in Allen's work. He's made endless jokes about sex. He's talked about it endlessly. He's told us everything we wanted to know but were afraid to ask. But he's never shot actual sex

scenes before, such as the one that transpires between Nola and Chris in a wet field, one afternoon, where they entwine like two snakes taking time off from climbing ladders.

The film shares their duplicity. Before you know it, this glossy entertainment has downshifted into Hitchcock territory, dark with remembrance of Allen's own *Crimes and Misdemeanors*, in which a mistress proved so bothersome as to drive a man to murder. Quite why murder should have replaced masturbation as the favorite activity of the Woody Allen male is something for Allen's analyst to answer, although Freud was not the first to insist on the hostility lurking beneath humor in *Jokes and Their Relation to the Unconscious*. In his 1651 book *Leviathan*, Thomas Hobbes

defined humor as "the sudden glory arising from the sudden conception of some eminency in ourselves, by comparison with the infirmity of others"—the flash of superiority when the other guy slips on the banana skin and we don't. Even the language—"punch line," "killing" the audience, "slaying" them—is violent. When we laugh we show our teeth.

The murderousness in Allen's later work picks up the dramatic slack left by absent punch lines. Instead *Match Point* resolves itself around the wrong end of a double-barreled shotgun. "This is a champagne cocktail laced with strychnine," wrote A. O. Scott in the *New York Times*. "You would have to go back to the heady, amoral heyday of Ernst Lubitsch or Billy Wilder to find cynicism so deftly turned

Above: Allen's filmmaking entered new territory with this rain-soaked sex scene.

Right: *Match Point* was the first film Allen made with Scarlett Johansson, but it would not be the last.

into superior entertainment." In *Entertainment Weekly*, Owen Gleiberman called it "the most vital return to form for any director since Robert Altman made *The Player*." The film got a rougher ride from British critics eager to engage in turf warfare with regard to matters of location and idiom. The *Guardian*'s Peter Bradshaw commented that "the dialogue is composed in a kind of Posh English that Allen seems to have learned from a Berlitz handbook," while the *Observer*'s Jason Solomons complained that the film "takes place in a London that's recognizable but doesn't really exist." To which one can only say: Welcome to the club. They've been saying that about Woody Allen's New York for decades. It didn't seem to hurt him any.

"There is sexuality without showing any real sex. You get the idea. That's more fun. Real sex, you can see that all you want. It looks like pistons, or a pneumatic drill, but is rarely sexy."

Scoop

2006

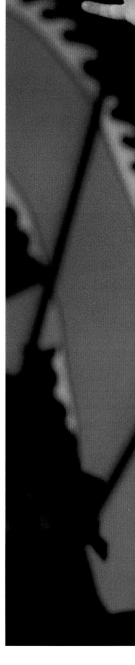

Left: Sid Waterman (Woody Allen) and Sondra Pransky (Scarlett Johansson) with their chief suspect, Peter Lyman (Hugh Jackman), in what Allen described as "a trivial little Kleenex of a film."

Right: Allen has written numerous magicians into his films, but The Great Splendini was the first one he played himself.

"Oh, Scarlett leaves me for dead," said Allen of working with Scarlett Johansson. "I mean, she's one of those people that always—offstage or on—always tops me. No matter how good a line I come up with—when we're putting each other down, teasing each other, whatever—she always nails me last, and best. Of course, that, to me, earns a lot of respect. Because I always think that I'm quick and witty, and so when someone outguns me consistently, I'm just amazed by it. But it's true—and everyone on the set will tell you that."

Written primarily to chase the chemistry Allen discovered with the actress while shooting *Match Point*, *Scoop* saw him return to the screen for the first time since *Anything*

Else to play Sid Waterman, aka The Great Splendini, an old-school magician whose stage act becomes the means by which the ghost of a recently deceased journalist, Joe Strombel (Ian McShane), delivers his final scoop, the identity of a serial killer, to a junior-league American journalist in London, Sondra Pransky (Johansson). An unpretentious *divertissement*, modeled as was *Manhattan Murder Mystery* on the old "Thin Man" movies with Myrna Loy and William Powell, *Scoop* is appealing without being especially funny, and peaks early with a scene in which Sid and Sondra must pass themselves off as plutocrats at an English garden party—"I must find out who does your hedges," quips Sid.

"My topiary moose is beginning to look a little shabby around the antlers." Allen's ability to do a panic-stricken nonchalance, leaking credibility with every gulp and wave, remains intact, even if the film doesn't find much else for him to do. *Scoop* is notable chiefly for the brief respite it gives Johansson from playing sirens. It suits her. Dressed in nerdy sweaters and spectacles, her hair pulled back into a ponytail, she peers up at Hugh Jackman's possibly guilty aristo and peppers him with questions, seemingly unaware of the effect she has on him—Johansson is playing a variant of one of the old screwball heroines, brainy but oblivious to her own sexual potency.

The movie was a sizable hit, taking in $39 million worldwide on a $4 million budget, even if Allen was quick to accept the middling critical verdict on it. "Allen doesn't seem to be working terribly hard in *Scoop*, and while that makes for some apparent goofs and lots of ragged edges, it gives the whole thing a pleasantly carefree vibe," wrote Manohla Dargis in the *New York Times*. "This goes back to funny concepts not scoring," said Allen. "*Scoop* proceeds laugh by laugh but the concept—which is witty—counts for little." Johansson did not share his opinion. "I don't think anything's played out," she said. "I'm waiting for him to write my *Citizen Kane*."

Cassandra's Dream

2007

Above: On set with Hayley Atwell (Angela) in the last of three consecutive films made in the United Kingdom.

Opposite: "Once you cross the line there's no going back." Brothers Ian and Terry (Ewan McGregor and Colin Farrell) lie in wait for their target.

"I wanted to make the main plot between men," Allen said of *Cassandra's Dream*, which had its origins in his 2004 play *A Second Hand Memory* for New York's Atlantic Theater Company. The subject, once again, was murder. Two brothers in London, one, called Terry, a garage mechanic and compulsive gambler, the other, Ian, a restaurateur trying to quit the business by investing in a Californian hotel, go to their wealthy uncle for a loan. He agrees to help them if they will commit a murder for him. "In my play he [the uncle] doesn't have any favors he wants to give out," said Allen. "He comes with his girlfriend and one of the brothers gets

involved with the girlfriend—it's a different kind of story. But in this case what occurred to me is, What if the uncle had a favor to ask—a favor that brought up a strong moral issue, a crisis of conscience? That gave me an interesting idea for a movie that could be suspenseful and tense, with a crime plot that could be entertaining."

Casting director Juliet Taylor suggested Ewan McGregor and Colin Farrell for the brothers. Allen wasn't sure at first, having envisaged younger actors in the roles, and met with Farrell for a grand total of sixty seconds.

"Hi," Farrell said, "Here I am. OK, I guess you want me to go now?"

"Yes," replied Allen, laughing. Once the actor had left, Allen said to Taylor, "He's perfect."

McGregor relished his first exposure to Allen's working method. "Most of the scenes play out in a single frame," he said. "There is a lot of dialogue. There are not many takes—it's wonderful. You get home at four thirty in the afternoon. You can have a life." Farrell later worked out that he did as many takes for the whole film as he did for one scene in the movie version of *Miami Vice*. For the score, Allen turned to Philip Glass—one of the few times the director has commissioned original music for a film. "In this one, I couldn't think of what to do, and then the idea of Philip Glass came up," said Allen. "I called him and he was very interested. I wanted something that complemented the tragedy of the story. He came in—and, of course, his music is so heavy, so ominous. He's a genius. He came in with an enormously ominous, heavy piece of music, and I said, 'My God, this is so ominous and peculiar—giving the audience the whole content of the

"Out of crime ideas, invariably, one is led to moral decisions. And those give the films more substance than just murder mysteries and whodunits."

story,' and he said, 'Oh no, that's the *love* theme—when he meets the girl. I haven't put the ominous part in yet.'"

The film suffers from the over-telegraphing of theme to which Allen's later films are sometimes prone. If we didn't get the message from the dire arpeggios of Glass's score, Allen lays on a crack of thunder to underline Uncle Howard's proposal of murder: Beware! Faustian Pact Approaching! "The stakes are enormous but I shouldn't have to talk to you about betting on risks!" says Ian (Ewan McGregor) in the bald, on-the-nose expository style that is the crutch of second-rate playwrights everywhere. "I'm just a two-bit player myself who plays the big shot in borrowed cars!" Allen found a snug fit for himself amid the drinking dens and gentleman's clubs of Belgravia in *Match Point*—parvenus are the same the world over, apparently—but stubs his toe on the

English working class. Only Sally Hawkins, reprising her role as the cheerful cockney from Mike Leigh's *Happy-Go-Lucky*, manages to invest his dialogue with the flavor of speech. His brothers sound like cockneys but think like Americans, dreaming of yachts, vintage cars, and lunch at Claridge's, when a Bentley Continental, an Xbox, and Arsenal season tickets would be closer to the mark. They are Runyonesque grifters in Mike Leigh clothes.

"You don't feel the human sweat and strain in *Cassandra's Dream*, despite game work from Farrell and McGregor," wrote Michael Phillips in the *Chicago Tribune*. "Like many of his later films, *Cassandra's Dream* feels too lightly polished and often rushed, as if he had directed it with a stopwatch," said Manohla Dargis in the *New York Times*. Allen's extended English tour seemed to have come to an end.

On set with Javier Bardem (Juan Antonio), Penélope Cruz (Maria Elena), and Scarlett Johansson (Cristina).

Vicky Cristina Barcelona

2008

"I started out with Barcelona, with Penélope, and in the back of my mind I was going to go to Scarlett," said Allen of *Vicky Cristina Barcelona*, a project initiated after Spanish financiers asked if Allen would like to make a picture in Barcelona with a little financial help from the government of Catalonia. "I had no idea for anything for it and then about a week or two later I got a call from Penélope Cruz. I didn't know her; she wanted to meet and she was in New York. I had only seen her in *Volver* and nothing else ever. I thought she was great in it, and she said that she knew I was doing a film in Barcelona and she would like to participate…Then I heard Javier was interested, so gradually it took shape. I put the thing together for the people almost."

Allen was initially reluctant to cast Johansson again so soon after *Match Point* and *Scoop*. "Even though he was crazy about her and I think really wanted to use her, we sort of thought better of it," said Juliet Taylor. "We felt we should do something different, that it shouldn't be so fast on the heels of the other movies. So we really, really looked around to see if we could cast someone else. And at a certain point, we felt like we were just going around in circles, because we were looking at people who were so much less interesting, who just couldn't bring as much to it."

Shooting in Spain drew enormous crowds. Much energized by his young cast and by the pleasures of filming in Barcelona, Allen kept a spoof diary for the *Guardian*, the first time he had done this kind of piece since writing about the shoot of *Love and Death* for *Esquire*:

5 June

Shooting got off to a shaky start. Rebecca Hall, though young and in her first major role, is a bit more temperamental than I thought and had me barred from the set. I explained the director must be present to direct the film. Try as I may,

Some time after their romantic evening in Oviedo, Juan Antonio gives Vicky (Rebecca Hall) another chance for something special.

"You could put this film together to emphasize the comedy or the drama, but basically it's a romance and it remains a romance. It's hard to explain. It's a dramatic film, but there are laughs in it and a lot of romance."

I could not convince her and had to disguise myself as a man delivering lunch to sneak back on the set.

His friskiness is evident in the finished film, whose honeyed views and heated couplings invest it with a sensuality nobody familiar with the clenched coolness of, say, *Interiors* could ever have predicted. Vicky (Rebecca Hall) is a levelheaded, cerebral graduate student working on her Master's degree in Catalan culture who is engaged to a nice, sensible young man: The comforts of a secure future beckon. Cristina (Scarlett Johansson), by contrast, is an impetuous thrill-seeker who looks for passion and excitement above all else; overhearing of the messy divorce of a local Catalan painter, Juan Antonio (Javier Bardem), her ears prick up. When he approaches and propositions the two of them one evening in a restaurant—"Life is short, life is dull, life is full of pain," he reasons, "and this is a chance for something special"—Vicky scoffs at his effrontery while Cristina pouts her pillowy lips and eats the swarthy suitor with her eyes.

What follows is a rueful, libidinous comedy about the pleasures and pitfalls of expat epicureanism—Henry James by way of Éric Rohmer—in which the two women are made, oh so gradually, to swap their respective positions. With Cristina indisposed by a stomach bug, it is the sensible Vicky to whom Juan Antonio first turns his attention, luring her to bed with soulful conversation, guitar, and copious swigs of red wine. Upon the arrival of her fiancé, he turns his attention back to Cristina, who finds all her dreams of the bohemian life turning on her as she is drawn into a messy *ménage à trois* with Juan Antonio and his volcanic, unstable ex-wife, Maria Elena (Penélope Cruz). Narrowing her eyes, Cruz delivers cascading tirades through artfully tousled L'Oréal tresses. She's playing a type—the Latin siren in all her unmedicated glory, Anna Magnani in the age of Prozac—but does so with such fire, smoke, and gusto that she punches the character into life, much as Mira Sorvino did in *Mighty Aphrodite*. She was rewarded in the same way: with an Oscar for Best Supporting Actress.

The film's moral is easily flagged—beware the lure of romantic bohemianism—but Allen the moralist is counterbalanced by Allen the late-blooming sensualist. "Let's not get into one of those turgid categorical-imperative arguments," pleads Vicky at one point, Hall's own free-spiritedness pushing past her beautifully wary intelligence. As always with Allen's soul-swap movies you get the feeling he is drawing two distinct parts of himself into a conversation. He is both women, sensible Vicky and impetuous Cristina, and could no more resist the temptation to seduce one than he could to rid the other of her illusions. Juan Antonio coils and enwraps both women with guileful ease, while cinematographer Javier Aguirresarobe bathes locations and actors alike in a honeyed, sun-glazed glow. Try resisting *this*, the film seems to say. The ripeness of *Vicky Cristina Barcelona* is quite a development from the man who once wrote a movie called *Anhedonia*, about the inability to experience pleasure. Allen had always known how to pleasure audiences, growing as lonely as a gigolo in the process. Relatively late in life, he seemed to have discovered something equally remarkable: how to enjoy himself.

Maria Elena and Juan Antonio
find an unconventional form
of domestic harmony with
Cristina (above), but when she
leaves, the tempestuous couple
are soon back at each other's
throats (left).

Left: Living with Maria Elena
and Cristina sparks Juan
Antonio's creativity.

Below: Cruz does not appear
until more than halfway
through the film, but the effect
of her arrival is electrifying.

Opposite: Facing the press
with Hall and Cruz.

"Really my heart is in it more when I'm writing for women. I don't know why, but I remember when that transformation took place from an inability to write a credible woman. I couldn't write anything but a one-dimensional woman. Then I was writing for women all the time."

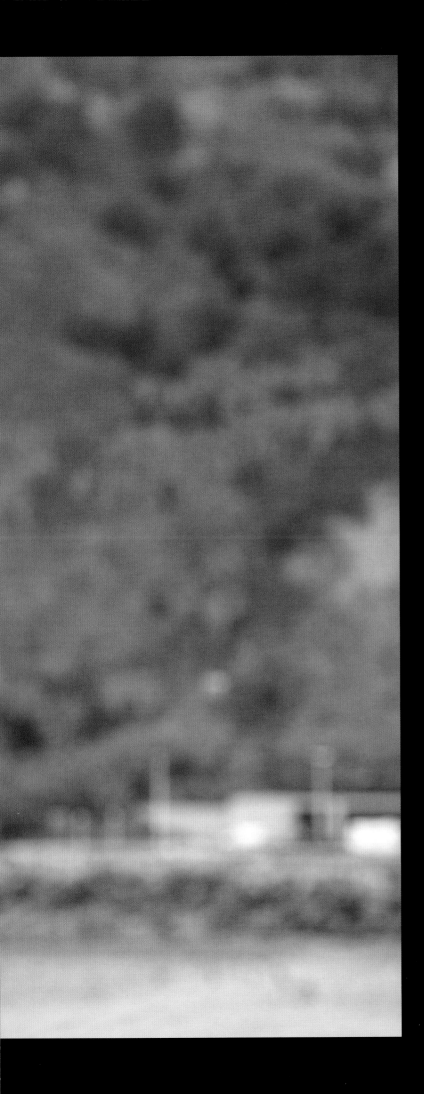

"You're always searching for control, and in the end, you're at the mercy of the hoisted piano not falling on your head."

Attending the San Sebastián Film Festival, where *Vicky Cristina Barcelona* received its Spanish premiere. Portrait by Alice Erardy, 2008.

Whatever Works

2009

Originally written in the 1970s for Zero Mostel around the time of *Annie Hall*, *Whatever Works* was dusted off as a vehicle for Larry David. It was actually David's third appearance in a Woody Allen film after bit parts in *Radio Days*—"All you got was my bald head," said David—and Allen's "Oedipus Wrecks" segment from *New York Stories* in 1989. He didn't hear from Allen again until the script for *Whatever Works* arrived with a cover letter attached. "I thought the script was brilliant," said David. "But I had my doubts as to whether or not I could do it. Because it's not the kind of thing I normally do. I generally just play myself."

Allen was insistent. "There's something obviously built into him that audiences like," he said. "You know, Groucho Marx had this. They were never offended by Groucho, they were offended if he didn't insult them, he told me once."

He reassured David, telling him it was nothing he couldn't handle, encouraging him to leap away from the screenplay and improvise, as he usually did. David nonetheless arrived determined to stick to the script, retreating to his trailer to memorize lines between scenes. "I didn't rewrite anything for Larry," said Allen. "When I took the script out of the drawer I did have to rewrite it because it had been lying there, you know, for a long time. Dormant, sort of. And I had to freshen it up and jazz it up a little bit to make it more contemporary. But I never changed it for Larry. Larry just seemed to fit it like a glove."

Whatever Works begins with a straight-to-camera address, with the misanthropic Boris Yellnikoff (David) delivering a monologue about cosmic injustice, his failure to win the Nobel Prize ("It's all politics, like any other phony honor"), global warming, terrorism, "the family value morons, and the gun morons," while his companions at a coffeehouse scratch their heads. Does he think he's talking to someone? It's a neat trick, lifted from *Annie Hall*, but where Allen cut from Alvy Singer's monologue to scenes from his present and past—in a schoolroom, at the movies, during lunch with Annie's family—shaking up the character's narcissism, here he just lets Boris rattle on, and not even David can raise a laugh with the material. He's meant for harangues, as *Curb Your Enthusiasm* showed, but only when barking at the feet of an unheeding universe. *Whatever Works* heeds him very closely: He's the only character given any depth.

One night, he finds on his doorstep a pretty young runaway from Mississippi named Melody (Evan Rachel Wood) whose intelligence he so enjoys impugning ("Inchworm!") that he lets her move in and finally marries her, in what is the most overtly patronizing of Allen's May-to-December romances: Wood cannot do anything with this dim-bulb Lolita. She

bounds into scenes, ponytail bouncing, the game object of Boris's condescension, but the comeuppance you are certain is heading his way never arrives. The exact opposite happens. Melody's mother, Marietta (Patricia Clarkson), turns up at their door and is at first horrified by her daughter's marriage ("He's not a husband," she says of Boris, "he's more of an outpatient") only to be converted, under his Jewish-atheist influence, to the ways of liberal-intellectual orthodoxy, eventually putting on a show of nude photographs and living in a *ménage à trois*. Clarkson is so vivacious and amiable she almost steals the picture, but the script's aged genesis shows. Allen had not yet learned how to creatively disagree with himself—to allow opposing characters to walk off with the drama. The film is a nod of agreement delivered to the mirror—the Alvy Singer story before Annie Hall showed up.

"You know, at one point I was going to call this film The Worst Man in the World. I thought it would be a funny character—a guy who is the quintessence of misanthropy and who can't fit in, doesn't want to fit in, rejects everything, just isn't someone who can deal with life or wants to deal with it."

You Will Meet a Tall Dark Stranger

2010

In 1969, Allen filmed a variety show for CBS in which he interviewed Billy Graham. It was an interestingly civil encounter, touching on religion, morality, the meaning of life, which left Allen with a grudging respect for the American preacher. "I was taking this bleak outlook position and Billy Graham was saying to me that even if I was right and he was wrong and there was no meaning to life and it was a bleak experience and there was no God and no afterlife or no hope or anything, that he would still have a better life than me because he believed differently. Even if he was a hundred percent wrong, our lives would both be completed and I would've had a miserable life wallowing in a bleak outlook and he would have had a wonderful life confident that there was more."

The comment stayed with Allen and many years later became the basis for *You Will Meet a Tall Dark Stranger*, a film about the value of unfounded faith. The production found him back in London with some Spanish financing and an international cast that included Anthony Hopkins as Alfie, a tan, silver-haired businessman who fights off impending mortality by leaving his wife of forty years, Helena (Gemma Jones), and marrying a fun-loving, long-limbed hooker named Charmaine (Lucy Punch), whom he buys with furs, jewels, and a spectacular apartment overlooking the Thames. The rejected Helena sips Scotch and falls under the sway of a fortune-teller (Pauline Collins), who convinces her she is receiving enormous waves of positive energy—an idea scoffed at by her unhappily married daughter Sally (Naomi Watts), whose boorish husband, Roy (Josh Brolin), a struggling writer, deals with the rejection of his new novel by starting an affair with a beautiful young woman (Freida Pinto) he sees in a window across the street.

Everyone except Helena chases what they don't have, and all end up with less than they had at the beginning in this not-quite-comedy about the folly of getting what you wish for. The more internalized the performer, the better the performance. Sporting a haircut seemingly styled in the late 1970s and a vocabulary to match, Brolin is noisy and overwrought. Watts gets one lovely, wordless moment in the car with her married boss, a debonair art-gallery owner played by Antonio Banderas, although in the movie's moral schema, her desires, too, turn to ashes. It is Hopkins who comes through most vividly. Coming good on the connection first established by Michael Caine in *Hannah and Her Sisters* between Allen's own emotional ambivalence and the British temperament at its most diffident, Hopkins distills all of his director's frets and fevers into his barrel-chested plutocrat, intelligent enough to know his dignity is being forsaken but too panicked by his own mortality to divert his own restless desires. Look for the apologetic little moue Alfie makes while waiting for some Viagra to kick in. "Three minutes," he says, tapping his watch, a member of the damned whiling away eternity.

"In the past, Allen made movies that echo Chekhov and Bergman, and this is a pass at Balzac: The world is ruled by egocentricity and meanness, and much of what we do approaches grubby comedy," wrote A. O. Scott in the *New York Times*. What a strange, fascinating place late Woody Allen was turning out to be: hints of farce, stabs of melodrama, some great-looking real estate, drawing-room dialogue, a smattering of O. Henry-ish twists, all served up with wry, sententious amusement at the sorry spectacle of human desire.

Above: An on-set discussion with Anthony Hopkins (Alfie). Allen said it required "years of disillusionment" to come up with this cautionary tale about the folly of getting what you wish for.

Left: Alfie's daughter, Sally (Naomi Watts), flirts with her tall, dark boss, Greg (Antonio Banderas).

Midnight in Paris

2011

"I had no idea for Paris at all—none," said Allen when first approached by French producers to make a movie set in the French capital. He asked himself what first came to mind when he thought of Paris—romance, of course—and hit on the title, *Midnight in Paris*, before he had so much as an inkling for a story to go with it. "And I'm thinking to myself for months, well, what happens at midnight in Paris? Does someone meet and fall in love? Are two people having an affair? And then one day it came to me that somebody visiting Paris is walking around at night, and it's midnight, and suddenly a car pulls up and he gets in and it takes him on a real adventure."

He attempted to shoot the film in 2006, only to have to abandon it as too expensive. It wasn't until France introduced a tax rebate for international productions in 2009 that Letty Aronson, Allen's sister now acting as his producer, was able to bring the budget down to a manageable $18 million. The lead, Gil, was originally an East Coast intellectual until Juliet Taylor suggested Owen Wilson who "belongs very much at home on a beach or with a surfboard," said Allen, who rewrote the script to make him a Los Angelino without too much difficulty. For Gil's difficult and demanding fiancée, Inez, he always had Rachel McAdams in mind. Marion Cotillard was slotted into place much as Javier Bardem and Penélope Cruz had been in *Vicky Cristina Barcelona*, almost as a matter of French national pride, while newcomer Corey Stoll was cast as Ernest Hemingway after Allen saw him in the Arthur Miller play *A View from the Bridge*, opposite Scarlett Johansson. "He handed me a couple of pages of Hemingway dialogue," said Stoll. "It burned through my fingers, I was so excited to see Hemingway on the page."

The shoot was brisk—just thirty-five days over seven weeks in the summer of 2010, with Allen delighting in the

Writer Gil Pender (Owen Wilson) is transported back to 1920s Paris, where he meets Adriana (Marion Cotillard), one of Picasso's muses.

"Matisse said that he wanted his paintings to be a nice easy chair that you sit down in, and enjoy. I feel the same way: I want you to sit back, relax, and enjoy the warm color, like take a bath in warm color."

Above: Gil is whisked away on the stroke of midnight in a time-traveling town car full of flappers.

Right: "Have you ever made love to a truly great woman?" Corey Stoll reveled in Allen's pastiche of Ernest Hemingway.

overcast weather and wet pavements. "I just wanted to put people in the *mood* of Paris," he said, and had discussions with his cinematographer Darius Khondji about shooting the 1920s sequences in black and white, but they eventually decided to go with color. "There's always a sense that if you could have lived in a different time, things would have been more pleasant. One thinks back, for instance, to *Gigi*, and you think, well, this is Belle Époque Paris, they have horses and carriages and gas lamps and everything is beautiful. Then you start to realize that if you went to the dentist, there was no novocaine, and that's just the tip of the iceberg. Women died in childbirth—there were all kinds of terrible problems. If you were an aristocratic gentile living in Paris at that time, that was a step forward. If you were not upper class, or you were Jewish, it would not have been such a dream existence. But you block that out."

The real wonder is not that Woody Allen should have a hit, in 2011, with a movie about the pleasures and pitfalls of nostalgia, but that he hadn't done so before. Of all the scripts he wrote for foreign commission, *Midnight in Paris* is the one that feels like it could have come from almost any point in his career. The idea speaks to the high-concept comedies he wrote in the 1980s when he imagined himself hobnobbing with the Fitzgeralds as Zelig; stretching back as far as his stand-up days he had riffed about hanging out with Hemingway. "Hemingway had just finished two short stories about prize fighting, and while Gertrude Stein and I both thought they were decent, we agreed they still needed much work," he wrote in his short story, "A Twenties Memory," published in the 1971 collection *Getting Even*. "We laughed a lot and had fun and then we put on some boxing gloves and he broke my nose."

"When I'm a grandmother I'd like to be able to say I made a film with Woody Allen." Carla Bruni-Sarkozy, wife of French president at the time, Nicolas Sarkozy, fulfilled her ambition with a minor role as a museum guide.

Above: On set with Wilson and Bruni-Sarkozy.

Right: Gil and his demanding fiancée, Inez (Rachel McAdams), stroll through the palace gardens at Versailles.

The plot's McGuffin goes beautifully unexplained, as it was in both *Zelig* and *The Purple Rose of Cairo*. There is explanation enough in Owen Wilson's face as he gazes in wonder at a dancing Josephine Baker, or lights up with the thought of giving Hemingway his novel to read. Wilson manages what so few actors have, which is to do justice to the hesitant rhythms of Allen's writing, while making Gil's mixture of befuddlement and enchantment all his own. "Wilson is wide-eyed without being fatuous, and lines that could sound like lazily reflexive, Yiddish-inflected gripes become philosophical and urgent," wrote David Edelstein in *New York* magazine. "The stammer is never shtick."

Scott Fitzgerald (Tom Hiddleston) and Zelda (Alison Pill) fall foul of Allen's slightly haphazard dramaturgy—shunted off stage almost as soon as they are summoned to it—but maybe he was just impatient to get to Corey Stoll's Hemingway, unfurling page after page of pitch-perfect parody ("All cowardice comes from not loving or loving too well, which is the same thing…") in the low murmur of someone noodling with his own chest hair. Marion Cotillard seems a little awkward as the film's Designated Area of Outstanding Natural Beauty—she's essentially reliving her role as the siren of *Inception*, coaxing Gil ever further into a dream-within-a-dream. She's not helped by Allen's slightly gloopy editing rhythms: Her scenes with Wilson are so slow they sometimes seem like they were patched together from separate shoots. In his mid-seventies, Allen shoots romance as if trying not to startle any nearby deer.

No matter. This was the first Woody Allen film to gross over $100 million worldwide and it was still in the Top Ten seven weeks after release, causing no end of boggle-eyed

think pieces from bloggers asking "How the heck did that happen?" Perhaps even more historic than the box office—adjusted for inflation, *Midnight in Paris* wound up clocking in at a respectable number seven in the director's career list, ahead of *Bananas* but behind *Love and Death*—is the undiluted pleasure Allen took from the movie's success, as it became his most Oscar-nominated film since *Bullets over Broadway*, garnering four and winning one, for Best Original Screenplay. With this, his third win from sixteen nominations, he became both the oldest winner ever to take

the award and the first person to win it three times. In the past such success would have been more than enough for Allen to disown the film in a fit of disgust and complain about how the happy ending was foisted on him by his psyche in a weak moment, while making preparations for his next film: a rancorous satire of the petty demagoguery of popular taste. Instead, we got a modest, queenly wave of assent to the people's wishes. "Nothing pleases me more than knowing people have gotten pleasure out of it," he told the *Hollywood Reporter*. "That's always a nice bonus."

To Rome with Love

2012

A genial traffic cop, standing on a pedestal in the Piazza Venezia, introduces the characters. In the film's weakest segment, newlyweds Antonio (Alessandro Tiberi) and Milly (Alessandra Mastronardi) lose one another in the city and face temptation, she in the form of a balding Casanova movie star, and he in the form of a prostitute called Anna (Penélope Cruz). Pouring into and out of a voluptuous red dress, Cruz channels Sophia Loren, but the story mechanics are a heavy trade for a few of Allen's remaining hooker jokes. Slightly better is the story in which Allen himself plays a retired American opera impresario, vacationing in Rome with his psychiatrist wife, who discovers, in the form of his daughter's prospective father-in-law, a mortician who can sing Puccini magnificently—but only in the shower. There are shades of Danny Rose, as Allen's newly revitalized impresario tries to get the man's career off the ground.

In the third segment a nervy, nerdy architecture student, Jack (Jesse Eisenberg), falls for an aggressively narcissistic actress (Ellen Page), while Alec Baldwin, playing a much older architect who sees himself in the young man, counsels wisdom from the sidelines. "Oh God, here comes the bullshit," he sighs, "I will allow you your moment but remember I know how it turns out." The conceit is rather like Bogart's walk-ons in *Play It Again, Sam*, except Baldwin's character goes largely ignored, and his ever more cynical interjections verge on sour grapes. In the fourth and most successful segment, Roberto Benigni plays an anonymous office worker called Leopoldo Pisanello who wakes up one morning to find himself inexplicably famous, pursued by photographers and camera crews reporting solemnly on everything from his shaving habits ("We're covering the shave live, from the first to the last stroke") to his preferences at breakfast (buttered toast) for millions of viewers. The

Allen went through two great titles—*The Bop Decameron* and *Nero Fiddled*—before he came up with one that suited Sony, a sure sign of the more relaxed, lackadaisical approach he took as he traversed his eighth decade. "I was trying to think about what it is about Rome that hits me," said Allen, again writing to commission for foreign financiers, "how it's so energetic and chaotic, with a ton of traffic and cars and people mingling, and some places with no sidewalks—the way everyone is out on the streets, sitting on steps or in cafés, the constant motion, the great flair for living with food and fashion and movies, and I couldn't convey it with one story. I wanted to write about tourists, and people who live there, and people coming from small towns, with all the romance and chaos and emotion. So, it needed a number of stories."

material that Allen played for sour farce in *Stardust Memories* and *Celebrity* here becomes inspiration for a delightful extended skit on modern celebrity, set in the birthplace of the paparazzi no less, and doing much to fill in the longueurs of *To Rome with Love* with a sense of cavalier, exuberant gaiety.

Opening in Italy several months earlier than anywhere else, the film was one of the country's most popular movies of 2012, grossing $9.5 million. "We're in the realm of miraculous transformation—transformation through sex, ambition, chance, and fame that suddenly and unaccountably lands on someone's shoulders like a ton of baked lasagna," wrote David Denby in the *New Yorker*, highlighting the theme running through all four stories. "What holds the pieces together formally is the idea of seizing the moment, the magic you make for yourself by not being afraid." After three films shot overseas, rebuilding his relationship with the audience, restoring his reputation at the box office, Allen was once again ready to return to American soil.

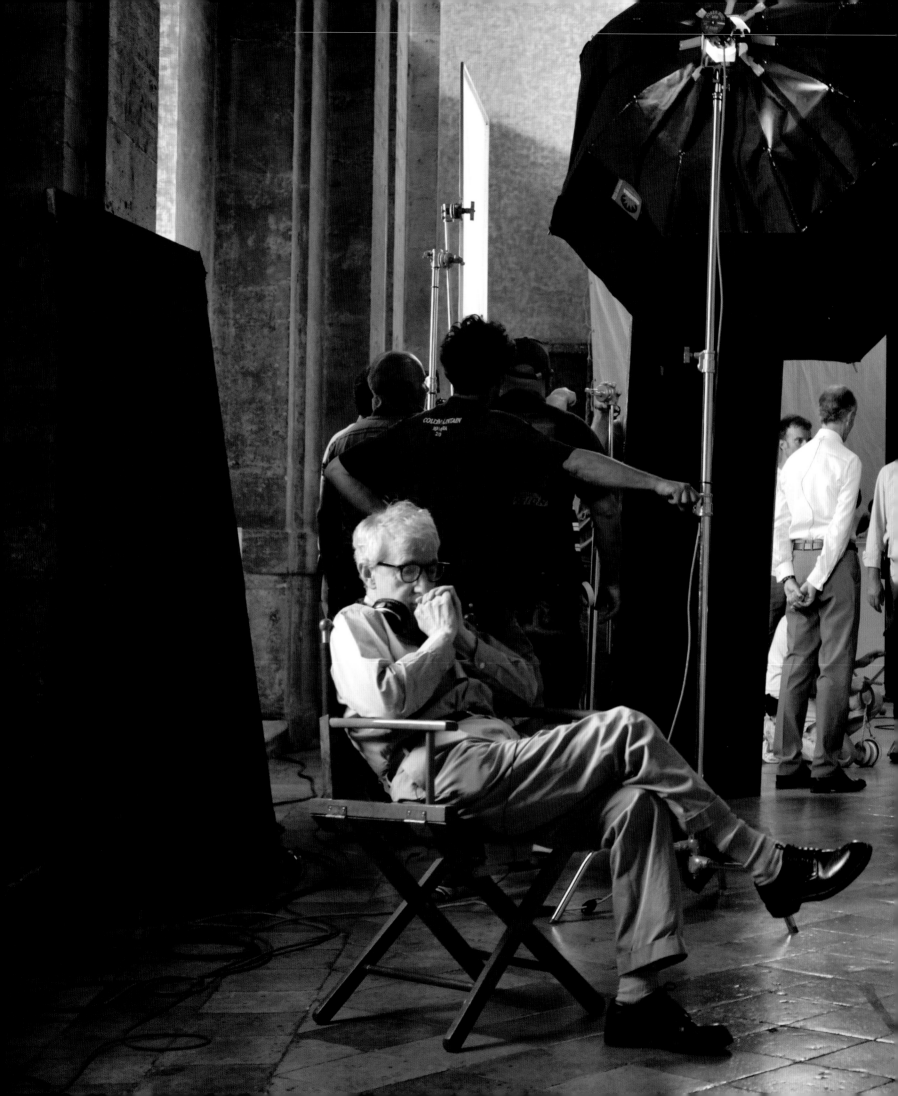

Blue Jasmine

2013

Above: "She's not just broke. She's all screwed up." Jasmine (Cate Blanchett) seeks refuge with her understanding sister Ginger.

Opposite: Happier times with her husband, Hal (Alec Baldwin).

The idea came from Soon-Yi, Allen's wife now of sixteen years, who told him about the friend of a friend—the wife of a financier who went into free fall after learning her husband was unfaithful and involved in a Ponzi-ish fraud. "She went from someone with charge accounts every place and a limitless amount of money, virtually, to someone who had to shop in bargain places and even get a job," said Allen, who thought it was "an interesting psychological situation for a woman to be in … if there was some way that she brought it on herself, it could fulfill some of those Greek requirements."

He found it in a pivotal scene—Allen called it a "tantrum"—in which she went on the warpath, bringing ruin upon both

herself and her husband. "She could have gotten a divorce, forgiven him, had a talk with him, moved out of the house. But she just hit the ceiling blindly and went on a rampage that brought destruction upon her whole household. She never stopped to think about the consequences of her raging moment. You see tantrums in adults all the time. You're driving on the highway and a car bumps you and the driver gets out and he's ready to tear your head off."

He wrote the character with Cate Blanchett in mind. The actress almost said yes to the role even before reading the script. "I'd given up hope," she explained. "So many people I'd known had worked with him, and I thought, 'Well, not every filmmaker's interested in every actress,' so I kind of accepted it. I was very surprised when I got the call. It was a very short call—about two-and-a-half minutes. He said he was interested in sending me a script, and was I interested in reading it? And I said, 'Yes, of course, Mr. Allen.' He sent it and asked me to give him a call when I read it. I read it straightaway and it was an incredible opportunity, of course. So I called him back and we spoke for about forty-five seconds. I said, 'I'd like to do it,' and he said, 'Great, I'll see you in San Francisco.'"

Blanchett arrived expecting the usual one or two takes per scene and was surprised to find Allen putting her through as many as eight takes. "I looked over at the monitor and he was smacking his head. And he came over and said to me, 'It's awful. It's awful. You look like an actor saying my lines, I don't believe a thing you're saying, it's awful.' He was shaking his head in disbelief, like a rabbi. And Peter [Sarsgaard] and I just burst out laughing. Ultimately, we cut that scene. He rewrote it and made it much shorter and in a different location. So it was partly he didn't like what we were doing, and partly he didn't like the location, and he felt the scene was too labored. So you can't take it personally.

In a way, that made me feel very safe. He'll absolutely come and say, in the most brutal, frank, direct way, when something's not working. So when he didn't say anything, you knew that either he had to go to dinner or you were doing OK."

"Woody really put Cate through the machine, because she's so talented," said Alec Baldwin, who played Jasmine's husband in what was now his third film with the director. "Take after take after take of very exhausting, emotional scenes. I sat there at the end of the day and thought, 'She is unbelievable.'"

A woman in her early forties sits talking to the passenger sitting next to her on a plane. She is glamorously dressed in Chanel, an Hermès handbag on her lap, gilded by the sunlight pouring through her window and there is a tinkle in her voice as she recounts the charming story of how she met her husband. She keeps up her monologue on the airport walkway and escalator and at the baggage claim, by which time her talk has turned from first meeting to marriage to sex—"not that I care to get too graphic"—her voice ratcheting

up its desperation levels as she goes. Her elderly listener has begun to get a panicked look in her eye: This woman won't shut up. The sequence is a beautifully modulated thumbnail not just of Blanchett's performance to come, but of Jasmine's journey to this point, the fall from grace of this Park Avenue wife after her husband, Hal, a Bernie Madoff–style swindler, is caught and jailed. Now she must go to live with her working-class sister Ginger (Sally Hawkins) in a cramped San Francisco apartment. If the film charts her fall, the art of Blanchett's performance lies in her failure to acknowledge it.

Allen borrows his setup from *A Streetcar Named Desire*, but his eye for class distinctions, no doubt sharpened by his spell in Europe, has never been sharper or more stringent. The two sisters are almost strangers to one another—Ginger

cheerful, chatty and bearing her sister's condescension with the same good nature that has made her the dupe of a succession of boyfriends, one of whom, Augie (Andrew Dice Clay), lost a $200,000 windfall through their investment with Hal. We find all this out through an elaborate flashback structure that is a marvel of dramatic construction, moving with the urgency and confidence of Allen's best work. Here finally was a film for all those who felt cheated by previous reports of Allen's comeback—more than a return to form, a revelation of entirely new form, in which the comic strains of his work were successfully subsumed within a larger tragic pattern, not in a spirit of faux-glumness or art-house piety, but because it now more fully represented Allen's current creative North. It marked quite a turnaround for the

dramatist who had labored so over *Interiors* and *September*: *Blue Jasmine* has the easy, room-temperature assurance of a fully engaged talent doing what comes most naturally. Allen's tragic muse was now the equal of, if not stronger than, his comic one.

"Much of this plays as farce, but the sting of suspicion and social loathing animates scene after scene," wrote David Denby in the *New Yorker*. "Allen, who's now seventy-seven, has become flintier as he has got older. His men and women tell one another off; the social clashes among people from different ways of life can be harsh and unforgiving. The movie is curt and decisive—a 'late' style, if there ever was one." Dropping her voice to its lowest, smokiest register, Blanchett holds herself like a statue, as Jasmine blinks and

drinks away the world and such inconvenient details as her husband's larceny. Did she know something was going on? Unequivocally yes. She knew and turned away. Blanchett's performance rests on Jasmine's subsequent inability to ever really look anyone straight in the eye. She either looks down at people, or up at them through pounding temples, her gaze performing immaculate swan-dives into the abyss. But face to face with her suitor Dwight (Peter Sarsgaard) she glazes over, her eyes swimming with the lies she is preparing to tell. It's exactly the kind of performance that wins an Oscar, as it did for Blanchett: a study in denial that is ninety-nine percent successful, bedeviled by the one percent that is not.

A biographical reading of the final reel is tempting: After discovering his affair with a teenage member of their household, Jasmine rains down legal hell on her husband.

That is her fatal flaw, her refusal to forgive, for it brings her crashing down, too. But if there is an echo of Mia Farrow in Jasmine's fury, there is an echo, too, of Allen himself, who knew only too well what it felt like to have your world shattered, to lose a family, to be rejected by your own children. His identification with Blanche DuBois goes all the way back to *Sleeper*, when he cast himself as Blanche opposite Diane Keaton's Stanley Kowalski in their *Streetcar* skit. During the shooting of *Blue Jasmine*, Blanchett asked him, "'How would you do this, Mr. Allen?' And he said, 'Well, if I were playing the role,' and I turned to him with a backward grin and said, 'You know, you could have played this role.'" Allen paused and thought about it "for a good minute and a half, and then he said, 'No, it would have been too comic.'"

Above: A romance with Dwight (Peter Sarsgaard), a wealthy widower, offers Jasmine a possible escape.

Opposite: "Who do I have to sleep with around here to get a Stoli martini with a twist of lemon?"

The truth, perhaps, is that Jasmine is both of them—that Allen had brought off his most sustained piece of tragic writing by an act of imaginative sympathy which illuminated the complicity between deceiver and deceived, victim and victimizer. In everything, it's opposite. "The wildest and most moving dramas are played not in the theater but in the hearts of ordinary men and women who pass by without exciting attention, and who betray to the world nothing of the conflicts that rage within them except possibly by a nervous breakdown," wrote Jung in his 1912 essay "New Paths in Psychology." He was explaining his theory of the Shadow archetype, but he could have been describing the end of *Blue Jasmine*, with Blanchett nattering to herself on a park bench, still chasing the dream of a world in which she is blameless, an origami woman lost in her own folds and corners.

"A cautionary fable? No. I just thought it was an interesting psychological situation for a woman to be in. This is not a character I'd have written forty years ago. I wouldn't have had the skill to do it, and I didn't come in contact with this type of woman until I got older, because I live in an upscale neighborhood in New York."

Magic in the Moonlight

2014

Above: Colin Firth (Stanley Crawford) unburdens himself.

Opposite: Wealthy heir Brice Catledge (Hamish Linklater) attempts to woo Sophie Baker (Emma Stone) with his ukulele (above). The young American medium also captivates Stanley (below), despite his skepticism.

"I'm like Blanche DuBois," declared Allen while shooting *Magic in the Moonlight* on location on the French Riviera. "I hope in life that there's a certain amount of magic. Unfortunately, there's not enough. There are little, sporadic things one could think of as magical. But for the most part, it's grim reality. If you're the kind of person that finds it hard to deceive yourself—even though it's seductive to believe the other thing—then you're stuck with it. The overwhelming amount of logic and evidence is that we're all victims of a bad deal." If *Blue Jasmine* told the story of someone unable to rid herself of her illusions, *Magic in the Moonlight* flips the equation on its back, as it concerns someone who must ultimately acquire illusions if he is to stand any chance of happiness. After a tragedy of radical disillusion, a comedy about illusion's necessity.

Colin Firth plays a 1920s stage magician named Stanley Crawford, who knows only too well how easily audiences are deceived; as a sideline he exposes frauds, and is summoned to the south of France to investigate the charms of a beautiful young American medium, Sophie Baker (Emma Stone), who along with her mother (Marcia Gay Harden) has taken up residence with the wealthy Catledge family, mesmerizing them with news of their dearly departed. Screwing up her nose and cradling the air with her hands, carny fashion, Sophie's green eyes seem to well with emotion. "The more I watch her, the more I'm stumped," confesses Stanley, who falls in love, as he must. After a rain-soaked dash to an observatory at the summit of Mont Gros—a cupid's stratagem reprised from *Manhattan*—Stanley begins to wonder if there aren't more things in heaven and earth than are dreamt of in his dry, rationalist philosophy.

It's a theme that Allen has been cogitating since *A Midsummer Night's Sex Comedy*, in which José Ferrer's pompous scholar was bewitched with midsummer madness, and more recently in films such as *Scoop*, *The Curse of the Jade Scorpion*, and *You Will Meet a Tall Dark Stranger*, in which the dramatist in him delighted in twitting the rationalist. In *Magic in the Moonlight* he beguiles us with cinematic pixie dust—we get lawns and tennis courts, trellised walkways and road trips around the Riviera all shot on 35 mm by Darius Khondji who seems to catch every speck in the diffuse lemony light. "You're most beautiful at this time of day," says Stanley. "What time is that?" asks Sophie, "In case I ever go on a job interview." The film takes

"I'd just done Blue Jasmine and wanted to do something more romantic, less gritty."

too long to trot through its rather rote romance, whose May-to-December undertones are kept from intruding by Firth's brand of chivalry. It's his performance that is the marvel here. He's like a cross between Henry Higgins and Mr. Darcy, all crusty distemper longing to be set free from its own rigid confines. There's a wonderful moment in which Stanley, frightened, prays to God for the first time, only to stop, disgusted with himself. You couldn't ask for a more distinctive Allen gesture: a yank of the rug beneath a self-doubting Prospero, too skeptical to allow himself to believe, too smitten with the possibilities of his own magic not to.

Irrational Man

2015

"In everybody's life, there are times when suddenly you realize that something momentous can possibly happen if you make a choice," said Woody Allen in Cannes of his forty-fifth film, a slight existential teaser in the Hitchcockian-Dostoyevskian manner which saw the director once again chewing over the topic of crime and punishment that has so exercised him since *Crimes and Misdemeanors.* Joaquin Phoenix plays Abe Lucas, a philosophy professor whose arrival on a Rhode Island campus sets tongues wagging. Seducer of students, depressive, frequently drunk, Abe is exactly the kind of lost soul who has ensnared those willing to mistake a career in nursing for romance in Allen's work ever since he and Diane Keaton swapped prescriptions in *Play It Again, Sam.*

Here the Nightingales include Parker Posey as Rita, an unhappily married science lecturer who slips between Abe's sheets with a bottle of cognac. "You're blocked," she whispers, "I'm going to unblock you." Posey is a natural Allen performer, and she finds brittle, urgent humor in this woman's rapaciousness. Less happily we have Emma Stone, last seen as the apple of Colin Firth's eye in *Magic in the Moonlight* and here stifling her discomfort to play Jill, the impressionable college student who also swoons for Abe and his romantic-tragic worldview. "He's so damn fascinating and so vulnerable," she says in voiceover, "so brilliant and so complicated," and again: "so destructive but so brilliant." It's never wise to ask one of your leads to spend half her time extolling the intellect of the other. You listen to Abe in class dismissing the entirety of Western Philosophy as "verbal masturbation" and hear less a genius at work and more an echo of Alvy Singer's famous dismissal of Annie Hall's classes in Russian literature as so much "mental masturbation"—the familiar streetwise rhythm of Allen vs. the pseuds.

Abe's cobwebbed gloom seems less to do with Kierkegaard and more to do with the hip flask in his pocket. Or, as he puts it, "I'm a passive intellectual who can't fuck." In the old days, it would have been a woman who pulled Abe out of his funk. Here, as with so much of Allen's later work, it is a murder. One day, Abe and Jill overhear a distraught woman telling her friends in a restaurant about the judge making her life a misery in a custody battle and Abe's face lights up: What if he were to kill her nemesis for her? This idea of the perfect murder being that of someone completely unknown to the murderer goes back to Hitchcock's *Strangers on a Train*; here, the completed act soon proves just the thing to pull Abe out of his funk. Soon he is writing, and conducting affairs with both Rita and Jill, and rhapsodizing, at length, on the existential tonic of murder. *Irrational Man* features not just one but two voiceovers, heavy with references to Kant, Heidegger, and Sartre, which feeds the suspicion that Allen is

fonder of ruminating on the significance of his tale than the telling of it: too many thought balloons, not enough rope.

That the movie doesn't float off altogether is largely down to Phoenix, who appears to have looked at the impossibly high bar set before his character and decided, nyah, then walked *around* it, hip flask and pot belly first. The role suits his sauntering, rum-soaked rhythms down to the ground, as well as his natural ability to portray men caught in a vice of their own devising: There is something like real hellfire in his eyes as he walks away from the scene of the crime. Late in his career, Allen's kinship with the great moralists of European cinema—Bergman, Rohmer—seems stronger than ever. If he began his career with comic-picaresque portraits of men getting away with everything—from Virgil Starkwell in *Take the Money and Run* to Fielding Mellish in *Bananas*, skipping merrily past jail, revolution, and death—here comes late Allen to trip up his rogues and tighten the noose around their necks.

Woody Allen: Actor

Side by side with Zero Mostel in *The Front* (1976).

So much of Woody Allen's early material depended on audiences underestimating the little shrimp they saw sweating in the lights in front of them—and to a large extent we still do. We know his mannerisms as a screen performer so well—the gulps, stutters, and gesticulations, the handwringing and hyperventilation, all the means by which he gives himself away when lying, or attempting breeziness—that he has become his own cartoon. His face, like Chaplin's, has an almost pictographic simplicity: the steepled brow, the frown lines, the ovoid face, the glasses which, when removed, give him the aspect of a recently shelled tortoise. Self-deprecation is so baked into his persona both on and off the screen, it is still hard to see him for what he is: one of the great screen actors, as studiously casual as Brando or Bogart, who, like many a comic, turned his personal predilection for glumness

into its own fretful comedy, but succeeded more than anyone before or since in turning introversion into its own form of exhibitionism. Genghis Khan should be so bashful.

Allen's acting work, away from his own films, tends toward streetwise, Runyonesque hustle-and-jivers, but the films themselves are a mixed bunch. He appeared in *The Front* (1976) as a smalltime bookie who agrees to let Zero Mostel, a blacklisted writer, use his name on TV scripts, only to become the hottest name in show business—shades of both Mostel in *The Producers* and Allen's own *Bullets over Broadway*. He seems as mystified as anyone by his uncredited cameo in the farrago of Godard's *King Lear* (1987), playing a film editor reciting Shakespearean sonnets. He hits an immediate, needling rhythm watching his marriage to Bette Midler unspool in Paul Mazursky's *Scenes from a Mall*

"I've always liked to act, and when I write a script and I look at it, if there's a part that I can play, I play it… I've always been open to acting in other people's films, but no one has ever asked me to be in their films, only two or three times in thirty years. When John Turturro asked me to be in Fading Gigolo, I said, 'Sure.'"

Above: Starring opposite Bette Midler as an unfaithful husband and wife in *Scenes from a Mall* (1991).

Left: Talking business with John Turturro in *Fading Gigolo* (2013).

(1991), while a venting of black humor appears to have been the main, possibly only, reason behind his appearance as a butcher who cuts up his unfaithful wife in the woeful *Picking Up the Pieces* (2000).

On the other hand, his voice acting in the DreamWorks animation *Antz* (1998), playing a timid, neurotic worker ant named Z who leads his fellow ants to a Marxist-style revolution, may even count as a career highlight, so deftly does the Weitz brothers' screenplay touch on the range of Allen's interests and obsessions: romantic attraction, career disenchantment, existential wit. Similarly, *Fading Gigolo* (2013) was tailor-written by John Turturro with Allen in

mind as the bookstore owner who plays pimp to his friend, a local florist, when his business goes under. "Directing him took a little getting used to," says Turturro. "The rough cut was very daunting. He said to me right before, 'Do you want my criticism? You know I am going to be brutal.' I watched it sat a few seats from him. He does not really laugh, if he does laugh he laughs quietly. I went to the bathroom in the middle and was like, 'Oh my God, why did I do this?' At the end of the movie he says to me, 'It is way more serious than I thought it would be… but in a good way.' I said, 'What do you think about your performance? Are you happy?' He said, 'I *always* love my performance.'"

Fast Forward

Woody Allen will be eighty in December 2015, but then when has he not been? He always *acted* eighty, fretting about death while still in school, spending his twenties and thirties mourning America's twenties and thirties. You have to look at photographs to remind yourself that he really was once younger, the hair thicker and sandy-red, and his skin less freckled. Now that he actually *is* eighty, he seems to have caught up with himself. There is a youthful hunger to his recent globe-trotting, in *Match Point*, *Vicky Cristina Barcelona*, and *To Rome with Love*, together with a contentment to let a younger generation of actors take their moment in the sun. There is a return to youthful preoccupations, too, in the theme of magic, always a thread in Allen's work since The Great Persky sent Professor Kugelmass into a novel of his choosing in the short story "The Kugelmass Episode." The dead speak in *Match Point*. They plot their comeback in *Scoop* and send messages to the living in *Magic in the Moonlight*. All artists turn into Prospero if they stick around long enough.

Entering his ninth decade, Allen's industry continues to approximate that of a young, go-getting bee. "He secretes movies like honey," as his longtime collaborator Marshall Brickman once put it. The year 2015 brought news not just of a new film, starring Jesse Eisenberg, Kristen Stewart, Bruce Willis, and Blake Lively, which he may shoot in digital as an experiment ("It is more than the wave of the future," he said in Cannes, "it's the wave of the present, really"), but a groundbreaking deal to write a full season of thirty-minute TV shows for Amazon Prime, to be available for streaming in 2016, even though he doesn't own a computer and doesn't understand what streaming is. "I never knew what Amazon was. I've never seen any of those series, even on cable. I've never seen *The Sopranos*, or *Mad Men*. I'm out

Portrait by Carlo Allegri, 2010.

every night and when I come home, I watch the end of the baseball or basketball game, and there's Charlie Rose and I go to sleep. Amazon kept coming to me and saying, please do this, whatever you want. I kept saying I have no ideas for it, that I never watch television. I don't know the first thing about it. Well, this went on for a year and a half, and they kept making a better deal and a better deal. Finally, they said, look, we'll do anything that you want, just give us six half hours … everybody around me was pressuring me, go ahead and do it, what do you have to lose? … I had the cocky

"I don't know what I'd do if I retired. I don't fish."

confidence, well, I'll do it like I do a movie—it'll be a movie in six parts. Turns out, it's not. For me, it has been very, very difficult. It's not a piece of cake. I'm earning every penny that they're giving me and I just hope that they don't feel, 'My God, we gave him a very substantial amount of money and freedom and this is what he gives us?'"

His first love, writing, remains his most true. As a film director, his days of experimentation may be behind him. As a comic performer, he may defer to the speedier synapses of a younger generation. But his Hemingway parody in

Midnight in Paris displayed the same perfect pitch he showed, decades before, in his *New Yorker* pieces; while the construction of *Blue Jasmine* easily matched that of *Hannah and Her Sisters* and *The Purple Rose of Cairo*. Embark on a weekend marathon of Woody Allen movies and you will emerge both blinking in the sunlight, like Allen himself in *Play It Again, Sam*, but also marveling over the scale, pace, and consistency of his imagination, that indefatigable silkworm spinning script after script, year after year. It remains one of the marvels of the medium.

Filmography

Release/broadcast dates are for the United States unless stated.

FEATURE FILMS

What's New Pussycat?
(Famous Artists Productions)
Opened June 22, 1965, 108 minutes
Directors: Clive Donner, Richard Talmadge
Screenplay: Woody Allen
Cinematography: Jean Badal
Cast: Woody Allen (Victor), Peter Sellers (Dr. Fritz
Fassbender), Peter O'Toole (Michael James),
Romy Schneider (Carole), Capucine (Renée),
Paula Prentiss (Liz), Ursula Andress (Rita)

What's Up, Tiger Lily?
(Benedict Pictures Corporation/National Recording
Studios/Toho Company)
Opened November 2, 1966, 80 minutes
Directors: Woody Allen, Senkichi Taniguchi
Screenplay: Woody Allen, Julie Bennett, Frank Buxton,
Louise Lasser, Len Maxwell, Mickey Rose,
Ben Shapiro, Bryna Wilson
Cinematography: Kuzuo Yamada
Cast: Dubbed voices of Woody Allen, Julie Bennett,
Frank Buxton, Louise Lasser, Len Maxwell,
Mickey Rose, Bryna Wilson

Casino Royale
(Columbia Pictures/Famous Artists Productions)
Opened April 28, 1967, 131 minutes
Directors: Ken Hughes, John Huston, Joseph McGrath,
Robert Parrish, Richard Talmadge
Screenplay: Wolf Mankowitz, John Law, Michael Sayers
Cinematography: Jack Hildyard
Cast: Woody Allen (Jimmy Bond), Peter Sellers (Evelyn
Tremble/James Bond 007), Ursula Andress (Vesper
Lynd/James Bond 007), David Niven (Sir James Bond),
Orson Welles (Le Chiffre)

Take the Money and Run
(ABC/Jack Rollins & Charles H. Joffe Productions/
Palomar Pictures International)
Opened August 18, 1969, 85 minutes
Director: Woody Allen
Screenplay: Woody Allen, Mickey Rose
Cinematography: Lester Shorr
Cast: Woody Allen (Virgil Starkwell), Janet Margolin
(Louise), Marcel Hillaire (Fritz), Jacquelyn Hyde
(Miss Blair), Louise Lasser (Kay Lewis)

Don't Drink the Water
(AVCO Embassy Pictures)
Opened November 11, 1969, 100 minutes
Director: Howard Morris
Screenplay: Woody Allen, R. S. Allen, Harvey Bullock

Cinematography: Harvey Genkins
Cast: Jackie Gleason (Walter Hollander), Estelle Parsons
(Marion Hollander), Ted Bessell (Axel Magee),
Joan Delaney (Susan Hollander), Michael Constantine
(Commissar Krojack)

Pussycat, Pussycat, I Love You
(Three Pictures)
Opened March 25, 1970, 99 minutes
Director: Rod Amateau
Screenplay: Woody Allen for his original screenplay
What's New Pussycat?, Rod Amateau
Cinematography: Tonino Delli Colli
Cast: Ian McShane (Fred C. Dobbs), John Gavin
(Charlie Harrison), Anna Calder-Marshall
(Millie Dobbs), Joyce Van Patten (Anna),
Severn Darden (Dr. Fahrquardt)

Bananas
(Jack Rollins & Charles H. Joffe Productions)
Opened April 28, 1971, 82 minutes
Director: Woody Allen
Screenplay: Woody Allen, Mickey Rose
Cinematography: Andrew M. Costikyan
Cast: Woody Allen (Fielding Mellish),
Louise Lasser (Nancy), Carlos Montalbán
(General Emilio Molina Vargas), Natividad Abascal
(Yolanda), Jacobo Morales (Esposito)

Play It Again, Sam
(Paramount Pictures/Rollins-Joffe Productions/
APJAC Productions)
Opened May 4, 1972, 85 minutes
Director: Herbert Ross
Screenplay: Woody Allen
Cinematography: Owen Roizman
Cast: Woody Allen (Allan), Diane Keaton (Linda),
Tony Roberts (Dick), Jerry Lacy (Bogart),
Susan Anspach (Nancy)

Everything You Always Wanted to Know About Sex*
(*But Were Afraid to Ask)
(Jack Rollins-Charles H. Joffe Productions/
Brodsky-Gould)
Opened August 6, 1972, 88 minutes
Director & Screenplay: Woody Allen
Cinematography: David M. Walsh
Cast: Woody Allen (Victor/Fabrizio/The Fool/Sperm),
John Carradine (Doctor Bernardo),
Lou Jacobi (Sam), Louise Lasser (Gina), Anthony Quayle
(The King), Tony Randall (The Operator),
Lynn Redgrave (The Queen)

Sleeper
(Jack Rollins & Charles H. Joffe Productions)

Opened December 17, 1973, 89 minutes
Director: Woody Allen
Screenplay: Woody Allen, Marshall Brickman
Cinematography: David M. Walsh
Cast: Woody Allen (Miles Monroe), Diane Keaton
(Luna Schlosser), John Beck (Erno Windt), Mary
Gregory (Dr. Melik), Don Keefer (Dr. Tryon)

Love and Death
(Jack Rollins & Charles H. Joffe Productions)
Opened June 10, 1975, 85 minutes
Director & Screenplay: Woody Allen
Cinematography: Ghislain Cloquet
Cast: Woody Allen (Boris), Diane Keaton (Sonja),
Georges Adet (Old Nehamkin), Frank Adu
(Drill Sergeant), Edmond Ardisson (Priest)

The Front
(Columbia Pictures/The Devon Company/
Persky-Bright Productions/Rollins-Joffe Productions)
Opened September 17, 1976, 95 minutes
Director: Martin Ritt
Screenplay: Walter Bernstein
Cinematography: Michael Chapman
Cast: Woody Allen (Howard Prince), Zero Mostel
(Hecky Brown), Herschel Bernardi (Phil Sussman),
Michael Murphy (Alfred Miller), Andrea Marcovicci
(Florence Barrett)

Annie Hall
(Rollins-Joffe Productions)
Opened April 20, 1977, 93 minutes
Director: Woody Allen
Screenplay: Woody Allen, Marshall Brickman
Cinematography: Gordon Willis
Cast: Woody Allen (Alvy Singer), Diane Keaton
(Annie Hall), Tony Roberts (Rob), Carol Kane (Allison),
Paul Simon (Tony Lacey), Christopher Walken
(Duane Hall)

Interiors
(Rollins-Joffe Productions)
Opened August 2, 1978, 93 minutes
Director & Screenplay: Woody Allen
Cinematography: Gordon Willis
Cast: Kristin Griffith (Flyn), Mary Beth Hurt (Joey),
Richard Jordan (Frederick), Diane Keaton (Renata),
E. G. Marshall (Arthur), Geraldine Page (Eve),
Maureen Stapleton (Pearl), Sam Waterston (Mike)

Manhattan
(Jack Rollins & Charles H. Joffe Productions)
Opened April 25, 1979, 96 minutes
Director: Woody Allen
Screenplay: Woody Allen, Marshall Brickman

Cinematography: Gordon Willis
Cast: Woody Allen (Isaac), Diane Keaton (Mary),
Michael Murphy (Yale), Mariel Hemingway (Tracy),
Meryl Streep (Jill)

Stardust Memories
(Rollins-Joffe Productions)
Opened September 26, 1980, 89 minutes
Director & Screenplay: Woody Allen
Cinematography: Gordon Willis
Cast: Woody Allen (Sandy Bates), Charlotte Rampling
(Dorrie), Jessica Harper (Daisy), Marie-Christine
Barrault (Isobel), Tony Roberts (Tony)

A Midsummer Night's Sex Comedy
(Orion Pictures)
Opened July 16, 1982, 88 minutes
Director & Screenplay: Woody Allen
Cinematography: Gordon Willis
Cast: Woody Allen (Andrew), Mia Farrow (Ariel),
José Ferrer (Leopold), Julie Hagerty (Dulcy),
Tony Roberts (Maxwell), Mary Steenburgen (Adrian)

Zelig
(Orion Pictures)
Opened July 15, 1983, 79 minutes
Director & Screenplay: Woody Allen
Cinematography: Gordon Willis
Cast: Woody Allen (Leonard Zelig), Mia Farrow
(Dr. Eudora Nesbitt Fletcher), Patrick Horgan (Narrator)

Broadway Danny Rose
(Orion Pictures)
Opened January 27, 1984, 84 minutes
Director & Screenplay: Woody Allen
Cinematography: Gordon Willis
Cast: Woody Allen (Danny Rose), Mia Farrow
(Tina Vitale), Nick Apollo Forte (Lou Canova)

The Purple Rose of Cairo
(Orion Pictures)
Opened March 1, 1985, 82 minutes
Director & Screenplay: Woody Allen
Cinematography: Gordon Willis
Cast: Mia Farrow (Cecilia), Jeff Daniels (Tom Baxter/
Gil Shepherd), Danny Aiello (Monk), Edward
Herrmann (Henry), Dianne Wiest (Emma)

Hannah and Her Sisters
(Orion Pictures/Jack Rollins & Charles H. Joffe
Productions)
Opened March 14, 1986, 103 minutes
Director & Screenplay: Woody Allen
Cinematography: Carlo Di Palma
Cast: Woody Allen (Mickey), Barbara Hershey (Lee),
Carrie Fisher (April), Mia Farrow (Hannah),
Michael Caine (Elliot), Dianne Wiest (Holly),
Maureen O'Sullivan (Norma), Daniel Stern (Dusty),
Max von Sydow (Frederick), Lloyd Nolan (Evan)

Radio Days
(Orion Pictures)
Opened January 30, 1987, 88 minutes
Director & Screenplay: Woody Allen
Cinematography: Carlo Di Palma
Cast: Woody Allen (Narrator), Mia Farrow (Sally
White), Seth Green (Young Joe), Julie Kavner (Mother),
Michael Tucker (Father), Dianne Wiest (Aunt Bea),
Danny Aiello (Rocco), Jeff Daniels (Biff Baxter),
Diane Keaton (New Year's Singer)

September
(Globo Video/MGM Home Entertainment/Orion
Pictures/RCA–Columbia Pictures International Video)
Opened December 18, 1987, 82 minutes
Director & Screenplay: Woody Allen
Cinematography: Carlo Di Palma
Cast: Denholm Elliott (Howard), Mia Farrow (Lane),
Elaine Stritch (Diane), Jack Warden (Lloyd),
Sam Waterston (Peter), Dianne Wiest (Stephanie)

King Lear
(The Cannon Group/Golan-Globus Productions)
Opened May 17, 1987 (Cannes Film Festival, France),
January 22, 1988 (United States), 90 minutes
Director: Jean-Luc Godard
Screenplay: Richard Debuisne, Jean-Luc Godard,
Norman Mailer, Peter Sellars
Cinematography: Sophie Maintigneux
Cast: Woody Allen (Mr. Alien), Freddy Buache
(Professor Quentin), Leos Carax (Edgar), Julie Delpy
(Virginia), Jean-Luc Godard (Professor Pluggy),
Burgess Meredith (Don Learo), Molly Ringwald
(Cordelia)

Another Woman
(Jack Rollins & Charles H. Joffe Productions)
Opened November 18, 1988, 81 minutes
Director & Screenplay: Woody Allen
Cinematography: Sven Nykvist
Cast: Gena Rowlands (Marion), Mia Farrow (Hope),
Ian Holm (Ken), Blythe Danner (Lydia),
Gene Hackman (Larry)

New York Stories
(anthology film with segments directed by Francis Ford
Coppola, Martin Scorsese, and Woody Allen)
(Touchstone Pictures)
Opened March 10, 1989, 124 minutes
Allen's segment: "Oedipus Wrecks"

Screenplay: Woody Allen
Cinematography: Speed Hopkins
Cast: Woody Allen (Sheldon), Marvin Chatinover
(Psychiatrist), Mae Questel (Mother), Mia Farrow (Lisa),
Molly Regan (Sheldon's secretary)

Crimes and Misdemeanors
(Jack Rollins & Charles H. Joffe Productions)
Opened October 13, 1989, 104 minutes
Director & Screenplay: Woody Allen
Cinematography: Sven Nykvist
Cast: Woody Allen (Cliff Stern), Alan Alda (Lester),
Claire Bloom (Miriam Rosenthal), Mia Farrow
(Halley Reed), Anjelica Huston (Dolores Paley),
Caroline Aaron (Barbara)

Alice
(Orion Pictures)
Opened December 25, 1990, 102 minutes
Director & Screenplay: Woody Allen
Cinematography: Carlo Di Palma
Cast: Mia Farrow (Alice), Joe Mantegna (Joe),
William Hurt (Doug), Blythe Danner (Dorothy),
Keye Luke (Dr. Yang)

Scenes from a Mall
(Touchstone Pictures/Silver Screen Partners)
Opened February 22, 1991, 89 minutes
Director: Paul Mazursky
Screenplay: Roger L. Simon, Paul Mazursky
Cinematography: Fred Murphy
Cast: Woody Allen (Nick Fifer), Bette Midler
(Deborah Fifer), Bill Irwin (Mime), Daren Firestone
(Sam), Rebecca Nickels (Jennifer), Paul Mazursky
(Dr. Hans Clava)

Shadows and Fog
(Orion Pictures)
Opened March 20, 1992, 85 minutes
Director & Screenplay: Woody Allen
Cinematography: Carlo Di Palma
Cast: Woody Allen (Kleinman), Kathy Bates (Prostitute),
John Cusack (Student Jack), Mia Farrow (Irmy),
Jodie Foster (Prostitute), Fred Gwynne (Hacker's
Follower), Julie Kavner (Alma), Madonna (Marie),
John Malkovich (Paul, the Clown)

Husbands and Wives
(TriStar Pictures)
Opened September 18, 1992, 108 minutes
Director & Screenplay: Woody Allen
Cinematography: Carlo Di Palma
Cast: Woody Allen (Gabe), Mia Farrow (Judy),
Judy Davis (Sally), Sydney Pollack (Jack),
Juliette Lewis (Rain), Liam Neeson (Michael)

Manhattan Murder Mystery
(TriStar Pictures)
Opened August 18, 1993, 104 minutes
Director & Screenplay: Woody Allen
Cinematography: Carlo Di Palma
Cast: Woody Allen (Larry Lipton), Diane Keaton (Carol Lipton), Alan Alda (Ted), Anjelica Huston (Marcia Fox), Jerry Adler (Paul Robert House), Lynn Cohen (Lillian Beale House)

Bullets over Broadway
(Miramax/Sweetland Films/Magnolia Productions)
Opened January 18, 1995, 98 minutes
Director: Woody Allen
Screenplay: Woody Allen, Douglas McGrath
Cinematography: Carlo Di Palma
Cast: John Cusack (David Shayne), Dianne Wiest (Helen Sinclair), Jennifer Tilly (Olive Neal), Chazz Palminteri (Cheech), Mary-Louise Parker (Ellen), Jim Broadbent (Warner Purcell)

Mighty Aphrodite
(Sweetland Films/Magnolia Productions/Miramax)
Opened January 11, 1996, 95 minutes
Director & Screenplay: Woody Allen
Cinematography: Carlo Di Palma
Cast: Woody Allen (Lenny), Mira Sorvino (Linda Ash), Helena Bonham Carter (Amanda), Claire Bloom (Amanda's mother), Michael Rapaport (Kevin), F. Murray Abraham (Leader), Olympia Dukakis (Jocasta), David Ogden Stiers (Laius), Jack Warden (Tiresias)

Everyone Says I Love You
(Miramax/Buena Vista Pictures/Magnolia Productions/Sweetland Films)
Opened January 3, 1997, 101 minutes
Director & Screenplay: Woody Allen
Cinematography: Carlo Di Palma
Cast: Woody Allen (Joe), Edward Norton (Holden), Drew Barrymore (Skylar), Alan Alda (Bob), Natalie Portman (Laura), Lukas Haas (Scott), Julia Roberts (Von), Gaby Hoffmann (Lane), Goldie Hawn (Steffi)

Deconstructing Harry
(Sweetland Films/Jean Doumanian Productions)
Opened December 12, 1997, 96 minutes
Director & Screenplay: Woody Allen
Cinematography: Carlo Di Palma
Cast: Woody Allen (Harry Block), Robin Williams (Mel), Eric Lloyd (Hilly), Julia Louis-Dreyfus (Leslie), Elisabeth Shue (Fay), Stanley Tucci (Paul Epstein), Demi Moore (Helen)

The Imposters
(First Cold Piece/Fox Searchlight Pictures)
Opened October 2, 1998, 101 minutes
Director & Screenplay: Stanley Tucci
Cinematography: Ken Kelsch
Cast: Oliver Platt (Maurice), Stanley Tucci (Arthur), Billy Connolly (Mr. Sparks, the Tennis Pro), Allison Janney (Maxine), Steve Buscemi (Happy Franks), Woody Allen (Audition Director)

Antz
(DreamWorks/Pacific Data Images/DreamWorks Animation)
Opened October 2, 1998, 83 minutes
Director: Eric Darnell, Tim Johnson
Screenplay: Todd Alcott, Chris Weitz, Paul Weitz
Cinematography: Kendal Cronkhite
Cast: Woody Allen (Z), Sylvester Stallone (Weaver), Jennifer Lopez (Azteca), Sharon Stone (Princess Bala), Christopher Walken (Colonel Cutter), Dan Aykroyd (Chip)

Celebrity
(Sweetland Films/Magnolia Productions)
Opened November 20, 1998, 113 minutes
Director & Screenplay: Woody Allen
Cinematography: Sven Nykvist
Cast: Hank Azaria (David), Kenneth Branagh (Lee Simon), Judy Davis (Robin Simon), Winona Ryder (Nola), Leonardo DiCaprio (Brandon Darrow), Melanie Griffith (Nicole Oliver), Joe Mantegna (Tony Gardella), Charlize Theron (Supermodel)

Sweet and Lowdown
(Sweetland Films/Magnolia Productions)
Opened December 3, 1999, 95 minutes
Director & Screenplay: Woody Allen
Cinematography: Zhao Fei
Cast: Sean Penn (Emmet Ray), Anthony LaPaglia (Al Torrio), Samantha Morton (Hattie), Uma Thurman (Blanche), Woody Allen as himself

Small Time Crooks
(DreamWorks/Sweetland Films)
Opened May 19, 2000, 94 minutes
Director & Screenplay: Woody Allen
Cinematography: Zhao Fei
Cast: Woody Allen (Ray), Tony Darrow (Tommy), Tracey Ullman (Frenchy), Hugh Grant (David), George Grizzard (George Blint), Elaine May (May Sloane)

Picking Up the Pieces
(Comala Films Productions/Kushner-Locke Company/Ostensible Productions)
First shown May 26, 2000 (TV premiere), 95 minutes
Director: Alfonso Arau

Screenplay: Bill Wilson
Cinematography: Vittorio Storaro
Cast: Woody Allen (Tex Cowley), Sharon Stone (Candy Cowley), Maria Grazia Cucinotta (Desi), Cheech Marin (Mayor Machado), David Schwimmer (Father Leo Jerome), Kiefer Sutherland (Officer Bobo)

Company Man
(Film Foundry Partners/GreeneStreet Films/Intermedia Films/SKE Films/Union Générale Cinématographique/Wild Dancer Productions)
Opened May 3, 2000 (France), March 9, 2001 (United States), 95 minutes
Directors & Screenplay: Peter Askin, Douglas McGrath
Cinematography: Russell Boyd
Cast: Alan Cumming (Gen. Batista), Anthony LaPaglia (Fidel Castro), Denis Leary (Officer Fry), Douglas McGrath (Alan Quimp), John Turturro (Crocker Johnson), Sigourney Weaver (Daisy Quimp), Woody Allen (Lowther)

The Curse of the Jade Scorpion
(DreamWorks/Perdido Productions)
Opened August 24, 2001, 103 minutes
Director & Screenplay: Woody Allen
Cinematography: Zhao Fei
Cast: Woody Allen (C. W. Briggs), Dan Aykroyd (Chris Magruder), Helen Hunt (Betty Ann Fitzgerald), Charlize Theron (Laura Kensington), David Ogden Stiers (Voltan)

Hollywood Ending
(DreamWorks/Gravier Productions/Perdido Productions)
Opened May 3, 2002, 112 minutes
Director & Screenplay: Woody Allen
Cinematography: Wedigo Von Schultzendorff
Cast: Woody Allen (Val), George Hamilton (Ed), Téa Leoni (Ellie), Debra Messing (Lori), Mark Rydell (Al), Tiffani Thiessen (Sharon Bates), Treat Williams (Hal)

Anything Else
(DreamWorks/Gravier Productions/Canal+/Granada Film Productions/Perdido Productions)
Opened September 19, 2003, 108 minutes
Director & Screenplay: Woody Allen
Cinematography: Darius Khondji
Cast: Woody Allen (David Dobel), Jason Biggs (Jerry Falk), Christina Ricci (Amanda Chase), Stockard Channing (Paula Chase), Danny DeVito (Harvey Wexler), Jimmy Fallon (Bob)

Melinda and Melinda
(Fox Searchlight Pictures/Gravier Productions/LF Hungary Film Rights Exploitation/Perdido Productions)

Opened September 17, 2004 (San Sebastián Film
Festival, Spain), March 18, 2005 (United States),
99 minutes
Director & Screenplay: Woody Allen
Cinematography: Vilmos Zsigmond
Cast: Chiwetel Ejiofor (Ellis Moonsong), Will Ferrell
(Hobie), Jonny Lee Miller (Lee), Radha Mitchell
(Melinda Robicheaux), Amanda Peet (Susan),
Chloë Sevigny (Laurel), Wallace Shawn (Sy)

Match Point
(BBC Films/Thema Production/Jada Productions/
Kudu Films)
Opened December 28, 2005, 124 minutes
Director & Screenplay: Woody Allen
Cinematography: Remi Adefarasin
Cast: Jonathan Rhys Meyers (Chris Wilton), Scarlett
Johansson (Nola Rice), Matthew Goode (Tom Hewett),
Emily Mortimer (Chloe Hewett Wilton), Brian Cox
(Alec Hewett), Penelope Wilton (Eleanor Hewett)

Scoop
(BBC Films/Ingenious Film Partners/Phoenix Wiley/
Jelly Roll Productions)
Opened July 28, 2006, 96 minutes
Director & Screenplay: Woody Allen
Cinematography: Remi Adefarasin
Cast: Woody Allen (Sid Waterman), Hugh Jackman
(Peter Lyman), Scarlett Johansson (Sondra Pransky), Ian
McShane (Joe Strombel), Charles Dance (Mr. Malcolm)

Cassandra's Dream
(Iberville Productions/Virtual Studios/Wild Bunch)
Opened June 18, 2007 (Spain), January 18, 2008
(United States), 108 minutes
Director & Screenplay: Woody Allen
Cinematography: Vilmos Zsigmond
Cast: Ewan McGregor (Ian), Colin Farrell (Terry),
Tom Wilkinson (Howard), Sally Hawkins (Kate),
Hayley Atwell (Angela)

Vicky Cristina Barcelona
(The Weinstein Company/Mediapro/
Gravier Productions)
Opened August 15, 2008, 96 minutes
Director & Screenplay: Woody Allen
Cinematography: Javier Aguirresarobe
Cast: Rebecca Hall (Vicky), Scarlett Johansson
(Cristina), Javier Bardem (Juan Antonio), Penélope Cruz
(Maria Elena), Patricia Clarkson (Judy), Kevin Dunn
(Mark), Chris Messina (Doug)

Whatever Works
(Sony Pictures Classics/Wild Bunch/
Gravier Productions/Perdido Productions)

Opened June 19, 2009, 92 minutes
Director & Screenplay: Woody Allen
Cinematography: Harris Savides
Cast: Ed Begley, Jr. (John), Patricia Clarkson (Marietta),
Larry David (Boris), Conleth Hill (Brockman), Michael
McKean (Boris's Friend), Evan Rachel Wood (Melody)

You Will Meet a Tall Dark Stranger
(Mediapro/Versátil Cinema/Gravier Productions/
Dippermouth Productions/Antena 3 Films)
Opened September 23, 2010, 98 minutes
Director & Screenplay: Woody Allen
Cinematography: Vilmos Zsigmond
Cast: Antonio Banderas (Greg), Josh Brolin (Roy),
Anthony Hopkins (Alfie), Gemma Jones (Helena),
Freida Pinto (Dia), Lucy Punch (Charmaine),
Naomi Watts (Sally)

Midnight in Paris
(Gravier Productions/Mediapro/Pontchartrain
Productions/Televisió de Catalunya/Versátil Cinema)
Opened June 10, 2011, 94 minutes
Director & Screenplay: Woody Allen
Cinematography: Darius Khondji
Cast: Kathy Bates (Gertrude Stein), Adrien Brody
(Salvador Dalí), Carla Bruni (Museum Guide),
Marion Cotillard (Adriana), Rachel McAdams (Inez),
Michael Sheen (Paul), Owen Wilson (Gil)

To Rome with Love
(Medusa Film/Gravier Productions/Perdido
Productions/Mediapro)
Opened July 6, 2012, 112 minutes
Director & Screenplay: Woody Allen
Cinematography: Darius Khondji
Cast: Woody Allen (Jerry), Alec Baldwin (John),
Roberto Benigni (Leopoldo), Penélope Cruz (Anna),
Judy Davis (Phyllis), Jesse Eisenberg (Jack),
Greta Gerwig (Sally), Ellen Page (Monica)

Paris-Manhattan
(Vendôme Production/France 2 Cinéma/SND)
Opened April 2, 2012 (Alliance Française French Film
Festival, Australia), 77 minutes
Director & Screenplay: Sophie Lellouche
Cinematography: Laurent Machuel
Cast: Alice Taglioni (Alice), Patrick Bruel (Victor),
Marine Delterme (Helen), Yannick Soulier (Vincent),
Woody Allen as himself

Blue Jasmine
(Gravier Productions/Perdido Productions)
Opened August 23, 2013, 98 minutes
Director & Screenplay: Woody Allen
Cinematography: Javier Aguirresarobe

Cast: Cate Blanchett (Jasmine), Alec Baldwin (Hal),
Louis C.K. (Al), Bobby Cannavale (Chili), Andrew Dice
Clay (Augie), Sally Hawkins (Ginger), Peter Sarsgaard
(Dwight), Michael Stuhlbarg (Dr. Flicker)

Fading Gigolo
(Antidote Films)
Opened September 7, 2013 (Toronto International
Film Festival, Canada), April 18, 2014 (United States),
90 minutes
Director & Screenplay: John Turturro
Cinematography: Marco Pontecorvo
Cast: Woody Allen (Murray), John Turturro
(Fioravante), Vanessa Paradis (Avigal), Liev Schreiber
(Dovi), Sharon Stone (Dr. Parker), Sofia Vergara
(Selima)

Magic in the Moonlight
(Dippermouth Productions/Gravier Productions/
Perdido Productions/Ske-Dat-De-Dat Productions)
Opened August 15, 2014, 97 minutes
Director & Screenplay: Woody Allen
Cinematography: Darius Khondji
Cast: Colin Firth (Stanley), Emma Stone (Sophie),
Hamish Linklater (Brice Catledge), Marcia Gay Harden
(Mrs. Baker), Jacki Weaver (Grace Catledge), Erica
Leerhsen (Caroline), Eileen Atkins (Aunt Vanessa),
Simon McBurney (Howard Burkan)

Irrational Man
(Annapurna Pictures/Gravier Productions/
Perdido Productions)
Opened July 24, 2015, 96 minutes
Director & Screenplay: Woody Allen
Cinematography: Darius Khondji
Cast: Joaquin Phoenix (Abe Lucas), Emma Stone (Jill),
Parker Posey (Rita)

TELEVISION

The Ed Sullivan Show (CBS/Sullivan Productions)
Member of the writing team, 1954

The Colgate Comedy Hour (Colgate-Palmolive
Peet/NBC) Member of the writing team, 1955

Stanley (Max Liebman Productions)
First broadcast September 24, 1956
Member of the writing team

The Sid Caesar Show (NBC)
First broadcast November 2, 1958. Co-writer

At the Movies (NBC)
First broadcast May 3, 1959. Co-writer

Hooray for Love (CBS)
First broadcast October 2, 1960. Co-writer

Candid Camera
(Allen Funt Productions/Bob Banner Associates)
Member of the writing team and performer, 1960–1967

The Garry Moore Show, episode #4.3 (CBS)
First broadcast October 10, 1961
Member of the writing team

The Laughmakers (ABC)
TV pilot filmed in 1962, but not broadcast. Writer

The Sid Caesar Show (ABC)
First broadcast October 3, 1963
Co-writer and performer

The Woody Allen Show (Granada Television)
First broadcast February 10, 1965 (UK)
Writer and performer

Gene Kelly in New York, New York (NBC)
First broadcast February 14, 1966
Co-writer and performer

The World: Color It Happy (Hanna-Barbera)
TV pilot filmed in 1967, but not broadcast
Member of the writing team and performer

The Kraft Music Hall: Woody Allen Looks at 1967
(Bob Banner Associates/Yorkshire Productions)
First broadcast December 27, 1967
Member of the writing team and performer

The Kraft Music Hall: The Woody Allen Special (CBS)
First broadcast September 21, 1969
Writer and performer

Hot Dog (Lee Mendelson-Frank Buxton
Joint Film Productions)
First broadcast September 12, 1970. Co-presenter

Men of Crisis: The Harvey Wallinger Story (WNET)
TV special filmed in 1971, but not broadcast
Writer, director, and actor

Don't Drink the Water (TV movie)
(Jean Doumanian Productions/Magnolia Productions/
Sweetland Films)
First broadcast December 18, 1994
Writer, director, and actor

Une aspirine pour deux (France 2)
First broadcast August 1, 1995 (France). Writer

The Sunshine Boys (Hallmark Entertainment/
Metropolitan Productions/RHI Entertainment)
First broadcast December 28, 1997. Actor

The Sorrow and the Pity (Télévision Rencontre/
Norddeutscher Rundfunk/Télévision Suisse-Romande)
First broadcast September 18, 1969 (West Germany),
rereleased July 7, 2000 (United States)
Presenter of the 2000 rerelease

Sounds from a Town I Love
(Short documentary segment for The Concert for
New York City)
First broadcast October 20, 2001. Writer and director

Barcelona, la Rosa de Foc (Mediapro)
First broadcast September 8, 2014 (Spain)
Narrator of the English version

THEATER

From A to Z
Musical revue containing sketches written by Woody Allen
Opened April 20, 1960 (Plymouth Theatre, New York City)

Don't Drink the Water
Opened November 17, 1966 (Morosco Theatre,
New York City)

Play It Again, Sam
Opened February 12, 1969 (Broadhurst Theatre,
New York City)

The Floating Light Bulb
Opened April 27, 1981 (Vivian Beaumont Theatre,
Lincoln Center, New York City)

Death Defying Acts
Anthology with short plays written by David Mamet
("An Interview"), Elaine May ("Hotline"), and
Woody Allen ("Central Park West")
Opened March 6, 1995 (Atlantic Theater Company,
New York City)

Writer's Block
Two one-act plays: "Riverside Drive" and
"Old Saybrook"
Opened May 15, 2003 (Atlantic Theater Company,
New York City)

A Second Hand Memory
Opened November 22, 2004 (Atlantic Theater Company,
New York City)

Relatively Speaking
Anthology with short plays written by Ethan Coen
("Talking Cure"), Elaine May ("George Is Dead"), and
Woody Allen ("Honeymoon Motel")
Opened October 20, 2011 (Brooks Atkinson Theatre,
New York City)

Bullets over Broadway: The Musical
Opened April 10, 2014 (St. James Theatre,
New York City)

BOOKS

Getting Even
New York: Random House, 1971

Without Feathers
New York: Random House, 1975

Side Effects
New York: Random House, 1980

**Three One-Act Plays: Riverside Drive, Old Saybrook,
Central Park West**
New York: Random House, 2004

Mere Anarchy
New York: Random House, 2007

The Insanity Defense: The Complete Prose
New York: Random House, 2007

"I've been telling people for my entire life in the movies that there's not a huge similarity between me on screen and me in real life, but for some reason they don't want to know that. And I think it even detracts from their enjoyment of the movie, and so they listen to me and nod benignly, but they don't really buy it."

Portrait by Jennifer S. Altman, 2011.

Select Bibliography

BOOKS

Allen, Woody. *The Insanity Defense: The Complete Prose.* New York: Random House, 2007.

Bach, Steven. *Final Cut: Art, Money, and Ego in the Making of Heaven's Gate, the Film that Sank United Artists.* New York: William Morrow, 1985.

Bailey, Peter J. *The Reluctant Film Art of Woody Allen.* Lexington, KY: University Press of Kentucky, 2001.

Bailey, Peter J., and Sam B. Girgus, eds. *A Companion to Woody Allen.* Chichester, West Sussex: Wiley-Blackwell, 2013.

Baxter, John. *Woody Allen: A Biography.* London: Harper Collins, 1998.

Benayoun, Robert. *Woody Allen: Beyond Words.* London: Pavilion, 1986.

Berger, Phil. *The Last Laugh: The World of Stand-up Comics.* New York: Cooper Square Press, 2000.

Björkman, Stig. *Woody Allen on Woody Allen.* New York: Grove Press, 1993 (revised 2005).

Brode, Douglas. *The Films of Woody Allen.* New York: Citadel, 1991.

Caine, Michael. *What's It All About?* London: Century, 1992.

De Navacelle, Thierry. *Woody Allen on Location.* New York: William Morrow, 1987.

Epstein, Lawrence J. *The Haunted Smile: The Story of Jewish Comedians.* Oxford: PublicAffairs, 2002.

Farrow, Mia. *What Falls Away: A Memoir.* New York: Doubleday, 1997.

Fox, Julian. *Woody: Movies from Manhattan.* London: Batsford, 1996.

Hirsch, Foster. *Love, Sex, Death, and the Meaning of Life: The Films of Woody Allen.* Cambridge, MA: Da Capo Press, 2001.

Kael, Pauline. *The Age of Movies: Selected Writings of Pauline Kael.* Edited by Sanford Schwartz. New York: Library of America, 2011.

Kapsis, Robert E., and Kathie Coblentz, eds. *Woody Allen: Interviews.* Jackson, MS: University Press of Mississippi, 2006.

Keaton, Diane. *Then Again: A Memoir.* New York: Random House, 2012.

Lax, Eric. *On Being Funny: Woody Allen and Comedy.* New York: Charterhouse, 1975

Lax, Eric. *Woody Allen: A Biography.* New York: Alfred A. Knopf, 1991.

Lax, Eric. *Conversations with Woody Allen.* New York: Alfred A. Knopf, 2007.

Lee, Sander H. *Anguish, God and Existentialism: Eighteen Woody Allen Films Analyzed.* Jefferson, NC: McFarland, 2002.

Meade, Marion. *The Unruly Life of Woody Allen.* London: Phoenix, 2001.

Rosenblum, Ralph., and Robert Karen. *When the Shooting Stops...the Cutting Begins: A Film Editor's Story.* New York: Viking, 1979.

Schickel, Richard. *Woody Allen: A Life in Film.* Chicago: Ivan R. Dee, 2003.

Sikov, Ed. *Mr. Strangelove: A Biography of Peter Sellers.* New York: Hyperion, 2002.

Silet, Charles L. P., ed. *The Films of Woody Allen: Critical Essays.* Lanham, MD: Scarecrow Press, 2006.

Wolcott, James. *Critical Mass: Four Decades of Essays, Reviews, Hand Grenades, and Hurrahs.* New York: Knopf Doubleday, 2013.

FEATURES AND INTERVIEWS

Abrams, Simon. "Simply Do It: Talking with Woody Allen about Directorial Style." rogerebert.com, July 24, 2014.

Allen, Woody. "Woody Allen's Diary." *Guardian,* January 12, 2009.

Andrew, Geoff. "Woody Allen: *Guardian* Interviews at the BFI." *Guardian,* September 27, 2001.

Barrett, Chris. "Jeff Daniels Talks about His Role in *The Purple Rose of Cairo.*" YouTube video, 2:19. Posted March 31, 2009. www.youtube.com/watch?v=NYVLHMZIftw

Billen, Andrew. Interview. *Observer,* April 16, 1995.

Blair, Iain. "Deconstructing Woody: The Director Considers Life, Art and Celebrity." http://dailytelegiraffe.tripod.com/celebritywoodyinterview.html

Blanchett, Cate. "In Conversation: Cate Blanchett Meets Woody Allen." *Harper's Bazaar,* December 2013.

Brooks, Richard. Interview. *Observer,* August 23, 1992.

Cadwalladr, Carole. "Woody Allen: 'My Wife Hasn't Seen Most of My Films...and She Thinks My Clarinet Playing Is Torture.'" *Observer,* March 13, 2011.

Calhoun, Dave. "Woody Allen: 'Making Films Is Not Difficult.'" *Time Out,* September 16, 2013.

Calhoun, Dave. "Woody Allen: 'I Was Happy Until I Was Five.'" *Time Out,* September 8, 2014.

Clark, John. "Citizen Woody." *Los Angeles Times,* December 1, 1996.

Cooney Carrillo, Jenny. "Allen, Woody: *Sweet and Lowdown.*" urbancinefile.com, July 13, 2000.

Cox, David. "Just Don't Ask Woody Allen What's Good about *Vicky Cristina Barcelona.*" *Guardian,* February 9, 2009.

Didion, Joan. "Letter from Manhattan." *New York Review of Books,* August 16, 1979.

Dowd, Maureen. "The Five Women of *Hannah and Her Sisters.*" *New York Times,* February 2, 1986.

Dowd, Maureen. "Diane and Woody, Still a Fun Couple." *New York Times,* August 15, 1993.

Ebert, Roger. "Woody Allen and *The Purple Rose of Cairo.*" *Chicago Sun-Times,* March 10, 1985.

Ebert, Roger. "Great Movies: *Annie Hall.*" *Chicago Sun-Times,* May 12, 2002.

Foundas, Scott. Interview. blogs.villagevoice.com, August 12, 2008.

Foundas, Scott. "Woody Allen on *Whatever Works,* the Meaning of Life (or Lack Thereof), and the Allure of Younger Women." blogs.villagevoice.com, June 18, 2009.

Foundas, Scott. "A Meeting of Minds." *DGA Quarterly,* Fall 2010.

Foundas, Scott. Interview. *Los Angeles Weekly,* May 19, 2011.

Franks, Alan. Interview. *Times,* February 15, 1997.

Fussman, Cal. "Woody Allen: What I've Learned." *Esquire,* September 2013.

Germain, David. "DreamWorks Signs Woody Allen." *Associated Press,* May 17, 2000.

Goldstein, Patrick. "What's the Buzz on Woody?" *Los Angeles Times,* May 21, 2000.

Gould, Mark R. "Woody Allen's *Manhattan* Tells Us Why Life Is Worth Living." atyourlibrary.org

Greenfield, Robert. "Seven Interviews with Woody Allen." *Rolling Stone,* September 30, 1971.

Gussow, Mel. "*Annie Hall:* Woody Allen Fights Anhedonia." *New York Times,* April 20, 1977.

Hillis, Aaron. "Woody Allen on *Cassandra's Dream.*" January 21, 2008.

Hiscock, John. Interview. *Telegraph,* September 29, 2009.

Hiscock, John. "Woody Allen: 'At Last, I'm a Foreign Filmmaker.'" *Telegraph,* September 14, 2012.

Husband, Stuart. "Woody Allen: 'I've Spent My Whole Life under a Cloud.'" *Telegraph,* September 24, 2013.

Itzkoff, Dave. "Annie and Her Sisters." *New York Times,* July 17, 2013.

Itzkoff, Dave. "A Master of Illusion Endures." *New York Times,* July 16, 2014.

Jagernauth, Kevin. "Scarlett Johansson Says She's Waiting for Woody Allen to Write Her *Citizen Kane.*" blogs.indiewire.com, November 1, 2011.

James, Caryn. "Auteur! Auteur!" *New York Times Magazine,* January 19, 1986.

Jeffreys, Daniel. Interview. *Independent,* October 24, 1996.

Jones, Kent. "Woody Allen: The *Film Comment* Interview (Expanded Version)." filmcomment.com, May/June 2011.

Kakutani, Michiko. "Woody Allen: The Art of Humor." *Paris Review,* Fall 1995.

Kilday, Gregg. "Woody Allen Reveals How He Conjured Up His Biggest Hit, *Midnight in Paris.*" *Hollywood Reporter,* January 7, 2012.

Lacey, Liam. "At Seventy-Six, Woody Allen Shows No Signs of Slowing Down." *Globe and Mail,* July 3, 2012.

Lahr, John. "The Imperfectionist." *New Yorker,* December 9, 1996.

Lax, Eric. "For Woody Allen, Sixty Days Hath *September.*" *New York Times,* December 6, 1987.

Lax, Eric. "Woody and Mia: A New York Story." *New York Times,* February 24, 1991.

Longworth, Karina. "Woody Allen on His New Film, *To Rome with Love,* and Some Very Old Themes." *Los Angeles Weekly,* June 21, 2012.

Lucia, Cynthia. "Contemplating Status and Morality in *Cassandra's Dream*: An Interview with Woody Allen." *Cineaste,* Winter 2007/Spring 2008.

MacNab, Geoffrey. "Why *Cassandra's Dream* Is Turning Out to Be Woody Allen's Nightmare." *Independent,* December 1, 2014.

Maslin, Janet. "How the Graphic Art Feats in *Zelig* Were Done." *New York Times,* August 1, 1983.

McGrath, Douglas. "If You Knew Woody Like I Knew Woody." *New York Magazine,* October 17, 1994.

Miller, Prairie. "*Sweet and Lowdown*: Woody Allen Interview." http://www.woodyallen.art.pl/eng/wywiad_eng_11.php

Acknowledgments

Mitchell, Sean. "Funny Isn't Good Enough: Woody Allen's Got Another Movie Coming Out, But There Are a Few Other Things on His Mind." *Los Angeles Times*, March 15, 1992.

Mottram, James. "'I Really Don't Care': After That Twitter Scandal, Actor Alec Baldwin Discusses Fatherhood, Working with Woody Allen and Being in the Public Eye." *Independent*, July 22, 2013.

Murray, Rebecca. *Vicky Cristina Barcelona* press conference: "Filmmaker Woody Allen Discusses *Vicky Cristina Barcelona*." movies.about.com, 2008.

Nesteroff, Kliph. "The Early Woody Allen 1952–1971." blog. wfmu.org, February 14, 2010.

Pond, Steve. "How Cate Blanchett Got Ready to Play a Boozer in Woody Allen's *Blue Jasmine*." *The Wrap*, July 26, 2013.

Prunner, Vifill. "Mariel Hemingway—*Manhattan*: The Birth of a Legend." thenewcinemamagazine.com, April 21, 2010.

Radish, Christina. "Woody Allen Talks *To Rome with Love*, the Importance of Music in His Films, How He Feels about Improvisation, and His Outlook on Retirement." collider. com, June 20, 2012.

Rhys, Tim. "Made in Manhattan." *MovieMaker*, Spring 2004.

Romney, Jonathan. "Scuzzballs Like Us." *Sight & Sound*, April 1998.

Ross, Scott. "The Night Woody Allen and Billy Graham Argued the Meaning of Life." nbcarea.com, May 30, 2012.

Rottenberg, Josh. "Woody Allen on His Prolific Career." *Entertainment Weekly*, December 16, 2005.

Shoard, Catherine. "Woody Allen on *Blue Jasmine*: 'You See Tantrums in Adults All the Time.'" *Guardian*, September 26, 2013.

Smithey, Cole. "Woody Allen Discusses *Melinda and Melinda*." filmcritic1963.typepad.com, May 7, 2005.

Szklarski, Stephen J. "Carlo Di Palma: An Interview." *Independent Film Quarterly*, Fall 2001.

Taylor, Juliet. Interview. *Observer*, May 21, 2000.

Verdiani, Gilles. "Woody Allen, C'est Moi." http://dailytelegiraffe.tripod.com/ celebrityinterviewfrenchpremiere.html

Wolfe, Tom. "The 'Me' Decade and the Third Great Awakening." *New York Magazine*, August 23, 1976.

Zuber, Helene. "*Spiegel* Interview with Woody Allen: 'Nothing Pleases Me More than Being Thought of as a European Filmmaker.'" *Der Spiegel*, June 20, 2005.

"Capone Interviews Woody Allen about *Cassandra's Dream*." aintitcool.com, January 20, 2008.

"Comedians: His Own Boswell." *Time*, February 15, 1963.

"Scoop: Q & A with Woody Allen." http://cinema.com/ articles/4167/scoop-q-and-a-with-woody-allen.phtml

WEBSITES

everywoodyallenmovie.com
woodyallenwednesday.com

DOCUMENTARIES

Kopple, Barbara. *Wild Man Blues*, 1997.
Weide, Robert B. *Woody Allen: A Documentary*, 2012.

PICTURE CREDITS

Every effort has been made to trace and acknowledge the copyright holders. We apologize in advance for any unintentional omissions and would be pleased, if any such case should arise, to add appropriate acknowledgment in any future edition of the book.

T: top; B: bottom; L: left; R: right; C: center

Getty Images: 2–3 (Nicholas Moore/Contour by Getty); 7, 288 (Arthur Schatz/The LIFE Premium Collection); 19 (Grey Villet/The LIFE Picture Collection); 26 (John Minihan/*Evening Standard*); 28 (Philippe Le Tellier); 30 (United Artists/AFP); 31 (American International Pictures); 33 (Columbia Pictures/Terry O'Neill); 69, 71, 73–74 (United Artists/Ernst Haas); 77, 78, 80–81, 94–95, 97–103, 108 B, 109 (United Artists/Brian Hamill); 87, 92–93, 230–231 (Brian Hamill); 117 (Hulton Archive); 123, 141, 158–159, 170 (Orion/Brian Hamill); 178, 182 (TriStar/Brian Hamill); 179 (Rose Hartman); 188, 191, 194–195 (Miramax/Brian Hamill); 211 (Hubert Fanthomme/*Paris Match*); 228–229 (Fox Searchlight/Brian Hamill); 257 (Miguel Medina/AFP); 258 (Bertrand Langlois/AFP); 285 (Jennifer S. Altman/ Contour by Getty); **The Kobal Collection:** 12 TL, 12 TC, 46, 49, 57, 58 B, 59–61, 63, 65–67, 83, 91, 106–107(Rollins-Joffe/United Artists); 12 BL, 13 TR, 124–125, 127, 130–131, 144 T, 149 B, 150–151, 160, 162, 168 (Orion/Rollins-Joffe/ Brian Hamill); 12–13 B, 180–181 (TriStar/Rollins-Joffe); 13 BR (Gravier Prods./Perdido Prods.); 39–40 (ABC/ Rollins-Joffe/Cinerama); 118–119 (Orion/Warner Bros./ Kerry Hayes); 152 (Orion); 164 (Orion/Brian Hamill); 176 (TriStar/Brian Hamill); 183 B (TriStar/Rollins-Joffe/Brian Hamill); 197 (Magnolia/Sweetland/Doumanian Prods./ Brian Hamill); 198, 212 (Magnolia/Sweetland/Doumanian Prods.); 206 (Sweetland/Doumanian Prods./John Clifford); 226 (DreamWorks/Gravier Prods./Brian Hamill); 233–234, 236–237 (Jada Prods./BBC Films/DreamWorks/Clive Coote); 238 (BBC Films/Focus Features); 241 (Perdido Prods./Wild Bunch); 242–244, 246 (Weinstein Co./ Mediapro/Gravier Prods.); 250, 254–255, 256 T, 258–259 (Gravier Prods.); 264–269 (Gravier Prods./Perdido Prods.); 271 (Dippermouth/Gravier Prods./Perdido Prods.); 275 B (Zuzu/Antidote Films); **The Ronald Grant Archive:** 12 BR (TriStar); 166–167 (Orion); 217 (Sony Pictures); **Rex:** 12–13 T, 138–139, 147 (Orion/Everett Collection); 13 BL (Miramax/Everett Collection); 34–35 (ABC/ Cinerama/Everett Collection); 53 B (Paramount/Everett Collection); 58 T, 70 (United Artists/Everett Collection); 75 (United Artists/Sipa Press); 136, 154, 165 (Orion/ Moviestore Collection); 161 (Orion/Snap Stills); 176–177 (TriStar/Snap Stills); 196 (Magnolia/Sweetland/Sipa Press); 208 (Alex Oliveira); 214, 215 T, 253 T, 270 (Sony Pictures/ Everett Collection); 218, 220 B, 221 (DreamWorks/Everett Collection); 238–239 (Focus Features/Everett Collection); 240, 245 B (Weinstein/Everett Collection); 253 B (Sony Pictures/Snap Stills); **Photofest:** 13 TL, 114–115, 118, 121, 126, 128–129, 132–135, 139–140, 142–143, 144 B, 145, 149 T, 150, 153, 155–156, 163, 169, 171–173 (Orion); 18 L, 20, 25 (© NBC); 38 (Cinerama Releasing Corporation); 48, 68, 72, 79, 82, 84, 88–90, 96 (United Artists); 52 (Paramount); 174–175, 190, 192–193, 199, 202, 203 B (Miramax); 207 (Fine Line Features); 213, 216 T, 256 B (Sony Pictures Classics); 220 T, 223 B, 235 (DreamWorks); 245 T (The Weinstein Company); 275 T (Buena Vista); **GlobePhotos:** 14; 64 (United Artists); **akg-images:** 17; 105 (Manuel Bidermanas); 108 T (United Artists/Album); **Corbis:** 11, 187 (Michael O'Neill/ Corbis Outline); 18 R (Bettmann); 32 (Columbia/Sunset Boulevard); 36 (Morton Beebe); 37 (ABC/Cinerama/ Sunset Boulevard); 56 (United Artists/Steve Schapiro); 110–111 (United Artists/Sunset Boulevard); 120 T (Orion/ Warner Bros./Sunset Boulevard); 120 B (Orion/Warner Bros./Bettmann); 208–209 (Miramax/Sunset Boulevard); 224–225 (Arnault Joubin/Corbis Outline); 272 (AKM-GSI/Splash News); 274 (Columbia/Steve Schapiro); 279 (Andrew Schwartz/Corbis Outline); **WA archive:** 17, 21; © **Rowland Scherman:** 22–23; **Image Courtesy of the Advertising Archives:** 24; **mptvimages.com:** 29, 62 (United Artists); 51 (Paramount); 183 T (TriStar); **Photoshot:** 41 (Cinerama); 47 (United Artists); 113 (Orion); 185 (TriStar); 55 (Paramount); 205 T (DreamWorks); 210 (Miramax); 215 B, 273 (Sony Pictures); 223 T (DreamWorks); **Magnum Photos:** 43 (Philippe Halsman); **TopFoto:** 44; © **Dennis Brack:** 50; **Alamy:** 53 T (Paramount/AF archive); 148 (Orion/AF Archive); 184 (TriStar/Pictorial Press Ltd); 216 B (Sony Pictures/Pictorial Press Ltd.); 219 (DreamWorks); 260 (Gravier Prods./Medusa Film/AF Archive); © **AP/PA Images:** 85; 261 B (Pier Paolo Cito); 276–277 (Carlo Allegri); **Camera Press London:** 146 (Orion/DDP); 204 (Miramax/DDP); 205 B (DreamWorks/ DDP); 232 (Jane Hodson); 248–249 (Starlitepics); **Mary Evans Picture Library:** 157 (Orion/Rue des Archives); **eyevine:** 200–201, 203 T (Graziano Arici); **ACE Pictures:** 227, 251; © **Walter McBride Photography:** 247; **Photo by Philippe Antonello:** 261 T, 262–263 (Medusa Film).

PUBLISHER'S ACKNOWLEDGMENTS

Palazzo Editions thanks Chloe Pew Latter for compiling the filmography and Matthew Coniam for sourcing of quotes.

Overleaf: Portrait by Arthur Schatz, 1967.

"I personally have no interest whatsoever in 'legacy'
because I'm a firm believer that when you're dead, naming
a street after you doesn't help your metabolism — I saw
what happened to Rembrandt and Plato and all those
other nice people. They just lie there."